Early Western Journals, 1748-1765

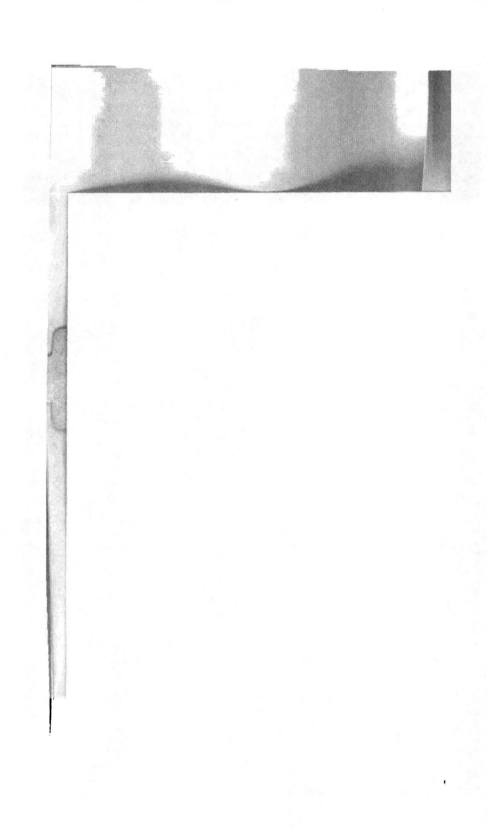

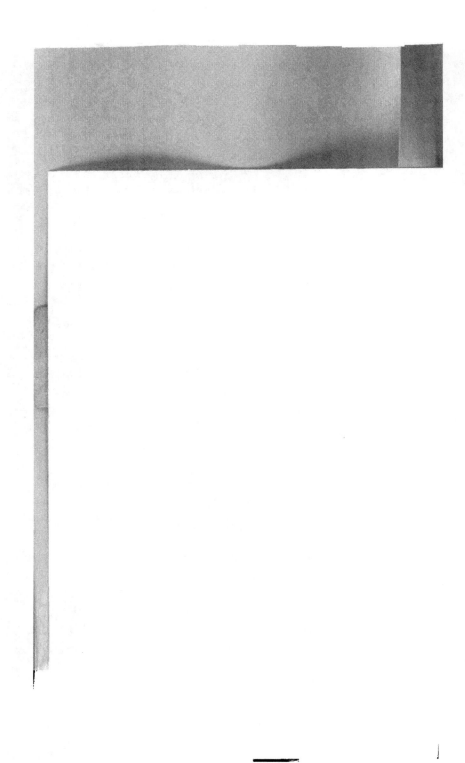

Early Western Travels
1748-1846

Volume I

Capt.ⁿ Thoˢ. Mewes.

f

Early Western Journals
1748-1765

By Conrad Weiser, 1748; George Croghan,
1750-1765; Frederick Post, 1758; and
Thomas Morris, 1764

Edited with Notes, Introductions, Index, etc., by

Reuben Gold Thwaites

Editor of "The Jesuit Relations and Allied Documents," "Wisconsin
Historical Collections," "Chronicles of Border Warfare,"
"Hennepin's New Discovery," etc.

(Separate publication from "Early Western Travels: 1748-1846,"
in which series this appeared as Volume I)

Cleveland, Ohio
The Arthur H. Clark Company
1904

I

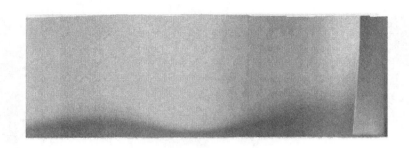

340162

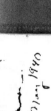

8 May 1940

CONTENTS OF VOLUME I

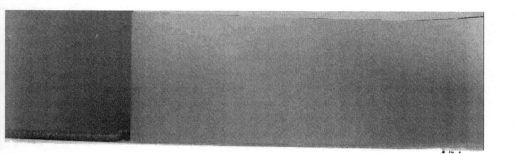

ILLUSTRATION TO VOLUME I

PORTRAIT OF CAPTAIN THOMAS MORRIS. *Photographic facsimile of steel plate in original edition of "Miscellanies in Prose and Verse."*

Frontispiece.

PREFACE TO VOLUME I

In planning for this series of reprints of Early Western Travels, we were confronted by an embarrassment of riches. To reissue all of the many excellent works of travel originally published during the formative period of Western settlement, would obviously be impossible. A selection had therefore to be made, both as to period and material. The century commencing with Conrad Weiser's notable journey to the Western Indians in 1748, set convenient limits to the field in the matter of time. The question of material was much more difficult.

It being unlikely that any two editors would choose the same volumes for reprint, criticism of our list will undoubtedly be made. It should, however, candidly be explained that the matter of selection has in each case necessarily been affected by two important considerations — (1) the intrinsic value of the original from the historical side, and (2) its present rarity and market value. The Editor having selected a list of items worthy of a new lease of life, the Publishers, from their intimate knowledge of the commercial aspect of rare Americana, advised which of these in their opinion were sufficiently in demand by libraries and collectors to render the enterprise financially productive. It is believed that this co-operative method has resulted in an interesting collection, and given point to the descriptive sub-title: ''Some of the best and rarest contemporary volumes of travel. . . in the Middle and Far West, during the period of early American settlement.''

The first volume of our series is necessarily more varied in composition than any of its successors, it having been deemed important to present herein several typical early tours into the Indian country west of the Alleghenies.

That of Conrad Weiser, occuŕring in August and September of 1748, was the first official journey undertaken at the instance of the English colonies, to the west of the mountain wall. His purpose was, to carry to the tribesmen on the Ohio a present from the Pennsylvania and Virginia authorities. The results were favorable to an English alliance, but they were partially neutralized by the French expedition headed by Céloron the following year.

The journals of George Croghan (1750-65) are an epitome of the Indian history of the time. The first three documents deal with the period of English progress— in 1750, Croghan was on the Ohio en route to the Shawnee towns and Pickawillany; the next season, he outwitted Joncaire on the Allegheny. The four succeeding documents are concerned with the period of hostility to the English — in 1754 he was on the Ohio after Washington had passed (December, 1753); the letter from Aughwick, in 1755, tells of affairs after Braddock's defeat; in 1756, we learn particulars of Indian affairs; and in 1757 is given a résumé of past events. The last two journals are the longest and most important — that of 1760-61 is concerned, topographically and otherwise, with the trip to Detroit via Lake Erie, in the company of Rogers's Rangers, and the return by land to Pittsburg; that of 1765, with a tour down the Ohio towards the Illinois, where the writer is captured and carried to Ouiatanon — in due course making a peace with Pontiac, and returning to Niagara.

The journals of Christian Frederick Post and Thomas

Morris are interludes, as to time, in the Croghan diaries.
Post's two journals cover the months of July to September, 1758, and October, 1758 to January, 1759. He
was at first sent out, by the northern trail, in midsummer,
as an official messenger to the hostiles, among whom he
succeeded in securing a kind of neutrality — a venturesome expedition into the neighborhood of Fort Duquesne,
whose French commandant offered a price upon his head.
The second journey, in the autumn, was undertaken to
carry the news of the treaty of Easton (October, 1758),
and pave the way for General Forbes's advance. In the
course of his journey he proceeded to the Indian towns
on the Ohio and its northern tributaries, and returned
to the settlements with Forbes's army.

Captain Morris accompanied Bradstreet (1764) on the
latter's expedition towards Detroit. Being dispatched
from Cedar Point on a mission to the French in the
Illinois, Morris was arrested and maltreated at the
Ottawa village at Maumee Rapids. He saw Pontiac,
went to Fort Miami, narrowly escaped being burned at
the stake, and finally made his escape through the woods
to Detroit. His journal presents a thrilling episode in
Western history.

It is our purpose, in these reprints, accurately to republish the original volumes, with all of their illustrations
and other features. While seeking to reproduce the old
text as closely as practicable, with its typographic and
orthographic peculiarities, it has been found advisable
here and there to make a few minor changes; these consist
almost wholly of palpable blemishes, the result of negli-
gent proof-reading — such as turned letters, transposed
letters, slipped letters, and mis-spacings. Such correc-
tions will be made without specific mention; in some

instances, however, the original error has for a reason been retained, and in juxtaposition the correction given within brackets. We indicate, throughout, the pagination of the old edition which we are reprinting, by inclósing within brackets the number of each page at its beginning, *e. g.* [24]; in the few instances where pages were, as the fruit of carelessness in make-up, misnumbered in the original, we have given the incorrect as well as the correct figure, *e. g.* [25, *i. e.* 125]. In two or three instances, where matter foreign to our purpose was introduced in the volume as originally published — such as the journal of a voyage not within our field, or an appendix of irrelevant or unimportant matter — we have taken the liberty of eliminating this; in such cases, however, especial attention will be called to the omission.

An analytical index to the series will appear in the concluding volume.

In the preparation of notes for the present volume, the Editor has been assisted by Louise Phelps Kellogg, Ph.D., of the Division of Maps and Manuscripts in the Wisconsin State Historical Library. He has also been favored with valuable information on various points, from Colonel Reuben T. Durrett of Louisville, Mr. Frank H. Severance of Buffalo, the Western Reserve Historical Society at Cleveland, and Dr. Ernest C. Richardson and Dr. John Rogers Williams of Princeton University.

R. G. T.

MADISON, WIS., January, 1904.

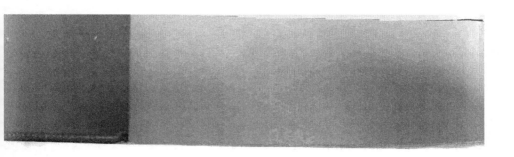

I

CONRAD WEISER'S JOURNAL OF A TOUR TO THE OHIO
AUGUST 11 – OCTOBER 2, 1748

SOURCE: *Pennsylvania Colonial Records*, v, pp. 348-358; with
variations from *Pennsylvania Historical Collections*, i, pp. 23-33.

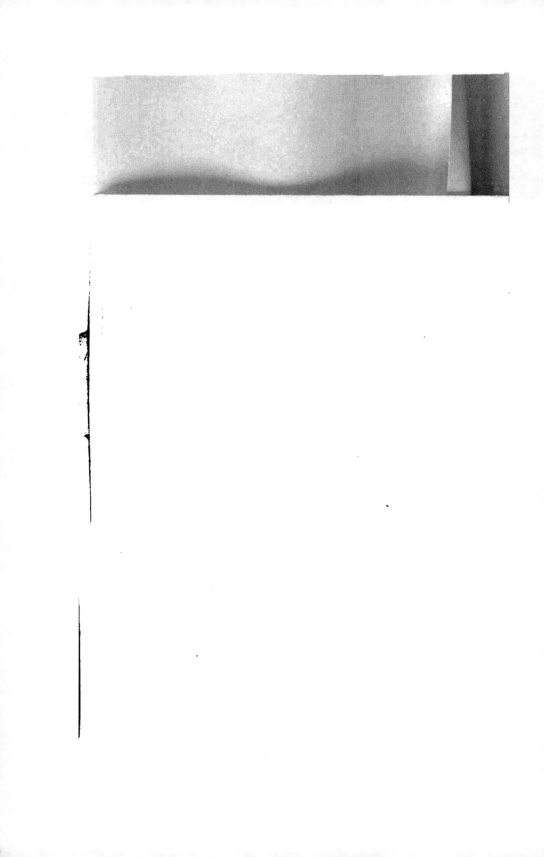

INTRODUCTORY NOTE

Conrad Weiser, one of the most prominent agents in the management of Indian affairs during the later French wars, was a native of Würtemberg, being born November 2, 1696. When Conrad was but fourteen years old, his father, John Conrad Weiser, led a party of Palatines to America where they lived four years on the Livingston manor in New York, and in 1714 removed to Schoharie. There young Weiser came in close contact with the Mohawk Indians, was adopted into their tribe, and living among them for some years became master of their language.

In 1729, he and his family, consisting of a wife and five young children, removed to Berks (then Lancaster) County, Pennsylvania, where a number of Weiser's countrymen had preceded them. The new homestead was a mile east of the present town of Womelsdorf, and became the centre of an extended hospitality both for Pennsylvania Germans and visiting Indians. When Reading was laid out (1748), Weiser was one of the commissioners for that purpose, building therein a house and store that are still standing.

His first employment as an interpreter was in 1731, when forty shillings were allotted him for his services. From this time forward he was official interpreter for Pennsylvania, and for thirty years was employed in every important Indian transaction. The Pennsylvania Council testified in 1736 "that they had found Conrad faithfull and honest, that he is a true good Man & had Spoke their words [the Indians'] & our Words, and not his own."[1] Again in 1743, the governor of Virginia requested the province of Pennsylvania to send their "honest interpreter," Conrad Weiser, to adjust a difficulty with the Iroquois Indians; whereupon he proceeded to Onondaga with a present of £100 on the part of Virginia, and made peace for the English colonists.[2] The following year, Weiser was chief interpreter at the important treaty of Lancaster; and throughout King George's War was occupied with negotiations with the Six Nations, detaching them from the French influence, and keeping the Pennsylvania Delawares quiet "upon their mats."

After the journey to the Ohio, described in the following diary, Weiser's Indian transactions were largely confined to the province of Pennsylvania; Montour and Croghan taking over the business with the Ohio Indians until the outbreak of the French and Indian War. Weiser now assumed duties in a military capacity. He raised a company of soldiers for the Canadian expedition (1755), and later was made lieutenant-colonel, with the care of the frontier forts under his charge. At the same time the New York authorities besought his influence with the Mohawks and Western Iroquois; and he assisted in arranging the treaty at Easton, which prepared the way for the success of Forbes's expedition (1758).

Weiser was the most influential German of his section, possibly of all Pennsylvania; but his religious affiliations and enmities interfered with his political ambitions. Originally a Lutheran, in 1735 he became concerned with the movement of the Seventh Day Baptists, which

---

[1] *Pennsylvania Colonial Records* (Harrisburg, 1851), iv, p. 88.
[2] *Ibid.*, pp. 660-669, for journal of this tour.

led to the establishment of the community at Ephrata, where he was known as Brother Enoch, and consecrated to the priesthood. These sectaries charged that the bribe of official position tempted him to forsake his vows; certain it is that in 1741 he was appointed justice of the peace for Berks County, and left Ephrata, later (1743) sending a letter requesting his former brethren to consider him a "stranger." The opposition of this sect of Germans, the indifference of the Moravians, and the alienation of his earlier Lutheran friends, lost him his coveted election for the assembly; and he afterwards withdrew from politics to remain the trusted adviser of the government upon Indian and local affairs. His sincerity, honesty, and trustworthiness made him greatly respected throughout the entire province, and his death, July 13, 1760, was considered a public calamity.

The journey undertaken to the Ohio, which the accompanying journal chronicles, was the first official embassy to the Indians who lived beyond the Alleghenies, and was undertaken for the following reasons.

The efforts of the English traders to push their connections among the "far Indians" had been increasingly successful, during the decade 1738-48, and the resulting rivalry with the French had reached an intense stage. The firm hold of the latter on the Indian nations of the "upper country" had been shaken by a long series of wars with the Foxes and Chickasaws, accompanied by humiliating defeats. In 1747, the most faithful of the French Indians — those domiciled at Mackinac and Detroit — had risen in revolt; and George Croghan sent word to the council at Philadelphia that some nations along the shore of Lake Erie desired the English alliance, having as an earnest thereof sent a belt of wampum and a French scalp.[2] The Pennsylvania authorities voted them a present of £200, to be sent out by Croghan. About the same time, a deputation of ten Indians from the Ohio arriving in Philadelphia, the council considered this "an extraordinary event in the English favor," and not only secured a grant of £1,000 from the assembly, but applied to the governors of the Southern provinces to aid in this work; in accordance with which request, Virginia replied with an appropriation of £200.[4] Croghan set off in the spring of 1748, and informed the Allegheny Indians that Weiser, the official interpreter, would be among them during the summer. Meanwhile, the latter was detained by a treaty with the Twigtwee (Miami) Indians, who had come unexpectedly offering to the English the alliance of that powerful nation;[5] so that it was not until August that he was able to start on his mission to the Ohio.

In addition to the delivery of the present, he was also instructed to secure satisfaction for the attack of some Northern Indians upon the Carolina settlements; wherein one Captain Haig, with several others, had been carried off prisoners — supposedly by some Ohio Indians.[6] The success of this mission was most gratifying to the English and the frontier settlers. The Virginia authorities were more active than those of Pennsylvania in following up the advantage thus gained; and under the leadership of the Ohio Company sought to secure the Forks of the Ohio, with the ensuing consequences of the French and Indian War.

R. G. T.

---

[2] *Pennsylvania Colonial Records*, v, p. 72.
[4] *Ibid.*, pp. 121, 140, 145-152; 189, 190, 257.
[5] *Ibid.*, pp. 286-290, 307-319.
[6] *Ibid.*, pp. 290-293, 304.

THE JOURNAL· OF CONRAD WEISER, ESQR., INDIAN INTERPRETER, TO THE OHIO[7]

Aug" 11th. Set out from my House & came to James Galbreath[8] that day, 30 Miles.

12th. Came to George Croghans,[9] 15 Miles.

13th. To Robert Dunnings, 20 Miles.

14th. To the Tuscarroro Path, 30 Miles.

15th and 16th. Lay by on Account of the Men coming back Sick, & some other Affairs hindering us.

17th. Crossed the Tuscarroro Hill & came to the Sleeping Place called the Black Log, 20 Miles.

18th. Had a great rain in the afternoon; came within two Miles of the Standing Stone, 24 Miles.

19th. We travelled but 12 Miles;[10] were obliged to dry our Things in the afternoon.

[7] There appear to have been two copies of this journal prepared, one as the official report to the president and council of Pennsylvania, which was published in the *Pennsylvania Colonial Records*, v, pp. 348-358. A reprint from the same manuscript appeared in *Early History of Western Pennsylvania* (Pittsburg and Harrisburg, 1846), appendix, pp. 13-23. The other copy seems to have been preserved among the family papers; and was edited and published by a descendant of Weiser—Heister M. Muhlenberg, M.D., of Reading, Pennsylvania—in Pennsylvania Historical Society *Collections* (Philadelphia, 1851), i, pp. 23-33. We have followed the official copy, indicating by footnotes variations in the other account.— ED.

[8] Weiser's house was about one mile east of Womelsdorf, now in Berks County, Pennsylvania. James Galbreath was a prominent Indian trader, one of those licensed by the government of Pennsylvania.— ED.

[9] Croghan lived at this time just west of Harrisburg in Pennsboro Township, Cumberland County.—ED.

[10] There were three great Indian paths from east to west through Western Pennsylvania. The southern led from Fort Cumberland on the Potomac, westward through the valleys of Youghiogheny and Monongahela, to the Forks of

20th. Came to Franks Town, but saw no Houses or Cabins; here we overtook the Goods,[11] because four of George Croghan's Hands fell sick, 26 Miles.

21st. Lay by, it raining all Day.

---

the Ohio, and was the route taken by Washington in 1753, later by Braddock's expedition, and was substantially the line of the great Cumberland National Road of the early nineteenth century.

The central trail, passing through Carlisle, Shippensburg, and Bedford, over Laurel Mountain, through Fort Ligonier, over Chestnut Ridge, to Shannopin's Town at the Forks of the Ohio, was the most direct, and became the basis of General Forbes's road, and later of the Pennsylvania wagon road to the Ohio. Gist took this trail in 1750.— See Hulbert, *Old Glade Road* (Cleveland, 1903).

The northern, or Kittanning trail, was the oldest, and that most used by Indian traders. It is this route that Weiser followed. From Croghan's, he passed over into the valley of Sherman's Creek (in Perry County), crossed the Tuscarora Mountains at what was later known as Sterritt's Gap, and reached the Black Log sleeping place near Shade Valley in the southeastern part of Huntingdon County. This was a digression to the south, for in an extract from his journal in *Pennsylvania Archives*, ii, p. 13, Weiser says: "The Black Log is 8 or 10 miles South East of the Three Springs and Frank's Town lies to y[e] North, so that there must be a deduction of at least twenty miles." From here, following the valley of Aughwick Creek, he crossed the Juniata River, and approached the "Standing Stone." This was a prominent landmark of the region, and stood on the right bank of a creek of the same name, near the present town of Huntingdon. It was about 14 feet high, and six inches square, and served as a kind of Indian guidepost for that region. From this point, the trail followed the Juniata Valley, coinciding for a short distance with the line of the Pennsylvania Central Railway, but turning off on the Frankstown branch of the Juniata at the present town of Petersburg.

There was also a fourth trail, still farther north, by way of Sunbury and the west branch of the Susquehanna to Venango. This was Post's route in 1758.— ED.

[11] Frankstown was an important Indian village in the county of Blair, near Hollidaysburg. The present town of this name lies on the north side of the river, whereas the Indian town appears to have been on the south bank. Remains of the native village were in existence in the early part of the nineteenth century. The Indian name was "Assunepachla," the title "Frankstown" being given in honor of Stephen Franks, a German trader who lived at this place.— See Jones, *History of Juniata Valley* (Harrisburg, 1889, and ed.), pp. 298-303. The cause of its desertion when Weiser passed, is not known. The other edition of the journal says, "Here we overtook one half the goods," which seems more correct in view of the succeeding account.— ED.

22d. Crossed Alleghany Hill & came to the Clear Fields, 16 Miles.[12]

23d. Came to the Shawonese[13] Cabbins, 34 Miles.

24th. Found a dead Man on the Road who had killed himself by Drinking too much Whisky; the Place being very stony we cou'd not dig a Grave; He smelling very strong we covered him with Stones & Wood & went on our Journey; came to the 10 Mile Lick, 32 Miles.

25th. Crossed Kiskeminetoes Creek & came to Ohio that Day, 26 Miles.[14]

---

[12] Of the place where the Kittanning trail crosses the Allegheny Range, Jones writes (*op. cit.*), that the path is still visible, although filled with weeds in the summer. "In some places where the ground was marshy, close to the run, the path is at least twelve inches deep, and the very stones along the road bear the marks of the iron-shod horses of the Indian traders. Two years ago we picked up, at the edge of the run, a mile up the gorge, two gun-flints,— now rated as relics of a past age." Clear fields was at the head waters of Clearfield Creek, a branch of the Susquehanna River, in Clearfield Township, Cambria County. This is not to be confused with Clearfield (Chinkla-camoos), an important Indian town farther north. See Post's *Journal, post.*— Ed.

[13] The Shawnees (Fr., Chaouanons), when first known, appear to have been living in Western Kentucky; they were greatly harassed by the Iroquois, and made frequent migrations which are difficult to trace. In 1692, they made peace with the Iroquois and the English, and portions of the tribe settled in the Ohio country and Western Pennsylvania. Intriguing with both English and French, they were treacherous toward both nations. The location of the cabins mentioned here by Weiser is not positively known — it was in the northern part of Indiana County; somewhere on the Kittanning trail.— Ed.

[14] Weiser turned aside from the regular trail that ended at the Delaware Indians' town of Kittanning, and followed a branch of the path that turned southwest; crossed the Kiskiminitas Creek at the ford where the town of Saltzburg, Indiana County, now stands; and reached the Allegheny River (then called the Ohio) at Chartier's Old Town, now Chartier's Station, Westmoreland County. It was at this point that in 1749, the French explorer, Céloron de Blainville, met six traders with fifty horses laden with peltries, by these sending his famous message to the governor of Pennsylvania to keep his traders from that country, which was owned by the French. Weiser calculated the distance of his journey by land as one hundred and seventy miles, and by deducting twenty miles for the detour at Black Log, made the distance from the settlements one hundred and fifty miles.— Ed.

26th. Hired a Cannoe; paid 1,000 Black Wampum for the loan of it to Logs Town. Our Horses being all tyred, we went by Water & came that Night to a Delaware Town; the Indians used us very kindly.[16]

27th. Sett off again in the morning early; Rainy Wheather. We dined in a Seneka Town, where an old Seneka Woman Reigns with great Authority;[16] we dined at her House, & they all used us very well; at this & the last-mentioned Delaware Town they received us by firing a great many Guns; especially at this last Place. We saluted the Town by firing off 4 pair of pistols; arrived that Evening at Logs Town, & Saluted the Town as before; the Indians returned about One hundred Guns;[17] Great Joy appear'd in their Countenances.

---

[16] This was the Delaware village known as Shannopin's Town, from a chief of that name, who died in 1749. It was situated on the Allegheny River in the present city of Pittsburg, and contained about twenty wigwams, and fifty or sixty natives. See Darlington, *Gist's Journals* (Pittsburg, 1893), pp. 92, 93.—ED.

[16] The reference is to Queen Aliquippa, whose town, directly at the Forks of the Ohio, was called by Céloron "the written rock village." The writings proved on examination to be but names of English traders scrawled in charcoal on the rocks. See Father Bonnécamps's Relation, *Jesuit Relations* (Thwaites's ed., Cleveland, 1896-1902), lxix, p. 175. Céloron says of the Seneca queen: "She regards herself as a sovereign, and is entirely devoted to the English." Upon the advent of the French, she removed her village to the forks of the Monongahela and Youghiogheny, where she told Gist in 1753 she would never go back to the Allegheny to live, unless the English built a fort. Céloron says of the site of her first village: "This place is one of the most beautiful I have seen on the Beautiful River [la Belle Rivière, the French name for the Ohio]."— ED.

[17] Logstown (French, Chinnigné, Shenango) was the most important Indian trading village in that part of the country. It was a mixed village composed of Indians of several tribes — chiefly Iroquois, Mohican, and Shawnee. When Céloron visited it a year after Weiser's sojourn, he spoke of it as "a very bad village, seduced by the desire for the cheap goods of the English." He was near being attacked here, being saved by discovering the plot, and displaying the strength of his forces. Like Weiser, he was received with a salute of guns, but feared it was more a sign of enmity than amity. Later, the Indians of this village returned to the French alliance, and after the founding of Fort

From the Place where we took Water, *i. e.* from the old Shawones Town, commonly called Chartier's Town,[18] to this Place is about 60 Miles by Water & but 35 or 40 by Land.

The Indian Council met this Evening to shake Hands with me & to shew their Satisfaction at my safe arrival; I desired of them to send a Couple of Canoes to fetch down the Goods from Chartier's old Town, where we had been oblig'd to leave them on account of our Horses being all tyred. I gave them a String of Wampum to enforce my Request.[19]

28th. Lay still.

29th. The Indians sett off in three Canoes to fetch the Goods. I expected the Goods wou'd be all at Char-

---

Duquesne, houses were built by the French for its inhabitants. With the restoration of English interest, the importance of the place diminished, and by 1784 it is spoken of as a "former settlement." The site of Logstown is about eighteen miles down the river from Pittsburg, just below the present town of Economy, Pennsylvania. It was on a high bluff on the north shore. For the history of this place, see Darlington's *Gist*, pp. 95-100.— ED.

[18] There were two Indian towns called by this name — one at the mouth of Chartier's Creek, Allegheny County, three miles below Pittsburg; the other opposite the mouth of Chartier's Run, which falls into the Allegheny in Westmoreland County. Weiser refers to the latter of these. Chartier was a French-Shawnee half-breed that had much influence with his tribe. In 1745, he induced most of them to remove to the neighborhood of Detroit, on the orders of the governor of New France. See Croghan's *Journals, post.*—ED.

[19] The other edition of the journal adds, that the horses were "all scalled on their backs."

The importance of "wampum" in all Indian transactions cannot be over-estimated. It was used for money, as a much-prized ornament, to enforce a request (as at this time), to accredit a messenger, to ransom a prisoner, to atone for a crime. No council could be held, no treaty drawn up, without a liberal use of wampum. It was used also to record treaties, as the one described by Weiser between the Wyandots, Iroquois, and governor of New York. Hale —"Indian Wampum Records," *Popular Science Monthly*, February, 1897— thinks that it was a comparatively late invention in Indian development, and took its rise among the Iroquois. Weiser's list of the wampum used and received in this journey is to be found in *Pennsylvania Archives*, ii, p. 17.— ED.

tier's old Town by the time the Canoes wou'd get there, as we met about twenty Horses of George Groghan's at the Shawonese Cabbins in order to fetch the Goods that were then lying at Franks Town.

This Day news came to Town that the Six Nations were on the point of declaring War against the French, for reason the French had Imprison'd some of the Indian Deputies. A Council was held & all the Indians acquainted with the News, and it was said the Indian Messenger was by the way to give all the Indians Notice to make ready to fight the French.[20] This Day my Companions went to Coscosky, a large Indian Town about 30 Miles off.[21]

30th. I went to Beaver Creek, an Indian Town about 8 Miles off, chiefly Delawares, the rest Mohocks, to have some Belts of Wampum made.[22] This afternoon Rainy Wheather set in which lasted above a Week. Andrew

---

[20] The French had retained the Iroquois deputies in order to secure from them the French prisoners in their hands. La Galissonière, the governor wrote to his home government in 1748, that he should persist in retaining their (the Iroquois) people, until he recovered the French. The governor of New York demanded the Mohawks, on the ground of their being British subjects, a claim the French refused to admit. The matter was finally adjusted without an Indian war, although it caused much irritation. See O'Callaghan (ed.), *New York Colonial Documents* (Albany, 1858), x, p. 185.— ED.

[21] Kuskuskis was an important centre for the Delaware Indians, on the Mahoning Branch of Beaver Creek, in Lawrence County, Pennsylvania. It consisted of separate villages scattered along the creek, one of which, called "Old Kuskuskis," was at the forks, where New Castle now stands. See Post's *Journal, post.*— ED.

[22] The Indian town at the mouth of Beaver Creek, where the town of Beaver now stands, was known indifferently as King Beaver's, or Shingas's Old Town (from two noted Delaware chiefs), or Sohkon (signifying "at the mouth of a stream"). This was a noted fur-trading station, and after the building of Fort Duquesne, the French erected houses here, for the Indians. It was the starting place for many a border raid, that made Shingas's name "a terror to the frontier settlements of Pennsylvania." See Post's experiences at this place in 1758, *post.*— ED.

Montour[22] came back from Coscosky with a Message
from the Indians there to desire of me that the ensuing
Council might be held at their Town.   We both lodged
at this Town at George Croghan's Trading House.

31st. Sent Andrew Montour back to Coscosky with a
String of Wampum to let the Indians there know that it
was an act of their own that the ensuing Council must
be held at Logs Town, they had order'd it do last Spring
when George Croghan was up, & at the last Treaty in
Lancaster the Shawonese & Twightwees[24] have been
told so, & they stayed accordingly for that purpose, &
both would be offended if the Council was to be held at
Coscosky, besides my instructions binds me to Logs
Town, & could not go further without giving offence.

Sept[r]. 1. The Indians in Logs Town having heard of

[22] Andrew Montour was the son of a noted French half-breed, Madame
Montour, who being captured by the Iroquois in her youth married an Oneida
chief and was a firm adherent of the English. Montour's services for the English
were considerable. He was an expert interpreter, speaking the languages of
the various Ohio Indians, as well as Iroquois. First mentioned by Weiser in
1744, when he interpreted Delaware for his Iroquois, he assisted in nearly all
the important Indian negotiations from that time until the treaty of Fort Stanwix
in 1768, being employed in turn by the Pennsylvania, Virginia, and New York
governments, and the Ohio Company. In 1754, he was with Washington at
the surrender of Fort Necessity. Several times he warned the settlements of
impending raids, among other services bringing word of Pontiac's outbreak.
He accompanied Major Rogers as captain of the Indian forces, when the latter
went to take possession of Detroit; and in 1764 commanded a party against
the recalcitrant Delawares. He received for his services several grants of land
in Western Pennsylvania, as well as money. For a detailed biography see
Darlington's *Gist*, pp. 159-175.— ED.

[24] Twigtwees was the English name for the Miamis, a large nation of Algonquian Indians, that were first met by the seventeenth century explorers in
Northern Illinois. But later, they moved eastward into the present state of
Indiana, and settled on the Maumee and Wabash rivers, also on St. Josephs
River in Michigan. The French had had posts among them for two genera-
tions, but from 1723 the English traders had been seeking a foothold in their
midst. Their adherence to the English in 1748 was a blow to the French
trade.— ED.

the Message from Coscosky sent for me to know what I was resolv'd to do, and told me that the Indians at Coscosky were no more Chiefs than themselves, & that last Spring they had nothing to eat, & expecting that they shou'd have nothing to eat at our arrival, order'd that the Council should be held here; now their Corn is ripe, they want to remove the Council, but they ought to stand by their word; we have kept the Twightwees here & our Brethren the Shawonese from below on that account, as I told them the Message that I had sent by Andrew Montour; they were content.

2d. Rain continued; the Indians brought in a good deal of Venison.

3d. Set up the Union Flagg on a long Pole. Treated all the Company with a Dram of Rum; The King's Health was drank by Indians & white men. Towards Night a great many Indians arrived to attend the Council. There was great firing on both sides; the Strangers first Saluted the Town at a quarter of a Mile distance, and at their Entry the Town's People return'd the fire, also the English Traders, of whom there were above twenty. At Night, being very sick of the Cholick, I got bled.

4th. Was oblig'd to keep my bed all Day, being very weak.

5th. I found myself better. Scaiohady[25] came to see me; had some discourse with him about the ensuing Council.

6th. Had a Council with the Wondats, otherways called Ionontady Hagas, they made a fine Speech to

[25] Scarroyahy was an Oneida chief of great influence with the Ohio Indians, especially at Logstown. He remained firm in the English interest, and in 1754 moved to Aughwick Creek, to get away from the French influence, and to protect the settlements. His death the same year, was imputed by his friends to French witchcraft.— ED.

me to make me welcome, & appeared in the whole very
friendly.[16]   Rainy Wheather continued.

7th. Being inform'd that the Wondats had a mind to
go back again to the French, & had endeavour'd to
take the Delawares with them to recommend them to the
French, I sent Andrew Montour to Beaver Creek with
a string of Wampum to inform himself of the Truth of
the matter; they sent a String in answer to let me know
they had no correspondence that way with the Wondats,
and that the aforesaid Report was false.

8th. Had a Council with the Chiefs of the Wondats;
enquired their number, & what occasion'd them to come
away from the French, What Correspondence they had
with the Six Nations, & whether or no they had ever
had any Correspondence with the Government of New
York; they inform'd me their coming away from the
French was because of the hard Usage they received from
them; That they wou'd always get their Young Men to
go to War against their Enemies, and wou'd use them as
their own People, that is like Slaves, & their Goods
were so dear that they, the Indians, cou'd not buy them;
that there was one hundred fighting Men that came over

[16] The Wyandots, or Tobacco Hurons, or Petuns, were of Iroquois stock,
but nearly destroyed by that nation in the seventeenth century. Fleeing westward, they placed themselves under French protection, and, after its founding
in 1701, were settled chiefly about Detroit. In the early eighteenth century
they straggled eastward along the south shore of Lake Erie, and began to open
communication with their ancient enemies, the Iroquois. In 1747, occurred
the rebellion of their chief Nicholas, who built a fort in the marshes of the
Sandusky, and defied the French soldiers. The chiefs whom Weiser met,
were deputies from this party of rebels.

The other edition of Weiser's journal does not mention the "Wondats"
until September 7; and has the following entry for September 6: "One canoe
with goods arrived, the rest did not come to the river. The Indians that brought
the goods found our casks of whiskey hid by some of the traders; they had
drunk two and brought two to the town. The Indians all got drunk to-night,
and some of the traders along with them. The weather cleared up."— ED.

to join the English, seventy were left behind at another Town a good distance off, & they hoped they wou'd follow them; that they had a very good Correspondence with the Six Nations many Years, & were one People with them, that they cou'd wish the Six Nations wou'd act more brisker against the French; That above fifty Years ago they made a Treaty of Friendship with the Governor of New York at Albany, & shewed me a large Belt of Wampum they received there from the said Governor as from the King of Great Britain; the Belt was 25 Grains wide & 265 long, very Curiously wrought, there were seven Images of Men holding one another by the Hand, the 1st signifying the Governor of New York (or rather, as they said, the King of Great Britain), the 2d the Mohawks, the 3d the Oneidos, the 4th the Cajugas, the 5th the Onondagers, the 6th the Senekas, the 7th the Owandaets [Wyandots], the two Rows of black Wampum under their feet thro' the whole length of the Belt to signify the Road from Albany thro' the 5 Nations to the Owendaets; That 6 Years ago, they had sent Deputies with the same Belt to Albany to renew the Friendship.

I treated them with a quart of Whiskey & a Roll of Tobacco; they expressed their good Wishes to King George & all his People, & were mightily pleas'd that I look'd upon them as Brethren of the English.

This Day I desir'd the Deputies of all the Nations of Indians settled on the Waters of Ohio to give me a List of their fighting Men, which they promis'd to do. A great many of the Indians went away this Day because the Goods did not come, & the People in the Town cou'd not find Provision enough, the number was so great.

The following is the number of every Nation, given to

me by their several Deputies in Council, in so many
Sticks tied up in a Bundle:

The Senacas 163, Shawonese 162, Owendaets 100,
Tisagechroanú 40; Mohawks 74; Mohickons 15; Onondagers 35; Cajukas 20; Oneidos 15; Delawares 165; in
all 789."

9th. I had a Council with the Senakas, & gave them
a large String of Wampum, black & White, to acquaint
them I had it in Charge from the President & Council
in Philadelphia to enquire who it was that lately took
the People Prisoners in Carolina, one thereof being a
Great man, & that by what discovery I had already
made I found it was some of the Senekas did it; I therefore desir'd them to give me their Reasons for doing so,
& as they had struck their Hatchet into their Brethren's
Body they cou'd not expect that I could deliver my
Message with a good heart before they gave me Satisfaction in that Respect, for they must consider the English, tho' living in several Provinces, are all one People, &
doing Mischeif to one is doing to the other; let me have
a plain & direct answer.

10th. A great many of the Indians got drunk; one
Henry Noland had brought near 30 Gallons of Whiskey
to the Town. This Day I made a Present to the old
Shawonese Chief Cackawatcheky, of a Stroud, a Blanket,

" The Tisagechroanu were "a numerous Nation to the North of Lake
Frontenac; they don't come by Niagara in their way to Oswego, but right
across the Lake."— *Pennsylvania Colonial Records*, v, p. 85. Probably
they were a party of the Neutral Hurons.

The other edition adds after the Mohawks, "among whom there were 27
French Mohawks." The Mohicans were a wandering tribe, whose original
home was on the banks of the Hudson, and in the Connecticut Valley. Charlevoix found them in the far West in 1721. These on the Ohio were called
"Loups" by the French.— ED.

a Match Coat,[28] a Shirt, a Pair of Stockings, & a large
twist of Tobacco, & told him that the President &
Council of Philadelphia remember'd their love to him
as to their old & true Friend, & wou'd Cloath his Body
once more, & wished he might weare them out so as to
give them an opportunity to cloath him again.   There
was a great many Indians present, two of which were the
big Hominy & the Pride, those that went off with Chartier, but protested against his proceedings against our
Traders.   Catchawatcheky return'd thanks, & some of
the Six Nations did the same, & express'd their Satisfaction to see a true man taken Notice of, altho' he was
now grown Childish.

iith. George Croghan & myself staved an 8 Gallon
Cag of Liquor belonging to the aforesaid Henry Norland,
who could not be prevail'd on to hide it in the Woods,
but would sell it & get drunk himselfe.

I desir'd some of the Indians in Council to send some
of their Young Men to meet our People with the Goods,
and not to come back before they heard of or saw them.
I begun to be afraid they had fallen into the Hands of the
Enemy; so did the Indians.

Ten Warriors came to Town by Water from Niagara;.
We suspected them very much, & fear'd that some of their
Parties went to meet our People by hearing of them.[29]

12th. Two Indians and a white man[30] went out to meet
our People, & had Orders not to come back before they
saw them, or go to Franks Town, where we left the

[28] Stroud was a kind of coarse, warm cloth made for the use of the Indian
trade.   A match-coat was a large loose coat worn by the Indians, originally
made of skins, later of match-cloth.— Ed.

[29] The other edition adds, "coming down the river."— Ed.

[30] His name is given in the other edition as Robert Callender.   He accompanied Croghan and Gist on their journey to the Ohio in 1750-51.— Ed.

Goods. The same Day the Indians made answer to my Request concerning the Prisoners taken in Carolina: Thanayieson, a Speaker of the Senekas, spoke to the following purpose in the presence of all the Deputies of the other Nations (We were out of Doors): ''Brethren, You came a great way to visit us, & many sorts of Evils might have befallen You by the way which might have been hurtful to your Eyes & your inward parts, for the Woods are full of Evil Spirits. We give You this String of Wampum to clear up your Eyes & Minds & to remove all bitterness of your Spirit, that you may hear us speak in good Chear.'' Then the Speaker took his Belt in his Hand & said: ''Brethren, when we and you first saw one another at your first arrival at Albany we shook Hands together and became Brethren & we tyed your Ship to the Bushes, and after we had more acquaintance with you we lov'd you more and more, & perceiving that a Bush wou'd not hold your Vessel we then tyed her to a large Tree & ever after good Friendship continued between us; afterwards you, our Brethren, told us that a Tree might happen to fall down and the Rope rot wherewith the Ship was tyed. You then proposed to make a Silver Chain & tye your Ship to the great Mountains in the five Nations' Country, & that Chain was called the Chain of Friendship; we were all tyed by our Arms together with it, & we the Indians of the five Nations heartily agreed to it, & ever since a very good Correspondence have been kept between us; but we are very sorry that at your coming here we are oblig'd to talk of the Accident that lately befell you in Carolina, where some of our Warriors, by the Instigation of the Evil Spirit, struck their Hatchet into our own Body like, for our Brethren the English & we are of one Body, &

what was done we utterly abhor as a thing done by the
Evil Spirit himself; we never expected any of our People
wou'd ever do so to our Brethren. We therefore remove
our Hatchet which, by the influence of the Evil Spirit, was
struck into your Body, and we desire that our Brethren
the Gov'. of New York & Onas[21] may use their utmost
endeavours that the thing may be buried in the bottomless
Pit, that it may never be seen again — that the Chain of
Friendship which is of so long standing may be preserv'd
bright & unhurt." Gave a Belt. The Speaker then
took up a String of Wampum, mostly black, and said:
"Brethren, as we have removed our Hatchet out of your
Body, or properly speaking, out of our own, We now
desire that the Air may be clear'd up again & the wound
given may be healed, & every thing put in good understanding, as it was before, and we desire you will assist
us to make up everything with the Gov'. of Carolina;
the Man that has been brought as a Prisoner we now
deliver to You, he is yours" (lay'd down the String, and
took the Prisoner by the Hand and delivered him to
me).[22] By way of discourse, the Speaker said, "the
Six Nation Warriors often meet Englishmen trading to
the Catawbas, & often found that the Englishmen
betrayed them to their Enemy, & some of the English
Traders had been spoke to by the Indian Speaker last
Year in the Cherrykees[23] Country & were told not to do

[21] "Onas" was the Indian term for the governor of Pennsylvania — first
used for Penn in his treaty with the Delawares, in 1682.— Ed.

[22] Apparently this was a lad named William Brown, whom Croghan sent
to the settlements, October 20, 1748.— *Pennsylvania Archives*, ii, p. 17.— Ed.

[23] The Catawbas were a powerful Indian tribe of South Carolina, thought
by Powell — "Indian Linguistic Families of North America," in U. S. Bureau
of Ethnology *Report*, 1885-86 — to be of Siouan stock. They inhabited the
western portion of the Carolinas, and were traditional enemies of the Iroquois.
The Cherokees were a settled tribe in North Carolina and Tennessee, and at
this time in the English interest.— Ed.

so; that the Speaker & many others of the Six Nations
had been afraid a long time that such a thing wou'd be
done by some of their Warriors at one time or other."

13th. Had a Council with the Senekas and Onontagers about the Wandots, to receive them into our
Union. I gave a large Belt of Wampum and the Indians
gave two, & everything was agreed upon about what
sho'd be said to the Wandots. The same Evening a
full Council was appointed & met accordingly, & a
Speech was made to the Wandots by Asserhartur, a
Seneka, as follows:

"Brethren, the Ionontady Hagas:[34] last Spring you
sent this Belt of Wampum to Us (having the Belt then in
his hand) to desire us and our Brethren, the Shawonese &
our Cousins the Delawares, to come & meet you in your
retreat from the French, & we accordingly came to your
Assistance & brought you here & received you as our
own flesh. We desire you will think you now join us, &
our Brethren, the English, & you are become one People
with us"— then he lay'd that Belt by & gave them a
very large String of Wampum.

The Speaker took up the Belt I gave & said: "Brethren: the English, our Brothers, bid you welcome & are
glad you escaped out Captivity like: You have been
kept as Slaves by Onontio,[35] notwithstanding he call'd
You all along his Children, but now You have broke the
Rope wherewith you have been tyed & become Freemen,
& we, the united Six Nations, receive you to our Council
Fire, & make you Members thereof, and we will secure
your dwelling Place to You against all manner of danger."
— Gave the Belt.

[34] "Ionontady Hagas" was the Iroquois phrase for the Wyandot or Huron
Indians.— ED.

[35] "Onontio" was the Indian term for the governor of Canada.— ED.

"Brethren: We the Six United Nations & all our Indian Allies, with our Brethren the English, look upon you as our Children, tho' you are our Brethren; we desire you will give no ear to the Evil Spirit that spreads lyes & wickedness, let your mind by easy & clear, & be of the same mind with us whatever you may hear, nothing shall befall you but what of necessity must befall us at the same time.

"Brethren: We are extremely pleased to see you here, as it happened just at the same time when our Brother Onas is with us. We jointly, by this Belt of Wampum, embrace you about your middle, & desire you to be strong in your minds & hearts, let nothing alter your minds, but live & dye with us." Gave a Belt — the Council broke up.

14th. A full Council was Summon'd & every thing repeated by me to all the Indians of what pass'd in Lancaster at the last Treaty with the Twightwees.

The News was confirm'd by a Belt of Wampum from the Six Nations, that the French had imprisoned some of the Six Nations Deputies, & 30 of the Wandots, including Women & Children.

The Indians that were sent to meet our People with the Goods came back & did not see any thing of them, but they had been no further than the old Shawonese Town.

15th. I let the Indians know that I wou'd deliver my Message to morrow, & the Goods I had, & that they must send Deputies with me on my returning homewards, & wherever we shou'd meet the rest of the Goods I wou'd send them to them if they were not taken by the Enemy, to which they agreed.

The same Day the Delawares made a Speech to me & presented a Beaver Coat & a String of Wampum, &

said, "Brother: we let the President & Council of Phila. know that after the Death of our Chief Man, Olomipies, our Grand Children the Shawnese[36] came to our own Town to condole with us over the loss of our good King, your Brother, & they wiped off our Tears & comforted our minds, & as the Delawares are the same People with the Pennsylvanians, & born in one & the same Country, we give some of the Present our Grand Children gave us to the President & Council of Philda. because the Death of their good Friend & Brother must have affected them as well as us."— Gave the Beaver Coat & a String of Wampum.

The same Day the Wandots sent for me & Andrew & presented us with 7 Beaver Skins about 10 lbs. weight, & said they gave us that to buy some refreshments for us after our arrival in Pennsylvania, wished we might get home safe, & lifted up their Hands & said they wou'd pray God to protect us & guide us the way home. I desir'd to know their names; they behav'd like People of good Sense & Sincerity; the most of them were grey headed; their Names are as follows: Totornihiades, Taganayesy, Sonachqua, Wanduny, Taruchiorus, their Speaker. The Chiefs of the Delawares that made the above Speech are Shawanasson & Achamanatainu.[37]

16th. I made answer to the Delawares & said, "Brethren the Delawares: It is true what you said that the

[36] Olumpias was principal chief of the Delawares. He had formerly lived in the Schuylkill Valley, and signed the treaty of purchase by which the Germans came into possession of their lands in that region (1732). He died in the autumn of 1747, the president and council of Pennsylvania being asked to name his successor. The Delawares considered themselves the aborigines of Pennsylvania, and spoke of the Shawnees, whom they had permitted to come among them, as "grandchildren."— ED.

[37] These names are given in the other edition as "Shawanapon and Achamantama."— ED.

People of Pennsylvania are your Brethren & Countrymen; we are very well pleas'd of what your Children
the Shawonese did to you; this is the first time we had
publick Notice given us of the Death of our good Friend
& Brother Olomipies. I take this opportunity to remove the remainder of your Troubles from your Hearts
to enable you to attend in Council at the ensuing Treaty,
& I assure you that the President & Council of Pennsylvania condoles with You over the loss of your King our
good Friend and Brother."— Gave them 5 Strouds.

The two aforesaid Chiefs gave a String of Wampum &
desir'd me to let their Brethren, the President & Council,
know they intended a Journey next Spring to Philadelphia to consult with their Brethren over some Affairs of
Moment; since they are now like Orphan Children,
they hoped their Brethren wou'd let them have their
good Advice and Assistance, as the People of Pennsylvania & the Delawares were like one Family.

The same Day the rest of the Goods arriv'd   the Men
said they had nine Days' Rain & the Creeks arose, &
that they had been oblig'd to send a sick Man back from
Franks Town to the Inhabitants with another to attend
him.

The neighboring Indians being sent for again, the
Council was appointed to meet to-morrow. It rain'd again.

17th. It rained very hard, but in the Afternoon it held
up for about 3 hours; the Deputies of the several Nations
met in Council & I delivered them what I had to say
from the President & Council of Pennsylvania by Andrew
Montour.

"Brethren, you that live on Ohio: I am sent to You
by the President & Council of Pennsylvania, & I am
now going to Speak to You on their behalf I desire You

will take Notice & hear what I shall say."— Gave a
String of Wampum.

"Brethren: Some of You have been in Philadelphia
last Fall & acquainted us that You had taken up the
English Hatchet, and that You had already made use of
it against the French, & that the French had very hard
heads, & your Country afforded nothing but Sticks &
Hickerys which was not sufficient to break them. You
desir'd your Brethren wou'd assist You with some Weap-
ons sufficient to do it. Your Brethren the Presid'. &
Council promis'd you then to send something to You
next Spring by Tharachiawagon,[18] but as some other
Affairs prevented his Journey to Ohio, you receiv'd a
Supply by George Croghan sent you by your said Brethren; but before George Croghan came back from Ohio
News came from over the Great Lake that the King of
Great Britain & the French King had agreed upon a
Cessation of Arms for Six Months & that a Peace was
very likely to follow. Your Brethren, the President &
Council, were then in a manner at a loss what to do. It
did not become them to act contrary to the command of
the King, and it was out of their Power to encourage you
in the War against the French; but as your Brethren
never miss'd fulfilling their Promises, they have upon
second Consideration thought proper to turn the intended
Supply into a Civil & Brotherly Present, and have
accordingly sent me with it, and here are the Goods before
your Eyes, which I have, by your Brethren's Order,
divided into 5 Shares & layd in 5 different heaps, one
heap whereof your Brother Assaraquoa sent to You to
remember his Friendship and Unity with You; & as
you are all of the same Nations with whom we the Eng-

---

[18] This was Weiser's Indian name.— ED.

lish have been in League of Friendship, nothing need be
said more than this, that the President & Council &
Assaraquoa[99] have sent You this Present to serve to
strengthen the Chain of Friendship between us the
English & the several Nations of Indians to which You
belong. A French Peace is a very uncertain One, they
keep it no longer than their Interest permits, then they
break it without provocation given them. The French
King's People have been almost starv'd in old France
for want of Provision, which made them wish & seek
for Peace; but our wise People are of opinion that after
their Bellies are full they will quarrel again & raise a
War. All nations in Europe know that their Friendship
is mix'd with Poison, & many that trusted too much on
their Friendship have been ruin'd.

"I now conclude & say, that we the English are your
true Brethren at all Events, In token whereof receive
this Present." The Goods being then uncover'd I proceeded. "Brethren: You have of late settled the
River of Ohio for the sake of Hunting, & our Traders
followed you for the sake of Hunting also. You have
invited them yourselves. Your Brethren, the President
& Council, desire You will look upon them as your
Brethren & see that they have justice done. Some of
your Young Men have robbed our Traders, but you will
be so honest as to compel them to make Satisfaction.
You are now become a People of Note, & are grown
very numerous of late Years, & there is no doubt some
wise Men among you, it therefore becomes you to Act
the part of wise men, & for the future be more regular

[99] The Virginians were called by the Indians "Long Knives," or more
literally "Big Knives." Ash-a-le-co-a is the Indian form of this word, which
Weiser spells phonetically. He means that the present was sent by both
Pennsylvania and Virginia.— ED.

than You have been for some Years past, when only a few Young Hunters lived here."— Gave a Belt.

"Brethren: You have of late made frequent Complaints against the Traders bringing so much Rum to your Towns, & desir'd it might be stop't; & your Brethren the President & Council made an Act accordingly & put a stop to it, & no Trader was to bring any Rum or strong Liquor to your Towns. I have the Act here with me & shall explain it to You before I leave you;[40] But it seems it is out of your Brethren's Power to stop it entirely. You send down your own Skins by the Traders to buy Rum for you. You go yourselves & fetch Horse loads of strong Liquor. But the other Day an Indian came to this Town out of Maryland with 3 Horse loads of Liquor, so that it appears you love it so well that you cannot be without it. You know very well that the Country near the endless Mountain affords strong Liquor, & the moment the Traders buy it they are gone out of the Inhabitants & are travelling to this Place without being discover'd; besides this, you never agree about it — one will have it, the other won't (tho' very few), a third says we will have it cheaper; this last we believe is spoken from your Hearts (here they Laughed). Your Brethren, therefore, have order'd that every cask of Whiskey shall be sold to You for 5 Bucks in your Town, & if a Trader offers to sell Whiskey to You and will not let you have it at that Price, you may take it from him & drink it for nothing."— Gave a Belt.

"Brethren: Here is one of the Traders who you know to be a very sober & honest Man; he has been robbed of the value of 300 Bucks, & you all know by whom; let,

---

[40] For this proclamation against the sale of liquor to Indians, see *Pennsylvania Colonial Records*, v, pp. 194-196.— ED.

therefore, Satisfaction be made to the Trader."— Gave a String of Wampum.

"Brethren, I have no more to say."

I delivered the Goods to them, having first divided them into 5 Shares — a Share to the Senekas another to the Cajukas, Oneidos, the Onontagers, & Mohawks, another to the Delawares, another to the Owendaets, Tisagech̃roanu, & Mohickons, and the other to the Shawonese.

The Indians signified great Satisfaction & were well pleased with the Cessation of Arms. The Rainy Wheather hasted them away with the Goods into the Houses.

18th. The Speech was delivered to the Delawares in their own Language, & also to the Shawonese in their's, by Andrew Montour, in the presence of the Gentlemen that accompanied me.[a] I acquainted the Indians I was determined to leave them to-morrow & return homewards.

19th. Scaiohady, Tannghrishon, Oniadagarehra, with a few more, came to my lodging & spoke as follows:

"Brother Onas, We desire you will hear what we are going to say to You in behalf of all the Indians on Ohio; their Deputies have sent us to You. We have heard what you have said to us, & we return you many thanks for your kindness in informing us of what pass'd between the King of Great Britain & the French King, and in particular we return you many thanks for the large Presents; the same we do to our Brother Assaraquoa, who joined our Brother Onas in making us a Present. Our Brethren have indeed tied our Hearts to their's. We at present can but return thanks with an empty hand till another opportunity serves to do it sufficiently. We

---

[a] One of those who accompanied Weiser was William, son of Benjamin Franklin, who later became governor of New Jersey. See *Pennsylvania Archives*, ii, p. 15.— ED.

must call a great Council & do every thing regular; in
the mean time look upon us as your true Brothers.

"Brother: You said the other Day in Council if any
thing befell us from the French we must let you know of it.
We will let you know if we hear any thing from the French,
be it against us or yourself. You will have Peace, but it's
most certain that the Six Nations & their Allies are upon
the point of declaring War against the French. Let us
keep up true Corrispondence & always hear of one
another."— They gave a Belt.

Scaiohady & the half King, with two others, had inform'd me that they often must send Messengers to Indian
Towns & Nations, & had nothing in their Council Bag,
as they were new beginners, either to recompense a Messenger or to get Wampum to do the business, & begged
I wou'd assist them with something. I had saved a
Piece of Strowd, an half Barrell of Pow[d]er, 100 pounds
of Lead, 10 Shirts, 6 Knives, & 1 Pound of Vermillion, &
gave it to them for the aforesaid use; they return'd many
thanks and were mightily pleased.[a]

---

[a] Here occurs the following, in the other edition: "The old Sinicker Queen
from above, already mentioned, came to inform me some time ago that she
had sent a string of wampum of three fathoms to Philadelphia by James Dunnings, to desire her brethren would send her up a cask of powder and some
small shot to enable her to send out the Indian boys to kill turkeys and other
fowls for her, whilst the men are gone to war against the French, that they
may not be starved. I told her I had heard nothing of her message, but if
she had told me of it before I had parted with all the powder and lead, I could
have let her have some, and promised I would make inquiry; perhaps her
messenger had lost it on the way to Philadelphia. I gave her a shirt, a Dutch
wooden pipe and some tobacco. She seemed to have taken a little affront
because I took not sufficient notice of her in coming down. I told her she
acted very imprudently not to let me know by some of her friends who she was,
as she knew very well I could not know by myself. She was satisfied, and went
away with a deal of kind expressions. The same day I gave a stroud, a shirt,
and a pair of stockings to the young Shawano, King Capechque, and a pipe
and some tobacco."— ED.

The same Day I set out for Pennsylvania in Rainy Weather, and arrived at George Croghan's on the 28th Instant.[a]

CONRAD WEISER.

PENNSBURY, Septr. 29th, 1748.

[a] The following description of the homeward journey is contained in the other edition:

"The 20th, left a horse behind that we could not find. Came to the river; had a great rain; the river not rideable [fordable].

"The 21st, sent for a canoe about 6 miles up the river to a Delaware town. An Indian brought one, we paid him a blanket, got over the river about 12 o'clock. Crossed Kiskaminity creek, and came that night to the round hole, about twelve miles from the river.

"The 22d, the weather cleared up; we travelled this day about 35 miles, came by the place where we had buried the body of John Quen, but found the bears had pulled him out and left nothing of him but a few naked bones and some old rags.

"The 23rd, crossed the head of the West Branch of the Susquehanna; about noon came to the Cheasts [Chest creek, Cambria County]. This night we had a great frost, our kettle standing about four or five feet from the fire, was frozen over with ice thicker than a brass penny.

"The 24th, got over Allegheny hill, otherwise called mountains, to Frankstown, about 20 miles.

"The 25th, came to the Standing Stone; slept three miles at this side; about 31 miles.

"The 26th, to the forks of the wood about 30 miles; left my man's horse behind as he was tired.

"The 27th, it rained very fast; travelled in the rain all day; came about 25 miles.

"The 28th, rain continued; came to a place where white people now begin to settle, and arrived at George Croghan's in Pennsbury, about an hour after dark; came about 35 miles that day, but we left our baggage behind.

"The 29th and 30th, I rested myself at George Croghan's, in the mean time our baggage was sent for, which arrived.

"The 1st of October reached the heads of the Tulpenhocken.

"The 2nd I arrived safe at my house."— ED.

II

A SELECTION OF GEORGE CROGHAN'S LETTERS AND
JOURNALS RELATING TO TOURS INTO THE WESTERN
COUNTRY—NOVEMBER 16, 1750–NOVEMBER, 1765.

SOURCES: *Pennsylvania Colonial Records*, v, pp. 496-498, 530-
536, 539, 540, 731-735; vi, pp. 642, 643, 781, 782; vii, pp. 267-271.
Massachusetts Historical Collections, 4 series, ix, pp. 362-379. Butler's *History of Kentucky* (Cincinnati and Louisville, 1836), appendix, with variations from other sources. *New York Colonial
Documents*, vii, pp. 781-788.

INTRODUCTORY NOTE

Next to Sir William Johnson, George Croghan was the most prominent figure among British Indian agents during the period of the later French wars, and the conspiracy of Pontiac. A history of his life is therefore an epitome of Indian relations with the whites, especially on the borders of Virginia and Pennsylvania and in the Ohio Valley. A pioneer trader and traveller, and a government agent, no other man of his time better knew the West and the counter currents that went to make up its history. Not even the indefatigable Gist, or the self-sacrificing Post, travelled over so large a portion of the Western country, knew better the different routes, or was more welcome in the Indian villages. Among his own class he was the "mere idol of the Irish traders." Sir William Johnson appreciated his services, made him his deputy for the Ohio Indians, and entrusted him with the most delicate and difficult negotiations, such as those at Fort Pitt and Detroit in 1758-61; and those in the Illinois (1765) by which Pontiac was brought to terms.

Born in Ireland and educated at Dublin, Croghan emigrated to Pennsylvania at an early age and settled just west of Harris's Ferry in the township of Pennsboro, then on the border of Western settlement. The opportunities of the Indian trade appealed to his fondness for journeying and sense of adventure. His daring soon carried him beyond the bounds of the province, and among the "far Indians" of Sandusky and the Lake Erie region, where he won adherents for the English among the wavering

allies of the French. His abilities and his influence over
the Indians soon attracted the attention of the hard-headed
German, Conrad Weiser, who in 1747 recommended him
to the Council of Pennsylvania. In this manner he entered
the public service, and continued therein throughout the
active years of his life.

Croghan was first employed by the province in assisting Weiser to convey a present to the Ohio, whither he
preceded him in the spring of 1748.[1] The following year
he was sent out to report on the French expedition whose
passage down the Ohio had alarmed the Allegheny
Indians, and arrived at Logstown just after Céloron had
passed, thus neutralizing the latter's influence in that
region.[2]

The jealousy of the Indians over the encroachments of
the settlers upon their lands west of the mountains on the
Juniata, and in the central valleys of Pennsylvania,
determined the government to expel the settlers rather
than risk a breach with the Indians. In this task, which
must have been uncongenial to him, Croghan, as justice
of the peace for Cumberland County, was employed during
the spring of 1750.[3] The autumn of the same year,
found him beginning one of his most extensive journeys
throughout the Ohio Valley, as far as the Miamis and
Pickawillany, where he made an advantageous treaty
with new envoys of the Western tribes who sought his
alliance. To Croghan's annoyance, the Pennsylvania
government in an access of caution repudiated this treaty
as having been unauthorized.

---

[1] See Weiser's *Journal, ante*; and *Pennsylvania Colonial Records*, v, pp. 287, 295.

[2] *Ibid.*, v, p. 387; *Pennsylvania Archives*, ii, p. 31.

[3] *Pennsylvania Colonial Records*, v, pp. 432-449.

In 1751 Croghan was again upon the Allegheny, encouraging the Indians in their English alliance, and defeating Joncaire, the shrewdest of the French agents in this region, by means of his own tactics. The next year, he was pursuing his traffic in furs among the Shawnees, but without forgetting the public interest;[4] and the following year finds him assisting the governor and Council at the important negotiations at Carlisle.[5] This same year (1753) Croghan removed his home some distance west, and settled on Aughwick Creek upon land granted him by the Province. His public services were continued early in the next year by a journey with the official present to the Ohio, where he arrived soon after Washington had passed upon the return from the famous embassy to the French officers at Fort Le Bœuf.

The outbreak of the French and Indian War ruined Croghan's prosperous trading business, and brought him to the verge of bankruptcy. While at the same time a large number of Indian refugees, desiring to remain under British protection, sought his home at Aughwick, where he felt obliged to provision them, with but meagre assistance from the Province. To add to his troubles, the Irish traders, because of their Romanist proclivities, fell under suspicion of acting as French spies, and Croghan was unjustly eyed askance by many in authority.[6] Although he was granted a captain's commission to command the Indian contingent during Braddock's campaign, he resigned this office early in 1756, and retired from the Pennsylvania service.

About this time he paid a visit to New York, where his

[4] See *Pennsylvania Colonial Records*, v, p. 568.

[5] *Ibid.*, p. 665.

[6] *Pennsylvania Archives*, ii, pp. 114, 689.

distant relative, Sir William Johnson, appreciating his abilities, chose him deputy Indian agent, and appointed him to manage the Susquehanna and Allegheny tribes.[7] From this time forward he was engaged in important dealings with the natives, swaying them to the British interest, making possible the success of Forbes (1758), and the victory of Prideaux and Johnson (1759). After the capitulation of Montreal, he accompanied Major Rogers to Detroit. All of 1761 and 1762 were occupied with Indian conferences and negotiations, in the course of which he again visited Detroit, meeting Sir William Johnson en route.[8]

Late in 1763, Croghan went to England on private business, and was shipwrecked upon the coast of France;[9] but finally reached London, where he presented to the lords of trade an important memorial on Indian affairs.[10]

Upon his return to America (1765), he was at once dispatched to the Illinois. Proceeding by the Ohio River, he was made prisoner near the mouth of the Wabash, and carried to the Indian towns upon that river, where he not only secured his own release, but conducted negotiations which put an end to Pontiac's War, and opened the Illinois to the British.

A second journey to the Illinois, in the following year, resulted in his reaching Fort Chartres, and proceeding thence to New Orleans. No journal of this voyage has to our knowledge been preserved.

Croghan's part in the treaty of Fort Stanwix (1768) was

---

[7] *Pennsylvania Colonial Records*, vii, p. 355; *New York Colonial Documents*, vii, pp. 136, 174, 196, 211.

[8] Stone, *Life of Johnson*, ii, app., p. 457.

[9] *New York Colonial Documents*, vii, p. 624.

[10] *Ibid.*, p. 603.

rewarded by a grant of land in Cherry Valley, New York. Previous to this he had purchased a tract on the Allegheny about four miles above Pittsburg, where in 1770 he entertained Washington. At the beginning of the Revolution he appears to have embarked in the patriot cause,[11] but later was an object of suspicion; and in 1778 was proclaimed by Pennsylvania as a public enemy, his place as Indian agent being conferred upon Colonel George Morgan. He continued, however, to reside in Pennsylvania, and died at Passyunk in 1782.[12]

In our selection of material from the large amount of Croghan's published work, we have chosen that which exemplifies Western conditions under three aspects: First, the period of English ascendency on the Ohio, which is illustrated by three documents of 1750 and 1751. Secondly, the period of French ascendency, hostility toward the English, and war on the frontiers; for this epoch we publish four documents, ranging from 1754 to 1757. The third period, after the downfall of Canada, is concerned with the surrender of the French posts, and the renewed hostility of the Indians; the two journals we publish for this period present interesting material for the study of Western history. Each deals with a pioneer voyage, for Rogers and Croghan were the first Englishmen (except wandering traders or prisoners) to penetrate the Lake Erie region and reach Detroit. The voyage down the Ohio (1765), with its circumstantial account of the appearance of the country, and its description of Indian conditions and relations, is noteworthy.

Croghan was a voluminous writer. In addition to the official reports of his journeys, he evidently had

[11] Egle, *Notes and Queries* (Harrisburg, 1896) 3d series, ii, p. 348.

[12] For his descendants see Egle, *Notes and Queries*, 3d series, ii, p. 349.

the habit of noting down the events of the day in a simple, straightforward manner, so that many manuscripts of his were long extant, presenting often different versions of the same journey. The earlier antiquaries published these as chance brought them to their notice.[13] The official reports themselves were preserved in the colonial archives, and are published in the Pennsylvania and New York collections. It is believed that this is the first attempt to bring together a selection of Croghan material that in any adequate manner outlines his interesting career. The chronological extent of these journals (from 1750–1765) makes those which follow — Post's of 1758; and Morris's of 1764 — interludes in the events which Croghan describes, thus throwing additional light upon the same period and the same range of territory.

R. G. T.

[13] See Craig, *The Olden Time*, and the heterogeneous mass of Croghan's writings therein printed.

A SELECTION OF GEORGE CROGHAN'S LETTERS AND JOURNALS RELATING TO TOURS INTO THE WESTERN COUNTRY — NOVEMBER 16, 1750 - NOVEMBER, 1765

CROGHAN TO THE GOVERNOR OF PENNSYLVANIA[14]

LOGSTOWN ON OHIO,
December [November] the 16th, 1750.[15]

SIR: Yesterday Mr. Montour and I got to this Town, where we found thirty Warriors of the Six Nations going

[14] The following is reprinted from *Pennsylvania Colonial Records*, v, pp. 496-498; also printed in *Early History of Western Pennsylvania*, app., pp. 21-29. The circumstances under which it was written are as follows: In the autumn of 1750, Conrad Weiser reported to the governor of Pennsylvania that the French agent Joncaire was on his way to the Ohio with a present of goods, and orders from the governor of Canada to drive out all the English traders. Accordingly, Governor Hamilton detailed Croghan and Montour to hasten thither, and by the use of a small present, and the promise ʹof more, to try and counteract the intrigues of the French, and maintain the Indians in the English interest. Upon Croghan's arrival at Logstown, he sent back this reassuring letter. Proceeding westward to the Muskingum, where he had a trading house at a Wyandot village, Croghan met Christopher Gist, agent for the Ohio Company, and with him continued to the Scioto, thence to the Twigtwee town of Pickawillany (near the present Piqua, Ohio). All the way, Croghan held conferences with the Delawares, Shawnees, Wyandots, and Twigtwees, strengthening the English alliance, and promising a large present of goods to be furnished next spring at Logstown. At Pickawillany, he made an unauthorized treaty with two new tribes who sought the English alliance — the Piankeshaws and Weas (Waughwaoughtanneys, French Ouiatonons). Unfortunately no extant document by Croghan adequately chronicles this journey. Our knowledge of it is derived from the journal of Gist (*q. v.*); from incidental notices in the *Pennsylvania Colonial Records*, v, pp. 476, 485-488, 522-525; and from Croghan's brief account, see *post.*— ED.

[15] In the original publication the month was misprinted December for November. See *Pennsylvania Colonial Records*, v, p. 498, where the governor in a message to the Assembly speaks of Croghan's letter from the Ohio of the sixteenth of November. Cf. also, Gist's *Journal*, November 25, 1750, where he says that Croghan had passed through Logstown about a week before.— ED.

to War against the Catawba Indians; they told us that
they saw John Coeur about one hundred and fifty miles
up this River at an Indian Town, where he intends to
build a Fort if he can get Liberty from the Ohio Indians;
he has five canoes loaded with Goods, and is very generous in making Presents to all the Chiefs of the Indians
that he meets with; he has sent two Messages to this
Town desiring the Indians here to go and meet him and
clear the Road for him to come down the River, but they
have had so little Regard to his Message that they have
not thought it worth while to send him an answer as yet.[16]
We have seen but very few of the Chiefs of the Indians
they being all out a hunting, but those we have seen are of
opinion that their Brothers the English ought *to have
a Fort on this River* to secure the Trade, for they think
it will be dangerous for the Traders to travel the Roads
for fear of being surprised by some of the French and
French Indians, as they expect nothing else but a War
with the French next Spring. At a Town about three
hundred miles down this River, where the Chief of the
Shawonese live,[17] a Party of French and French Indians   ·

[16] Philippe Thomas Joncaire (John Cœur), Sieur de Chabert, was a French
officer resident among the Seneca Indians, to whose tribe his mother was said
to belong. Born in 1707, on the death of his father (1740) he succeeded to
the latter's influence and authority among the Iroquois, and made constant
efforts to neutralize the influence of Sir William Johnson, the English agent.
Joncaire had a trading house at Niagara, and his profits from the portage of
goods at that place were great. He accompanied Céloron's expedition in
1749; and in 1753 met Washington at Venango. It was chiefly due to his influence that the Ohio Indians deserted the English at the outbreak of the French
and Indian war. Joncaire led the Iroquois contingent in all the campaigns on
the Allegheny and in Western New York; and when Prideaux and Johnson
advanced against Niagara, he commanded an outpost at the upper end of the
portage. He signed the capitulation of Fort Niagara (1759), but after that
nothing further is known of him.— ED.

[17] The town mentioned here was at the mouth of the Scioto River, and
was known as "the lower Shawnee town."— ED.

surprised some of the Shawonese and killed a man and
took a woman and two children Prisoners; the Shawonese
pursued them and took five French Men and some
Indians Prisoners; the Twightwees likewise have sent
word to the French that if they can find any of their People, either French or French Indians, on their hunting
Ground, that they will make them Prisoners, so I expect
nothing else but a War this Spring; the Twightwees want
to settle themselves some where up this River in order
to be nearer their Brothers the English, for they are
determined never to hold a Treaty of Peace with the
French.   Mr. Montour and I intend as soon as we can
get the Chiefs of the Six Nations that are Settled here
together, to sollicit them to appoint a Piece of Ground
up this River to seat the Twightwees on and kindle a
Fire for them, and if possible to remove the Shawonese
up the River, which we think will be securing those
Nations more steady to the English Interest.   I hope the
Present of Goods that is preparing for those Indians
will be at this Town some time in March next, for the
Indians, as they are now acquainted that there is a Present
coming, will be impatient to receive it, as they intend to
meet the French next Spring between this and Fort De
Troit, for they are certain the French intend an Expedition against them next Spring from Fort De Troit.[18]

[18] Detroit was considered an important station by La Salle; but no permanent post was established there until 1701, when De la Mothe Cadillac built a
fort named Pontchartrain, and established the nucleus of a French colony.
Bands of Indians were induced to settle at the strait; and here (1712) took
place the battle of the Foxes with the Hurons and Ottawas. Detroit continued to be one of the most important French posts in the West until in 1760.
when it was transferred to an English detachment under command of Major
Rogers. See Croghan's *Journal, post.*
The siege of Detroit during Pontiac's War is one of the best known inci-

I hear the Owendaets [Wyandots] are as steady and well
attached to the English Interest as ever they were, so
that I believe the French will make but a poor hand of
those Indians. Mr. Montour takes a great deal of Pains
to promote the English Interest amongst those Indians,
and has a great sway amongst all those Nations; if your
Honour has any Instructions to send to Mr. Montour,
Mr. Trent will forward it to me.[19] I will see it delivered
to the Indians in the best manner, that your Honour's
Commands may have their full Force with the Indians.

I am, with due respects,

Your Honour's most humble Servant,

GEO. CROGHAN.

The Honoble. JAMES HAMILTON,[20] Esq.

———

dents in its history. During the Revolution, the British officials here were
accused of sending scalping parties against the frontier settlements; and in
1779 George Rogers Clark captured at Vincennes its "hair-buying" coms
mandant, General Henry Hamilton. In 1780, an expedition against Detroit wa-
projected by Clark, but failed of organization. Throughout the Indian wars
of the Northwest, Detroit was regarded with suspicion by the Americans, and
its surrender in 1796 secured a respite for the frontier. Its capitulation to the
British by Hull (1812) was a blow to the American cause, which was not repaired until after Perry's victory on Lake Erie, when Proctor evacuated Detroit,
which was regained by an American force (September 29, 1813). Cass was
then made governor. As American settlement came in, the importance of
Detroit as a centre for the fur-trade declined, and its career as a Western commercial city began.— ED.

[19] Captain William Trent was a noted Indian trader, brother-in-law and at
this time partner of Croghan. Although born in Lancaster, Pennsylvania (1715),
he served the colony of Virginia as Indian agent; and in 1752 its governor dispatched him to the Miamis with a present. See *Journal of Captain Trent*
(Cincinnati, 1871). The following year he was sent out by the Ohio Company
to begin a fortification at the Forks of the Ohio, from which in Trent's absence
(April, 1754), the garrison was expelled by a French force under Contrecœur.
Trent was with Forbes in 1758, and the following year was made deputy Indian
agent, assistant to Croghan, and aided at the conferences at Fort Pitt in 1760.
His trade was ruined by the uprising of Pontiac's forces, but he received repara-
tion at the treaty of Fort Stanwix (1768) by a large grant of land between the
Kanawha and Monongahela rivers, where he made a settlement. At the out-

break of the Revolution he joined the patriot cause, and was major of troops raised in Western Pennsylvania.— ED.

[90] Governor James Hamilton was the son of a prominent Philadelphia lawyer, and being himself educated for the legal profession, held several offices in the colony before he was appointed lieutenant-governor in 1748. His administration was a vigorous one, but owing to difficulties with the Quaker party he resigned in 1754. Five years later he was reinstated in the office, and served until the proprietor John Penn came over as governor (1763). His death occurred at New York during the British occupation (1783).— ED.

PROCEEDINGS OF GEORGE CROGHAN, ESQUIRE, AND MR.
ANDREW MONTOUR AT OHIO, IN THE EXECUTION OF
THE GOVERNOR'S INSTRUCTIONS TO DELIVER THE
PROVINCIAL PRESENT TO THE SEVERAL TRIBES OF
INDIANS SETTLED THERE:[21]

May the 18th, 1751.—I arrived at the Log's Town on
Ohio with the Provincial Present from the Province of
Pennsylvania, where I was received by a great number
of the Six Nations, Delawares, and Shawonese, in a very
complaisant manner in their way, by firing Guns and
Hoisting the English Colours. As soon as I came to the
shore their Chiefs met me and took me by the Hand
bidding me welcome to their Country.

May the 19th.— One of the Six Nation Kings from the
Head of Ohio came to the Logstown to the Council, he
immediately came to visit me, and told me he was glad to
see a Messenger from his Brother Onas on the waters of
the Ohio.

May the 20th.—Forty Warriors of the Six Nations

[21]This document is reprinted from *Pennsylvania Colonial Records*, v, pp.
530-536; a portion of it is also to be found in Craig, *The Olden Time* (Pittsburg,
1846), l, p. 136, and a reprint in *Early History of Western Pennsylvania*, app.,
pp. 26-34. As the result of Croghan's Western journey during the winter of
1750-51, and the desire of Pennsylvania to maintain its trade relations with
the Ohio Indians, the Assembly voted £700 to be employed in presents;
and the governor instructed Croghan and Montour to deliver the goods.—
See *Pennsylvania Colonial Records*, v, pp. 487, 518, 525, and Croghan's
account, *post*. The adroitness with which Croghan outwitted the French
officer and interpreter Joncaire, and his influence over the chiefs on the
Ohio, as well as the susceptibility of the Indian nature to the influence
of material goods, are all exemplified in this narrative. It did not result,
however, as Croghan and the governor wished, in inducing the Pennsylvania authorities to construct a fort on the Ohio. The beginnings of that
enterprise were left to the Virginians, but too late to secure the Forks of the
Ohio from being seized by the French.— ED.

came to Town from the Heads of Ohio, with Mr. Ioncoeur
and one Frenchman more in company.

May the 21st, 1751.—Mr. Ioncoeur, the French Interpreter, called a council with all the Indians then present
in the Town, and made the following Speech:

"CHILDREN: I desire you may now give me an answer
from your hearts to the Speech Monsieur Celeron (the
Commander of the Party of Two Hundred Frenchmen
that went down the River two Years ago) made to you.[22]
His Speech was, That their Father the Governor of
Canada desired his Children on Ohio to turn away the
English Traders from amongst them, and discharge
them from ever coming to trade there again, or on any
of the Branches, on Pain of incurring his Displeasure, and
to enforce that Speech he gave them a very large Belt of
Wampum. Immediately one of the Chiefs of the Six
Nations get up and made the following answer:

"FATHERS: I mean you that call yourselves our
Fathers, hear what I am going to say to you. You desire we may turn our Brothers the English away, and not
suffer them to come and trade with us again; I now tell
you from our Hearts we will not, for we ourselves brought
them here to trade with us, and they shall live amongst

---

[22] The commandant of this famous expedition (1749) was Pierre Joseph
Céloron, Sieur de Blainville, born in 1693, and having served a long apprentice-
ship in the posts of the upper country. He commanded an invasion of the
Chickasaw country (1739), and had charge of the post at Detroit in 1742-43,
and again in 1750-54. Fort Niagara was entrusted to him in 1744-47, whence
he was transferred to Crown Point, until his Ohio expedition took place. In
the French and Indian War he held the rank of major, and served on the staff
of the commander-in-chief. He died about 1777. In 1760, the Canadian
authorities characterized him as "poor and brave." Some question has
arisen, whether the leader of this expedition might not have been a younger
brother, Jean Baptiste. For Croghan's visit to the Ohio directly after Céloron's
expedition had passed, see *post*; also, *Pennsylvania Colonial Records*, v,
p. 387, and *Pennsylvania Archives*, ii, p. 31.— ED.

us as long as there is one of us alive. You are always
threatning our Brothers what you will do to them, and
in particular to that man (pointing to me); now if you
have anything to say to our Brothers tell it to him if you
be a man, as you Frenchmen always say you are, and the
Head of all Nations. Our Brothers are the People we
will trade with, and not you. Go and tell your Governor
to ask the Onondago Council If I don't speak the minds
of all the Six Nations;"[28] and then [he] returned the Belt.

I paid Cochawitchake the old Shawonese King a visit,
as he was rendered incapable of attending the Council
by his great age, and let him know that his Brother the
Governor of Pennsylvania was glad to hear that he was
still alive and retained his senses, and had ordered me to
cloathe him and to acquaint him that he had not forgot
his strict Attachment to the English Interest. I gave
him a Strowd Shirt, Match Coat, and a pair of Stockings,
for which he gave the Governor a great many thanks.

May the 22d.— A number of about forty of the Six
Nations came up the River Ohio to Logstown to wait on
the Council; as soon as they came to Town they came to
my House, and after shaking Hands they told me they
were glad to see me safe arrived in their Country after my
long Journey.

May the 23d.— Conajarca, one of the Chiefs of the
Six Nations, and a Party with him from the Cuscuskie,
came to Town to wait on the Council, and congratulated
me upon my safe arrival in their Country.

---

[28] The Onondaga Council was the chief governing body of the Six Nations,
or Iroquois, and since this confederacy assumed supremacy over the Ohio
Indians, it was the chief centre of Indian diplomacy. The council house was
situated on the site of the present town of Onondaga, New York, and was
about eighty feet long, with broad seats arranged on each side. For an early
description see Bartram, *Observations, etc.* (London, 1751), pp. 40, 41.— ED.

May the 24th.— Some Warriors of the Delawares came
to Town from the Lower Shawonese Town, and brought
a Scalp with them; they brought an Account that the
Southward Indians had come to the Lower Towns to
War, and had killed some of the Shawonese, Delawares,
and the Six Nations, so that we might not expect any
People from there to the Council.

May the 25th.— I had a conference with Monsieur
Ioncoeur; he desired I would excuse him and not think
hard of him for the Speech he made to the Indians requesting them to turn the English Traders away and not
suffer them to trade, for it was the Governor of Canada's
Orders[24] to him, and he was obliged to obey them altho'
he was very sensible which way the Indians would receive them, for he was sure the French could not accomplish their designs with the Six Nations without it could
be done by Force, which he said he believed they would
find to be as difficult as the method they had just tryed,
and would meet with the like success.

May the 26th.— A Dunkar from the Colony of Virginia
came to the Log's Town and requested Liberty of the
Six Nation Chiefs to make [a settlement] on the River
Yogh-yo-gaine a branch of Ohio, to which the Indians
made answer that it was not in their Power to dispose of
Lands; that he must apply to the Council at Onondago,

[24] Galissonière, the governor of Canada, who planned Céloron's expedition
to the Ohio, was superseded in the autumn of 1749 by Jacques Pierre de Taffanel,
Marquis de la Jonquière, who continued the policy of the former; he sent orders
to the commandants of the Western posts to arrest all British subjects found in
the Ohio Valley. La Jonquière, who was born in 1686, had served in the
French navy with distinction, and after his first commission as governor of
New France was captured by an English vessel (1747), and kept a prisoner for
more than a year, so that he did not reach his post until 1749. His term of
service was but two years and a half, being terminated by his death in May,
1752.— ED.

and further told him that he did not take a right method, for he should be first recommended by their Brother the Governor of Pennsylvania, with whom all Publick Business of that sort must be transacted before he need expect to succeed.[26]

May the 27th.— Mr Montour and I had a Conference with the Chiefs of the Six Nations, when it was agreed upon that the following Speeches should be made to the Delawares, Shawonese, Owendatts and Twightwees, when the Provincial Present should be delivered them in the Name of the Honourable James Hamilton, Esquire, Lieutenant Governor and Commander-in-Chief of the Province of Pennsylvania, and Counties of New Castle, Kent, and Sussex, on Delaware, in Conjunction with the Chiefs of the Six United Nations On Ohio:

A Treaty with the Indians of the Six Nations, Delawares, Shawonese, Owendatts and Twightwees.

In the Log's Town on Ohio,
Thursday the 28th May, 1751.

PRESENT:

Thomas Kinton,	Joseph Nelson,	
Samuel Cuzzens,	James Brown,	
Jacob Pyatt,	Dennis Sullavan,	Indian Traders.
John Owens,	Paul Pearce,	
Thomas Ward,	Caleb Lamb,	

The Deputies of the Six Nations, Delawares, Shawo-

[26] This Dunkar (or Dunker) was doubtless Samuel Eckerlin one of three brothers who migrated from Ephrata about 1745, and ultimately settled on the Monongahela about ten miles below Morgantown, West Virginia. The Dunkers were a sect of German Baptists that arose in the Palatine about 1708, and migrated to Pennsylvania in 1719. Their formal organization took place at a baptism on the banks of Wissahickon Creek (near Philadelphia) in 1723. There were several divisions of this sect, one of which founded the community

nese, Owendatts, and Twightwees; Mr. Andrew Montour, Interpreter for the Province of Pennsylvania;
Toanshiscoe, Interpreter for the Six Nations.

George Croghan made the following Speech to the
several Nations, when they were met in Council, in the
Name of the Honourable James Hamilton, Esquire,
Governor of the Province of Pennsylvania:

"FRIENDS AND BRETHREN:—I am sent here by your
Brother the Governor of Pennsylvania with this Present
of Goods to renew the Friendship so long subsisting
between Us, and I present you these four strings of Wampum to clear your Minds and open your Eyes and Ears
that you may see the Sun clear, and hear what your
Brother is going to say to you."— Gave 4 Strings of
Wampum.

A Speech delivered the Delawares — in answer to the
Speech they sent by Mr. Weiser three Years ago to his
Honour the Governor to acquaint him of the Death of
their Chief, King Oulamopess²⁶— by George Croghan:

"BRETHREN THE DELAWARES:— Three years ago
some of the Chiefs of your Nation sent me a Message by
Mr. Weiser to acquaint me of the Death of your King, a
man well beloved by his Brethren the English. You told
Mr. Weiser that you intended to visit me in order to
consult about a new Chief, but you never did it. I have
ever since condoled with you for the Loss of so good a
Man, and considering the lamentable Condition you were

of Ephrata. Their tenets were baptism by immersion, a celibate community
life, and refusal to bear arms. The Eckerlin brothers sought a solitary wilderness life, and at first were regarded with favor by the Ohio Indians. A massacre, however, demolished their settlement in 1757. Three of the party were
captured, and sent as prisoners to Canada, and later to France. For details
see Sachse, *German Sectarians of Pennsylvania* (Philadelphia, 1900), ii, pp.
340-359.— ED.

²⁶ For an account of this chief see Weiser's *Journal, ante*.— ED.

in for want of a Chief I present You this Belt of Wampum and this Present to wipe away your Tears, and I desire you may choose amongst Yourselves one of your wisest Counsellors and present to your Brethren the Six Nations and me for a Chief, and he so chosen by you shall be looked upon by us as your King, with whom Publick Business shall be transacted. Brethren, to enforce this on your Minds I present you this Belt of Wampum."— Gave a Belt of Wampum, which was received with the Yohah.[27]

A Speech delivered the Shawonese from the Honourable James Hamilton, Governor of Pennsylvania, by George Croghan:

"BRETHREN THE SHAWONESE:—Three years ago when some of your Chiefs and some Chiefs of the Six Nations came down to Lancaster with our Brethren the Twightwees, they informed me that your People that went away with Peter Chartier was coming back, and since that I hear that Part of them are returned. I am glad to hear that they are coming home to you again that you may become once more a People, and not as you were dispersed thro' the World. I do not blame you for what happened, for the wisest of People sometimes make mistakes; it was the French that the Indians call their Fathers that deceived You and scattered you about the Woods that they might have it in their Power to keep you poor. Brethren, I assure you by this Present that I am fully reconcil'd and have forgot any thing that you have done, and I hope for the future there will be a more free and open Correspondence between us; and now your Brethren

[27] Indians receive a speech with grunts of approval, which the French annalists spelled "ho-ho." Croghan is apparently giving the English rendering of this term.— ED.

the Six Nations join with me to remove any misunderstanding that should have happened between us, that we may henceforth spend the remainder of our days together in Brotherly Love and Friendship. Now, that this Speech which your Brothers the Six Nations joyn with me in may have its full Force on your minds, I present you this Belt of Wampum."— Gave a Belt of Wampum, Which was received with the Yo-hah.

A Speech delivered the Owendatts, from the Honourable James Hamilton, Governor of Pennsylvania, by George Croghan:

"BRETHREN THE OWENDATTS:— I receiv'd a Message by the Six Nations and another by Mr. Montour from you, by both which I understand the French, whom the Indians call their Father, wont let you rest in your Towns in Peace, but constantly threaten to cut you off. How comes this? Are you not a free and independent People, and have you not a Right to live where you please on your own Land and trade with whom you please? Your Brethren, the English, always considered you as a free Nation, and I think the French who attempt to infringe on your Liberties should be opposed by one and all the Indians or any other Nations that should undertake such unjust proceedings.

"Brethren: I am sorry to hear of your Troubles, and I hope you and your Brethren the Six Nations will let the French know that you are a free People and will not be imposed on by them. To assure you that I have your Troubles much at heart I present you this Belt and this Present of Goods to cloathe your Families."— Gave a Belt of Wampum, which was received with the Yo-hah.

A Speech delivered the Twightwees from the Honourable James Hamilton, Esquire, Governor Pennsylvania, by George Croghan:

"BRETHREN THE TWIGHTWEES:— As you are an antient and renowned Nation I was well pleased when you sent your Deputies now three years ago to sollicit our Alliance; nor did we hesitate to grant you your Request, as it came so warmly recommended to us by our Brethren the Six Nations, Delawares, and Shawonese. At your further Request we ordered our Traders to go amongst you and supply you with Goods at as reasonable rates as they could afford. We understand that in obedience to our Commands our Traders have given you full Satisfaction to your Requests. In one your Towns about three Months ago Mr. George Croghan likewise informs us that some more of your Tribes earnestly requested to become our Allies. He and Mr. Montour did receive a writing from you Certifying such your Request, and containing your Promises of Fidelity and Friendship, which we have seen and approve of. Brethren: we have recommended it to our Brethren the Six Nations to give you their advice how you should behave in your new Alliance with us, and we expect that you will follow it, that the Friendship now subsisting between Us, the Six Nations, Delawares, Shawonese, Owendatts, and you, may become as Strong as a great Mountain which the Winds constantly blow against but never overset. Brethren, to assure you of our hearty Inclinations towards you I make you this Present of Goods; and that this Speech which I make you now in Conjunction with the Six Nations may have its full Force on your minds, I present you this Belt of Wampum."— Gave a Belt, which was received with the Yo-hah.

A Speech made to the Six United Nations by George

Croghan in behalf of the Honourable James Hamilton, Esquire, Governor of the Province of Pennsylvania:

"BRETHREN THE SIX NATIONS: Hear what I am going to say to you. Brethren: it is a great while since we, your Brothers the English, first came over the great Water (meaning the Sea); as soon as our ship struck the Land you the Six Nations took hold of her and tyed her to the Bushes, and for fear the Bushes would not be strong enough to hold her you removed the Rope and tyed it about a great Tree; then fearing the winds would blow the Tree down, you removed the Rope and tyed it about a great Mountain in the Country (meaning the Onondago Country), and since that time we have lived in true Brotherly Love and Friendship together. Now, Brethren, since that there are several Nations joined in Friendship with you and Us, and of late our Brethren the Twightwees: Now, Brethren, as you are the Head of all the Nations of Indians, I warmly recommend it to you to give our Brethren the Twightwees your best advice that they may know how to behave in their New Alliance, and likewise I give our Brethren the Owendatts in charge to you, that you may Strengthen them to withstand their Enemies the French, who I understand treat them more like Enemies than Children tho' they call themselves their Father.

"Brethren: I hope we, your Brothers the English, and you the Six Nations, Delawares, Shawonese, Owendatts, and Twightwees, will continue in such Brotherly Love and Friendship that it will be as strong as that Mountain to which you tyed our Ship. Now, Brethren, I am informed by George Croghan that the French obstruct my Traders and carry away their Persons and Goods, and are guilty of many outrageous Practices,

Whereby the Roads are rendered unsafe to travel in, nor can we ask our Traders to go amongst you whilst their Lives and Effects are in such great Danger. How comes this to pass? Don't this proceed from the Pride of Onontio, whom the Indians call their Father, because they don't see his ill Designs? The strong houses you gave him Leave to erect on your Lands serve (As your Brethren the English always told you) to impoverish You and keep your Wives and Children always naked by keeping the English Traders at a Distance, the French well knowing the English sell their Goods cheaper than they can afford, and I can assure You Onontio will never rest while an English Trader comes to Ohio; and indeed if you don't open your Eyes and put a Stop to his Proceedings he will gain his Ends. Brethren: I hope you will consider well what Onontio means or is about to do. To enforce what I have been saying to you on your minds, I present this Belt of Wampum."— Gave a Belt. They received this Belt with Yo-hah.

The Speaker of the Six Nations made the following Speech to Monsieur Ioncoeur in open Council; he spoke very quick and sharp with the Air of a Warrior:

"FATHER — How comes it that you have broke the General Peace? Is it not three years since you as well as our Brother the English told Us that there was a Peace between the English and French, and how comes it that you have taken our Brothers as your Prisoners on our Lands? Is it not our Land (Stamping on the Ground and putting his Finger to John Coeur's Nose)? What Right has Onontio to our Lands? I desire you may go home directly off our Lands and tell Onontio to send us word immediately what was his Reason for using our Brothers so, or what he means by such Proceedings, that we may

know what to do, for I can assure Onontio that We the
Six Nations will not take such Usage. You hear what
I say, and that is the Sentiments of all our Nations; tell
it to Onontio that that is what the Six Nations said to
you."— Gave 4 Strings of black Wampum.

After which the Chief of the Indians ordered the Goods
to be divided, and appointed some of each Nation to
stand by to see it done, that those that were absent might
have a sufficient Share laid by for them.

After which the Chiefs made me a Speech and told me
it was a Custom with their Brothers whenever they went
to Council to have their Guns, Kettles, and Hatchets
mended, and desired I might order that done, for they
could not go home till they had that done. So Mr. Montour and I agreed to comply with their Request, and
ordered it done that they might depart well satisfied.

LETTER OF CROGHAN TO THE GOVERNOR, ACCOMPANYING THE FOREGOING TREATY [28]

PENNSBORO', June 10th, 1751.

MAY IT PLEASE YOUR HONOUR: Inclosed is a Copy of the Treaty held on Ohio by your Honour's Instructions on delivering your Honour's Present to the several Nations of Indians Residing there. I hope your Honour on perusing the Proceedings of the Treaty will find that I have observed your Honour's Instructions in every Speech that I delivered from your Honour. I took all the Pains I could to make the Present have its full Force and Weight with the Indians, and I have the Pleasure of assuring your Honour that the Indians were all unanimously well pleased at your Honour's Speeches, and likewise acknowledged it was a great Present, and the Chiefs of the Six Nations took great Pains with me in dividing it amongst the other nations, that it might have its full force with them, which I assure your Honour it had, for every man I saw there was well satisfied with his share of the Present; the Indians in general expressed a high Satisfaction at having the Opportunity in the Presence of Ionccœur of expressing their hearty Love and Inclinations towards the English, and likewise to assure your Honour what Contempt they had for the French, which your Honour will see by the Speeches they made. Ionccœur-Ionccœur has sent a Letter to your

---

[28] This letter accompanied the preceding journal, and was written on Croghan's return to the settlements. Pennsboro was the district in Cumberland County west of the Susquehanna, in which Croghan's home was at this time situated.— ED.

Honour, which I enclose here.[19] Mr. Montour has exerted himself very much on this occasion, and he is not only very capable of doing the Business, but look'd on amongst all the Indians as one of their Chiefs, I hope your Honour will think him worth notice, and recommend it to the Assembly to make him full Satisfaction for his Trouble, as he has employed all his Time in the Business of the Government. I hope your Honour will recommend it to the Government of Virginia to answer the Speech sent them now in answer to their own Speech sent last Fall, as soon as possible. May it please your Honour, I make bold to send down my Account against the Province for what Wampum I delivered Mr. Montour to make the Speeches last Fall and this Spring, delivered by your Honour's Instructions. Mr. Montour is at my House and will wait on your Honour when you Please to appoint the time. I hope what has been transacted at this Treaty will be pleasing to your Honour, as I am sure the Present had its full Force, and shall defer any farther Account till you have the opportunity of examining Mr. Montour.

    I am your Honour's most obedient, humble Servant,

                        GEORGE CROGHAN.

----

[19] The letter from Joncaire here referred to, is printed in French in *Pennsylvania Colonial Records*, v, p. 540. It consists merely of a statement of the French right to the Ohio Valley, and of the orders of the governor of Canada to permit no English to trade therein.— ED.

January 12th, 1754.— I arrived at Turtle Creek about eight miles from the Forks of Mohongialo, where I was

[20] This journal is reprinted from the *Pennsylvania Colonial Records*, v, pp. 731-735 (also found in *Early History of Western Pennsylvania*, app., pp. 50-53), and chronicles a material change of affairs on the Ohio since the last account written by Croghan. Then the English interests were in the ascendency, and the French were being flouted and driven from the headwaters of the Ohio. But the division in English councils, the supineness of the colonial assemblies, and the active preparation and determined advance of the French into the upper Ohio Valley had had its effect upon the Indian tribes. Two years before, Trent had reported all the Ohio tribes secure in the English interest; but the same year an expedition from Detroit had moved against the recalcitrant Miamis (Twigtwees), and after inflicting a severe chastisement had secured them again to the French control, as Croghan herein reports. Early the following year the French expedition under Marin had advanced to take forcible possession of the Ohio country, and begin the chain of posts necessary to its defense. Presqu'isle and Le Bœuf had been built, while a deputation under Joncaire had seized the English trader's house at Venango, and placed a French flag above it. A large number of the Indians, frightened at this show of force, yielded to the threatenings and cajoleries of the French officers. A small party, hoping to obtain aid from the English colonists, had sent off a deputation in the autumn of 1753 to meet the Virginia authorities at Winchester, and those of Pennsylvania at Carlisle, at both of which conferences Croghan was in attendance· The present which the Assembly of Pennsylvania had voted the preceding May (*Pennsylvania Colonial Records*, v, p. 617) was cautiously given out, most of it consisting of powder and lead; it was feared with reason, that it might be used to the disadvantage of the back settlements. Croghan himself, although using every endeavor to fortify the Indians in the English alliance, lost heart at the dilatoriness of the Pennsylvania Assembly, some of whose members even doubted whether the land invaded did not rightfully belong to the French. He could wish with all his "hart Some gentleman who is an Artist in Philadelphia, and whos Acount wold be Depended on, whould have ye Curiosety to take a Journay in those parts," in order to prove to the province (by means of a map) that the lands on which the French were building lay within their jurisdiction — (*Pennsylvania Archives*, ii, p. 132). Meanwhile, Washington had been sent out by Dinwiddie to summon the French to retire. Croghan, who reached this territory soon after Washington's return, reports in the following journal the conditions on the Ohio.— ED.

informed by John Frazier, an Indian Trader,[11] that Mr.
Washington, who was sent by the Governor of Virginia
to the French Camp, was returned. Mr. Washington
told Mr. Frazier that he had been very well used by the
French General; that after he delivered his Message the
General told him his Orders were to take all the English
he found on the Ohio, which Orders he was determined
to obey, and further told him that the English had no
business to trade on the Ohio, for that all the Lands of
Ohio belonged to his Master the King of France, all
to Alegainay Mountain. Mr. Washington told Mr.
Frazier the Fort where he was is very strong, and that
they had Abundance of Provisions, but they would not
let him see their Magazine; there are about one hundred
Soldiers and fifty Workmen at that Fort, and as many
more at the Upper Fort, and about fifty Men at Weningo
with Jean Coeur; the Rest of their Army went home last
Fall, but is to return as soon as possible this Spring;
when they return they are to come down to Log's Town
in order to build a Fort somewhere thereabouts. This
is all I had of Mr. Washington's Journey worth relating
to your Honour.[12]

[11] A year and a half after this visit of Croghan's, Turtle Creek was the site
of Braddock's defeat. For a description of the battle, and the present appearance of the site, see Thwaites, *How George Rogers Clark won the Northwest
and other Essays in Western History* (Chicago, 1903), pp. 184, 185.

John Frazier, who had his house at the mouth of Turtle Creek, was a Pennsylvania trader, gunsmith, and interpreter, who had lived twelve years at Venango,
whence he was driven by the invading French expedition the summer previous.
He assisted Washington on his journey, and the next year (1754) was commissioned lieutenant of the militia forces under Trent's command, that were
to fortify the Forks of the Ohio.— ED.

[12] The journal of Washington on this journey was on his return printed in
Winchester (only two copies of which edition are known to be extant), also in
London (1754). Frequent reprints have been made, and the journal has been
edited by Sparks, Rupp, Craig, Shea, and Ford. The journal of Gist, who
accompanied Washington, is found in Darlington's *Gist*, pp. 80-87. Croghan
gives a concise summary of Washington's mission and its results.— ED.

On the thirteenth I arrived at Shanoppin's Town, where Mr. Montour and Mr. Patten overtook me.[32]

· On the fourteenth we set off to Log's Town, where we found the Indians all drunk; the first Salutation we got was from one of the Shawonese who told Mr. Montour and myself we were Prisoners, before we had time to tell them that their Men that were in Prison at Carolina were released, and that we had two of them in our Company. (The Shawonese have been very uneasy about those Men that were in Prison, and had not those Men been released it might have been of very ill consequence at this time; but as soon as they found their Men were released they seem'd all overjoyed, and I believe will prove true to their Alliance.[34])

(On the fifteenth Five Canoes of French came down to Log's Town in Company with the Half King[35] au.l some more of the Six Nations, in Number an Ensign, a Serjeant, and Fifteen Soldiers)

[32] John Patten was a Pennsylvania Indian trader, who was captured in the Miami towns by the order of the French governor (1750). He and two companions were carried to Canada, and afterwards sent to France, being imprisoned at La Rochelle, whence they appealed to the English ambassador who secured their release. See *New York Colonial Documents*, x, p. 241. Patten had at this time been sent to the Ohio with the Shawnee prisoners from South Carolina. See *Pennsylvania Colonial Records*, v, pp. 730, 731.— ED.

[34] Six Shawnee Indians had been arrested on suspicion of being concerned in a raid, and confined in the Charleston, South Carolina, jail. On the request of Governor Hamilton, two were released and sent to Philadelphia to be delivered to their kinsfolk. The other four made their escape. See *Pennsylvania Colonial Records*, v, pp. 696-700.— ED.

[35] The Half-King was a prominent Seneca or Mingo chief, whose home was at Logstown. He was faithful to the English interest, and accompanied Washington both on his journey of 1753 and his expedition of 1754; upon the latter, he claimed to have slain Jumonville with his own hand. He was decorated by the governor of Virginia in recognition of his services, and given the honorary name of "Dinwiddie" in which he took great pride. When the French secured the Ohio region, he removed under Croghan's protection to Aughwick Creek, where he died in October, 1756.— ED.

On the sixteenth in the morning Mr. Patten took a Walk to where the French had pitched their Tents, and on his returning back by the Officer's Tent he ordered Mr. Patten to be brought in to him, on which Word came to the Town that Mr. Patten was taken Prisoner. Mr. Montour and myself immediately went to where the French was encamped, where we found the French Officer and the Half King in a high Dispute. The Officer told Mr. Montour and Me that he meant no hurt to Mr. Patton, but wondered he should pass backward and forward without calling in. The Indians were all drunk, and seemed very uneasy at the French for stopping Mr. Patten, on which the Officer ordered his Men on board their Canoes and set off to a small Town of the Six Nations about two Miles below the Log's Town, where he intends to stay till the Rest of their Army come down. As to any particulars that pass'd between the Officer and Mr. Patten I refer your Honour to Mr. Patten.

By a Chickisaw Man who has lived amongst the Shawonese since he was a Lad, and is just returned from the Chickisaw Country[36] where he has been making a Visit to his Friends, we hear that there is a large Body of French at the Falls of Ohio, not less he says than a thousand Men; that they have abundance of Provisions and Powder and Lead with them, and that they are coming up the River to meet the Army from Canada coming down. He says a Canoe with Ten French Men in her came up to the

[36] The Chickasaws were a tribe of Southern Indians, domiciled in Western Tennessee and Northern Mississippi, who were traditional allies of the English and enemies of the French. After the Natchez War in Louisiana, the remnant of that tribe took refuge with the Chickasaws, who inflicted a severe defeat upon the French (1736), capturing and burning a Jesuit priest and several well-known officers.— ED.

Lower Shawonese Town with him, but on some of the English Traders' threatning to take them they set back that night without telling their Business.

By a message sent here from Fort De Troit by the Owendats to the Six Nations, Delawares, and Shawonese, we hear that the Ottoways are gathering together on this Side Lake Erie, several hundreds of them, in order to cutt off the Shawonese at the Lower Shawonese Town.[27] The French and Ottoways offered the Hatchet to the Owendats but they refused to assist them.

We hear from Scarrooyady that the Twightwees that went last Spring to Canada to counsel with the French were returned last Fall; that they had taken hold of the French Hatchet and were entirely gone back to their old Towns amongst the French.

(From the sixteenth to the twenty-sixth we could do nothing, the Indians being constantly drunk.

On the twenty sixth the French called the Indians to Council and made them a Present of Goods. On the Indians Return the Half King told Mr. Montour and me he would take an Opportunity to repeat over to Us what the French said to them.)

On the twenty-seventh We called the Indians to Council, and cloathed the Two Shawonese according to the Indian Custom, and delivered them up in Council with your Honour's Speeches, sent by Mr. Patten, which Mr. Montour adapted to Indian Forms as much as was in his Power or mine.

On the twenty-eighth We called the Indians to Council

---

[27] The Ottawas were an Algonquian tribe, domiciled in Michigan about the posts of Mackinac and Detroit. Faithful to the French interests, they were doubtless acting under the directions of their commandants in gathering to attack the Shawnees on the Scioto.— ED.

again, and delivered them a large Belt of Black and White Wampum in Your Honour's and the Governor of Virginia's Name, by which we desired they might open their Minds to your Honour, and speak from their Hearts and not from their Lips; and that they might now inform your Honour by Mr. Andrew Montour, whom You had chosen to transact Business between You and your Brethren at Ohio, whether that Speech which they sent your Honour by Lewis Montour was agreed on in Council or not, and assured them they might freely open their Minds to their Brethren your Honour and the Governor of Virginia, as the only Friends and Brethren they had to depend on.   Gave the Belt.

After delivering the Belt Mr. Montour gave them the Goods left in my Care by your Honour's Commissioners at Carlisle, and at the same time made a Speech to them to let them know that those Goods were for the Use of their Warriors and Defence of their Country.

As soon as the Goods were delivered the Half King made a Speech to the Shawonese and Delawares, and told them as their Brother Onas had sent them a large Supply of Necessaries for the Defence of their Country, that he would put it in their Care till all their Warriors would have Occasion to call for it, as their Brethren the English had not yet got a strong House to keep such Things safe in.

The Thirty-First A Speech delivered by the Half King in Answer to your Honour's Speeches on delivering the Shawonese:

"BROTHER ONAS:— We return You our hearty Thanks for the Trouble You have taken in sending for our poor Relations the Shawonese, and with these four Strings of Wampum we clear your Eyes and Hearts, that You

may see your Brothers the Shawonese clear as You used
to do, and not think that any small Disturbance shall
obstruct the Friendship so long subsisting between You
and us your Brethren, the Six Nations, Delawares, and
Shawonese. We will make all Nations that are in Alliance with Us acquainted with the Care You have had of
our People at such a great distance from both You and
Us."— Gave Four Strings of Wampum.

A Speech Delivered by the Half King

"Brethren the Governors of Pennsylvania and Virginia: You desire Us to open our Minds to You and to
speak from our Hearts, which we assure You, Brethren, we
do. You desire We may inform you whether that Speech
sent by Lewis Montour was agreed on in Council or not,
Which we now assure You it was in part; but that Part
of giving the Lands to pay the Traders' Debts We know
nothing of it; it must have been added by the Traders
that wrote the Letter;[38] but we earnestly requested by
that Belt, and likewise we now request that our Brother
the Governor of Virginia may build a Strong House at
the Forks of the Mohongialo, and send some of our young
Brethren, their Warriors, to live on it; and we expect
our Brother of Pennsylvania will build another House
somewhere on the River where he shall think proper,
where whatever assistance he will think proper to send

[38] Lewis Montour, a brother of Andrew, had come the previous autumn to
the governor of Pennsylvania, with a message purporting to have been sent by
the Ohio Indians; they were represented as requesting help against the French,
and the building of forts on the river, and as offering all the lands east of the
river to pay the debts of the traders. As the character of those who claimed to
have obtained this treaty was open to suspicion, the governor had sent Croghan
and Andrew Montour to ascertain the truth of the matter. The unauthorized
insertion of so great a land grant, is a good specimen of the methods by which
the unprincipled traders sought to take advantage of the Indians. See *Pennsylvania Colonial Records*, v, pp. 691-696.— ED.

us may be kept safe for us, as our Enemies are just at hand, and we do not know what Day they may come upon Us. We now acquaint our Brethren that we have our Hatchet in our Hands to strike the Enemy as soon as our Brethren come to our assistance."

Gave a Belt and Eight Strings of Wampum.

THE HALF KING,
SCARROOYADY,
NEWCOMER,
COSWENTANNEA,
TONELAGUESONA,
SHINGASS,
DELAWARE GEORGE.

After the Chiefs had signed the last Speech, the Half King repeated over the French Council, which was as follows:

"CHILDREN: I am come here to tell you that your Father is coming here to visit you and to take You under his care, and I desire You may not listen to any ill News You hear, for I assure you he will not hurt You; 'Tis true he has something to say to your Brethren the English, but do you sit still and do not mind what your Father does to your Brothers, for he will not suffer the English to live or tread on this River Ohio;"— on which he made them a Present of Goods.

February the First.— By a Cousin of Mr. Montour's that came to Log's town in company with a Frenchman from Weningo by Land, we hear that the French expect Four Hundred Men every Day to the Fort above Weningo, and as soon as they come they are to come down the River to Log's town to take possession from the English till the rest of the Army comes in the Spring.

The Frenchman that came here in company with Mr.

Montour's Cousin, is Keeper of the King's Stores, and I
believe the chief of his Business is to take a view of the
Country and to see what Number of English there is
here, and to know how the Indians are affected to the
French.

February the Second.—Just as we were leaving the
Log's Town, the Indians made the following Speech:

"Brethren the Governors of Pennsylvania and Virginia: we have opened our Hearts to You and let you
know our Minds; we now, by these two Strings of black
Wampum, desire You may directly send to our Assistance
that You and We may secure the Lands of Ohio, for there
is nobody but You our Brethren and ourselves have any
Right to the Lands; but if you do not send immediately
we shall surely be cut of[f] by our Enemy the French."—
Gave two Strings of black Wampum.

February the Second.— A Speech made by Shingass,
King of the Delawares.

"BROTHER ONAS: I am glad to hear all our People
here are of one mind; it is true I live here on the River
Side, which is the French Road, and I assure you by
these Strings of Wampum that I will neither go down or
up, but I will move nearer to my Brethren the English,
where I can keep our Women and Children safe from the
Enemy."[39]— Gave Three Strings of Wampum.

---

[39] Shingas, brother of King Beaver, was one of the principal leaders of the
Delaware Indians on the Ohio, where he had a town at the mouth of Beaver
Creek. Shortly after this meeting with Croghan, he deserted to the French,
and his braves were a terror to the border settlers. Governor Denny of Pennsylvania set a price of £200 upon his head. Post had a conference with Shingas
(1758), and persuaded him to return to the English alliance; nevertheless, at
the occupation of the Forks of the Ohio by the English, Shingas with his band
retreated to the Muskingum. The last mention of him seems to be in 1762
(*Pennsylvania Colonial Records*, viii, p. 690), and he appears to have died before
the conspiracy of Pontiac (1763), in which his tribe took part.— ED.

The above is a true account of our Proceedings, taken down by Your Honour's most obedient humble Servant.

GEORGE CROGHAN.

3d February, 1754.

The Honourable James Hamilton Esquire.

CROGHAN TO CHARLES SWAINE AT SHIPPENSBURG[40]

AUGHWICK, October 9th, 1755.

DEAR SIR: On my return home I met with an Indian from Ohio who gives me the following accounts: That about 14 days ago he left Ohio, at that time there was about 160 Men ready to set out to harrass the English which probably they be those doing the Mischiefs on Potomack. He says the French Fort is not very strong with men at present. He likewise says that he is of opinion the Indians will do no mischief on the Inhabitants of Pennsylvania till they can draw all the Indians out of the Province and off Sasquehanna, which they are now industriously endeavouring to do; and he desires me as soon as I see the Indians remove from Sasquehanna back to Ohio to shift my quarters, for he says that the French will, if possible, lay all the back frontiers in ruins this Winter.

This man was sent by a few of my old Indian Friends to give me this caution, that I might save my scalps, which he says would be no small Prize to the French;

[40] This letter is reprinted from *Pennsylvania Colonial Records*, vi, pp. 642 643. In the interval between this and the preceding document, momentous events, in which Croghan had a full share, had occurred on the Ohio. The governor of Virginia had engaged him to act as interpreter in Colonel Washington's army — see "Dinwiddie Papers," *Virginia Historical Collections* (Richmond, 1883-84), i, p. 187 — and he had been present at the affair of the Great Meadows. During the period between this and Braddock's expedition, Croghan had been busily employed in bringing over as many Indians as possible to the English cause, and he had led the Indian contingent to Braddock's aid (see *post*). After the battle of the Monongahela, Croghan returned to his home at Aughwick Creek, caring at his own expense for the few Indians who remained firm in the English interest, and planning to defend his settlement by a stockade fort. A bill for his relief (he had lost all of his trading equipment) passed the Pennsylvania Assembly. Although holding no provincial office, his knowledge of the frontier situation was much relied on in this extremity.— ED.

and he has ordered me to keep it private so that I don't
intend to communicate it to any body but you.   I don't
know whether the Governor should be made acquainted
with it or no; but if you judge it proper write the Governor the whole, but at the same time request him to keep
it a secret from whom he had his Information, for if it
should be made publick to the Interpreters or Indians it
may cost me and the man I had my Information from
our Lives; and, moreover, the best method to frustrate
their Designs will be for the Governor not to let the Indians
know that he is acquainted with their design, but to
conduct the affair privately, so as not to let the Indians
know he has any suspicion of them.   Indeed it is only
what I thought the Indians always aimed at, and what
I feared they would accomplish, for I see all our great
Directors of Indian affairs are very short sighted, and
glad I am that I have no hand in Indian affairs at this critical time, where no fault can be thrown on my shoulders.

I am, Dear Sir, Your most humble Servant,

GEO. CROGHAN.

To Mr. Charles Swaine.

P. S.— Sir, if you could possibly Lend me 6 guns with
powder, 20 of lead by the bearer, I will return them in
about 15 days, when I can get some from the Mouth of
Conegochege.   I hope to have my Stockade finished by
the middle of next week.[41]   G. C.

----

[41] This stockade fort was built on Aughwick Creek, where stands the present
town of Shirleysburg.   It was known first as Fort Croghan, then a private
enterprise; but later in the same year (1755), a fort was built on this site by
order of the government and named for General Shirley, commander-in-chief
of the British forces in North America.   Governor Morris wrote, after a visit
to this fort in January, 1756, that seventy-five men were garrisoned therein
(*Pennsylvania Archives,* ii, p. 556).   It was appointed as the rendezvous for
Armstrong's expedition against Kittanning in August of this same year; but by
October 15 the site had grown so dangerous that the governor ordered it abandoned.— ED.

A COUNCIL HELD AT CARLISLE, TUESDAY THE 13TH
JANUARY, 1756 [a]

Present:

The Honourable ROBERT HUNTER MORRIS,[a] Esq.,
Lieutenant Governor.

JAMES HAMILTON   WILLIAM LOGAN, } Esquires.
RICHARD PETERS,

JOSEPH FOX, Esquire, Commissioner,
MR. CROGHAN.

(Mr. Croghan having been desired by the Governor in
December last to do all in his Power to gain Intelligence
of the Motions and Designs of the Indians, and being
now in Town was sent for into Council, and at the Instance of the Governor gave the following Information,
viz: ''That he sent Delaware Jo, one of our Friendly
Indians, to the Ohio for Intelligence, who returned to his
House at Aucquick the eighth Instant, and informed
him that he went to Kittannin} an Indian Delaware Town
on the Ohio about forty Miles above Fort Duquesne, the

---

[a] This account of the situation on the Ohio, obtained from the journey of a
Delaware Indian, is reprinted from *Pennsylvania Colonial Records*, vi, pp. 781,
782. Since the last letter written by Croghan, the Assembly had passed a militia
bill (November, 1755), and Franklin had been commissioned to take charge of
the erection of a series of frontier forts. Croghan was commissioned captain,
and promptly raising a company, entered with zeal upon the work. For his
instructions, see *Pennsylvania Archives*, ii, p. 536.— ED.

[a] Robert Hunter Morris, son of Lewis Morris, prominent colonial statesman
and governor of New Jersey, was born at Morrisania, New York, about 1700.
Having been educated for the law, he became chief-justice of New Jersey (1738),
a position held until his death in 1764. The Pennsylvania proprietors chose
him as lieutenant-governor to succeed Hamilton in 1754; during his term of
office he vigorously defended the province, but engaged in constant disputes
with the Quaker party in the Assembly. The annoyance arising from this
caused him to resign in 1756.— ED.

Residence of Chingas and Captain Jacobs, where he found one hundred and forty Men chiefly Delawares and Shawonese, who had then with them above one hundred English Prisoners big and little taken from Virginia and Pennsylvania.

That there the Beaver," Brother of Chingas, told him that the Governor of Fort Duquesne" had often offered the French Hatchet to the Shawonese and Delawares, who had as often refused it, declaring they would do as they should be advised by the Six Nations; but that in April or May last a Party of Six Nation Warriors in Company with some Caghnawagos" and Adirondacks called at the French Fort in their going to War against the Southern Indians, and on these the Governor of Fort

---

" King Beaver (Tamaque) was head chief of the Delaware Indians on the Ohio, with headquarters at the mouth of Beaver Creek. He was somewhat half-hearted in the English service, but protested his desire to preserve the alliance until after Braddock's defeat, when he openly took the hatchet against the English settlements. Post met him upon the Ohio in 1758, and secured a conditional agreement to remain neutral; but after the English occupation of the Forks of the Ohio, he retreated to the Muskingum, where a town was named for him. He took part in the treaties with the English in 1760 and 1762; but was one of the ring-leaders in the conspiracy of Pontiac (1763). After Bouquet's advance into his territory, he reluctantly made peace, and delivered up his English prisoners. He died about 1770, having in his later years passed under the influence of the Moravian missionaries, and become one of their most eminent disciples.— ED.

" Fort Duquesne, built at the Forks of the Ohio in 1754, was first commanded by Contrecœur; but in the September following the battle of the Monongahela, Captain Dumas, who had distinguished himself at that engagement, was made commandant. He was an officer of great ability, and while he sent out parties against the frontier, his instructions to one subordinate (Donville, captured in 1756) were to use measures "consistent with honor and humanity." Dumas was superseded in 1756 by De Ligneris, who remained in command at Fort Duquesne until ordered to demolish the post, and retire before Forbes's advancing army (1758).— ED.

" The Caghnawagos (Caughnawagas) were the Iroquois of the mission village of that name, about six miles above Montreal.— ED.

Duquesne prevailed to offer the French Hatchet to the Delawares and Shawonese who received it from them and went directly against Virginia.

That neither the Beaver nor several others of the Shawonese and Delawares approved of this measure nor had taken up the Hatchet, and the Beaver believed some of those who had were sorry for what they had done, and would be glad to make up Matters with the English.

That from Kittannin he went to the Log's Town, where he found about one hundred Indians and thirty English Prisoners taken by the Shawonese living at the Lower Shawonese Town from the western Frontier of Virginia and sent up to Log's Town. He was told the same thing by these Shawonese that the Beaver had told him before respecting their striking the English by the advise of some of the Six Nations, and further he was informed that the French had sollicited the Indians to sell them the English Prisoners, which they had refused, declaring they would not dispose of them, but keep them until they should receive Advice from the Six Nations what to do with them.

That there are more or less of the Six Nations living with the Shawonese and Delawares in their Towns, and these always accompanied them in their Incursions upon the English and took Part with them in the War.

That when at Log's Town, which is near Fort Duquesne, on the opposite Side of the River, he intended to have gone there to see what the French were doing in that Fort, but could not cross the River for the driving of the Ice; he was, however, informed the Number of the French did not exceed four hundred.

That he returned to Kittannin, and there learned that Ten Delawares were gone to the Sasquehannah, and as he supposed to persuade those Indians to strike the English who might perhaps be concerned in the Mischief lately done in the County of Northampton.[47]

No more than Seven Indians being as yet come to Carlisle Mr. Croghan was asked the Reason of it; he said that the Indians were mostly gone an hunting, but he expected as many more at least would come in a day or two.

Mr. Weiser was then sent for and it was taken into Consideration what should be said to the Indians.

[47] This reference is to the massacre of the Moravian settlers at Gnaden-hütten, in November, 1755.— Ed.

In November 1748 Mr Hamilton arrived in Philadelphia, Governor of Pennsylvania. During the late war

[48] This paper is reprinted from *New York Colonial Documents*, vii, pp.
267-271. It accompanied a letter from Croghan to Sir William Johnson, in
which he says, "Inclosed you have a copy of some extracts from my old
journals relating to Indian Affairs, from the time of Mr. Hamilton's arrival
as Governour of this Province till the defeat of General Braddock; all which
you may depend upon are facts, and will appear upon the records of Indian
Affairs in ye several Governments."

After Croghan had been commissioned captain by the Pennsylvania authorities, "he continued in Command of one of the Companies he had raised, and
of Fort Shirley on the Western frontier about three months, during which
time he sent, by my direction, Indian Messengers to the Ohio for Intelligence,
but never procured me any that was very material, and having a dispute with
the Commiss[rs] about some accounts between them, in which he thought himself ill-used; he resigned his commission, and about a month ago informed me
that he had not received pay upon Gen[l] Braddock's warrant, and desired my
recommendation to Gen[l] Shirley, which I gave him, and he set off directly
for Albany, & I hear is now at Onondago with S[r] W[m] Johnson."—(Letter of
Governor Morris, July 5, 1756, in *Pennsylvania Archives*, ii, pp. 689, 690.)

Sir William Johnson, having more penetration than the Pennsylvania authorities as to the value of Croghan's services, immediately appointed him his
deputy, in which position he continued for several years. When he presented
himself to the governor's council in Philadelphia, December 14, 1756, "the
Council knowing Mr. Croghan's Circumstances was not a little surprised at
the Appointment, and desired to see his Credentials"— (*Pennsylvania Colonial
Records*, vii, p. 355). In regard to his services during this period, see *New
York Colonial Documents*, vii, pp. 136, 174, 175, 196, 211, 246, 277, 280; *Pennsylvania Colonial Records*, vii, pp. 435, 465, 484, 506; viii, 175; *Pennsylvania
Archives*, iii, pp. 319, 544.

Sir William Johnson was born in Ireland in 1715, came to New York at an
early age, and settled as a trader in the Mohawk Valley. He was adopted into
the Iroquois nation, and acquired power in their national councils, retaining
them in the English interest during the French and Indian War. After the
battle of Lake George, Johnson was rewarded with a baronetcy, and secured
the surrender of Niagara in 1759. From that time until his death in 1774, he
was occupied with Indian negotiations, chief of which was the treaty of Fort
Stanwix (1768).— ED.

all the Indian tribes living on the Ohio and the branches thereof, on this side Lake Erie, were in strict friendship with the English in the several Provinces, and took the greatest care to preserve the friendship then subsisting between them and us. At that time we carried on a considerable branch of trade with those Indians for skins and furrs, no less advantagious to them than to us. (We sold them goods on much better terms than the French, which drew many Indians over the Lakes to trade with us. The exports of skins and furs from this Province at that time will shew the increase of our trade in them articles.)

In August 1749. Governor Hamilton sent me to the Ohio with a message to the Indians, to notifie to them the Cessation of Arms, and to enquire of the Indians the reason of the march of Monsieur Celaroon with two hundred French soldiers through their country (This detachment under Monsieur Celaroon had passed by the Logs Town before I reached it.)

After I had delivered my message to the Indians, I inquired what the French Commander said to them. They told me he said he was only come to visit them, and see how they were cloathed, for their Father the Governor of Canada was determined to take great care of all his children settled on the Ohio, and desired they wou'd turn away all the English traders from amongst them, for their Father would not suffer them to trade there any more, but would send traders of his own, who would trade with them on reasonabler terms than the English.

I then asked them if they really thought that was the intention of the French coming at that time: They answered, yes, they believed the French not only wanted to drive the English traders off, that they might have the trade to themselves; but that they had also a further intention by their burrying iron plates with inscriptions on them in the mouth of every remarkable Creek, which we know is to steal our country from us. But we will go to the Onondago Council and consult them how we may prevent them from defrauding us of our land.

At my return I acquainted the Governor what passed between the Indians and me.

This year the Governor purchased a tract of land on the East of Susquehannah for the Proprietaries, at which time the Indians complained that the White People was encroaching on their lands on the West side of Susquehannah, and desired that the Governor might turn them off, as those lands were the hunting-grounds of the Susquehannah Indians.

At that time the Six Nations delivered a string of Wampum from the Connays, desiring their Brother Onas to make the Connays some satisfaction for their settlement at the Connay Town in Donegal,[49] which they had lately left and settled amongst the Susquehannah Indians which town had been reserved for their use at that time their Brother Onas had made a purchase of the land adjoining to that town.

In November [1750] I went to the country of the Twightwees by order of the Governor with a small present to renew the chain of friendship, in company

[49] Donegal was an old town on the east side of the Susquehanna, situated between the Conewago and Chiques creeks, in the northwestern angle of the county of Lancaster (Scull's *Map of Pennsylvania*), where these Indians have left their name to the Conoy, or as it is now called, Coney Creek. *Memoirs of the Pennsylvania Historical Society*, iv, part ii, p. 210. The Conoys were originally from Piscataway, in Maryland, whence they moved to an island in the Potomac, and, on the invitation of William Penn, removed to the Susquehanna — (*Pennsylvania Colonial Records*, iv, p. 657).— E. B. O'CALLAGHAN.

with Mr Montour Interpreter; on our journey we met M^r
Gist, a messenger from the Governor of Virginia, who
was sent to invite the Ohio Indians to meet the Commissioners of Virginia at the Logs town in the Spring
following to receive a present of goods which their father
the King of Great Britain had sent them.[60] Whilst I
was at the Twightwee town delivering the present and
message, there came several of the Chiefs of the Wawi-
oughtanes and Pianguisha Nations, living on Wabash,
and requested to be admitted into the chain of friendship
between the English and the Six Nations and their allies;
which request I granted & exchang'd deeds of friendship with them, with a view of extending His Majesty's
Indian interest, and made them a small present. On
my return I sent a coppy of my proceedings to the Governor. On his laying it before the House of Assembly, it
was rejected and myself condemned for bad conduct in

[60] Christopher Gist was of English descent, and a native of Maryland. In
early life he removed to the frontiers of North Carolina, where he became so
expert in surveying and woodcraft, that he was employed for two successive
years by the Ohio Company in inspecting and surveying the Western country.
It was on his first journey (1750-51) that he encountered Croghan, when they
travelled together to Pickawillany (the Twigtwee town), and Gist continued via the Scioto River and the Kentucky country back to Virginia. On
the second journey (1751-52), he explored the West Virginia region. His
most noted adventure was accompanying Major George Washington in
the autumn of 1753 to the French forts in Northwest Pennsylvania. Earlier
in the same year, Gist had made a settlement near Mount Braddock, Fayette
County, Pennsylvania, and under the auspices of the Ohio Company was en-
listing settlers for the region. Eleven came out in the spring of 1754, and a
stockade fort was begun. This was utilized during Washington's campaign,
but burned by the French after the defeat at Great Meadows. Gist later
petitioned the Virginia House of Burgesses for indemnity, but his request was
rejected. Both Gist and his son served with Braddock as scouts, and after
his defeat, raised a company of militia to protect the frontiers. After serving
for a time as deputy Indian agent for the Southern Indians, he died in 1759,
either in South Carolina or Georgia. One of his sons was killed at the battle
of King's Mountain (1780).— ED.

drawing an additionall expence on the Government, and the Indians were neglected.[61]

At the time that the Secretary, the provincial Interpreter, with the Justice of Cumberland County and the Sheriff were ordered to dispossess the people settled on the unpurchased lands on the West side of Susquehannah, and on their return to my house, they met a deputation of the Ohio Indians, who told the Secretary that they had heard of a purchase that the Governor had made on the East side of Susquehannah, and said they were intitled to part of the goods paid for that purchase, but had received none, that they were come now to desire the Governor to purchase no more lands without first acquainting them, for that the lands belonged to them as well as to the Onondago Council; on which they delivered a Belt of Wampum, and desired that the Governor might send that Belt to Onondago to let them know that the Ohio Indians had made such a complaint.

In April 1751 the Governor sent me to Ohio with a present of goods; the speeches were all wrote by the Provincial Interpreter M[r] Wiser. In one of the speeches was warmly expressed that the Gov[r] of Pennsylvania would build a fort on the Ohio, to protect the Indians, as well as the English Traders, from the insults of the French. On the Governor perusing the speech he thought it too strongly expressed, on which he ordered me not to make it, but ordered me to sound the Chief of the Indians on that head, to know whether it would be agreeable to them or not. Which orders I obeyed, and did in the presence of M[r] Montour sound the Half King Scarioa-

---

[61] For a copy of this treaty see *Pennsylvania Colonial Records*, v, pp. 522-525. In regard to the rejection thereof, note that the governor in the speech made to the Twigtwees says it is approved. See *ante.*— ED.

day and the Belt of Wampum, who all told me that the
building of a Trading House had been agreed on between
them and the Onondago Council, since the time of the
detachment of French, under the command of Mons'
Celaroon, had gone down the river Ohio, and said they
would send a message by me to their Brother Onas, on
that head.

After I had delivered the present and done the chief
of the business, the Indians in publick Council, by a
Belt of Wampum, requested that the Governor of Pennsylvania would immediately build a strong house (or Fort)
at the Forks of Monongehela, where the Fort Du Quesne
now stands, for the protection of themselves and the
English Traders.

But on my return this Government rejected the pro-
posal I had made, and condemned me for making such
a report to the government, alledging it was not the intention of the Indians. The Provincial Interpreter, who
being examined by the House of Assembly, denyed that
he knew of any instructions I had to treat with the Indians
for building a Trading House, though he wrote the speech
himself, and further said he was sure the Six Nations
would never agree to have a Trading House built there,
and Governor Hamilton, though he by his letter of instructions ordered me to sound the Indians on that head,
let the House know he had given me no such instructions: all which instructions will appear on the Records
of Indian Affairs.[52]

---

[52] The records appear to bear out Croghan's contention that he was given
instructions to discuss the erection of a fort.   See *Pennsylvania Colonial Records*,
v, pp. 522, 529. Historians admit that this neglect of the Indians' request was
attended with evil consequences to the English colonies, and Pennsylvania
in particular. Consult *Pennsylvania Colonial Records*, v, pp. 537, 547, for the
Indian demand and the Assembly's refusal.— ED.

The 12th June 1752, the Virginia Commissioners met the Indians at the Logs Town and delivered the King's present to them. The Indians then renewed their request of having a fort built as the government of Pennsylvania had taken no notice of their former request to them, and they insisted strongly on the government of Virginia's building one in the same place that they had requested the Pennsylvanians to build one; but to no effect.⁵³

In the year 1753 a French army came to the heads of Ohio and built fort Preskle on the Lake, and another fort at the head of Venango Creek, called by the French Le Buff Rivere.⁵⁴ Early in the fall the same year about one hundred Indians from the Ohio came from Winchester in Virginia, expecting to meet the Governor there who did not come, but ordered Coll. Fairfax to meet them. Here again they renewed their request of having a Fort built, and said altho' the French had placed themselves on the head of Ohio, that if their Brethren the English would exert themselves and sent out a number of men, that they would join them, & drive the French army away or die in the attempt.

From Winchester those Indians came to Cumberland County where they were met by Commissioners from Governor Hamilton, and promised the same which they had done in Virginia;⁵⁵ but notwithstanding the earnest solicitations of those Indians, the governments neglected building them a fort, or assisting them with men; believ-

⁵³ On this conference at Logstown see *Dinwiddie Papers*, i, pp. 6, 7, 11, 22; Trent's *Journals*, pp. 69-81; Gist's *Journals*, pp. 231-234.— ED.

⁵⁴ For the French sources of this expedition see *New York Colonial Documents*, x, pp. 255-257; *Pennsylvania Archives* (2d series), vi, pp. 161-164.— ED.

⁵⁵ On the conferences at Winchester and Carlisle (1753), see *Pennsylvania Colonial Records*, v, pp. 657, 665-684.— ED.

ing or seeming to believe that there was no French there; till the Governor of Virginia sent Col. Washington to the heads of Venango Creek, where he met the French General at a fort he had lately built there.

In February 1754, Captain Trent was at the mouth of Red Stone Creek, building a Store house for the Ohio Company, in order to lodge stores to be carried from there to the mouth of Monongehela, by water, where he had received orders in conjunction with Cresap[66] and Gist to build a fort for that Company. This Creek is about 37 miles from where fort Du Quesne now stands.

About the 10th of this month he received a Commission from the Governor of Virginia with orders to raise a Company of Militia, and that he would soon be joined by Col. Washington. At this time the Indians appointed to meet him at the mouth of Monongehela in order to receive a present which he had brought them from Virginia. Between this time and that appointed to meet the Indians he raised upwards of twenty men & found them with arms ammunition & provisions at his own expence. At this meeting the Indians insisted that he should set his men at work, which he did, and finished a Store House,

---

[66] Colonel Thomas Cresap was a Yorkshireman who came to Maryland at an early age. Having settled within the territory in dispute between Maryland and Pennsylvania, he became an aggressive leader of the forces of the former and was arrested by the Pennsylvania sheriff of Lancaster, where he spent several months in jail. Being released by an agreement between the proprietors of the two colonies (1739), he moved westward, and became the first permanent settler of Maryland beyond the mountains, taking up land at a deserted Shawnee village now called Oldtown. An active member of the Ohio Company, he was assisted by the Indian Nemacolin in blazing the first path west to the Ohio (1752). After the defeat on the Monongahela, Cresap moved back to the settlements on Conococheague Creek; but on the return of peace sought his former location, where he became a noted surveyor and frontiersman. His son Michael was likewise a well-known borderer and Indian fighter. For a complete biographical account, see Ohio Archæological and Historical *Publications* (Columbus, 1902), x, pp. 146-164.— ED.

and a large quantity of timber hew'd, boards saw'd, and shingles made. After finishing his business with the Indians he stayed some time in expectation of Col. Washington joining him, as several accounts came of his being there in a few days. As there was no more men to be had here at this time, there being no inhabitants in this country but Indian traders who were scattered over the country for several hundred miles, & no provisions but a little Indian corn to be had, he applied to the Indians, who had given him reason to believe they would join him and cut off the French on the Ohio, but when he proposed it to the Half-King, he told him that had the Virginians been in earnest they wou'd have had their men there before that time, and desired him to get the rest of his men and hurry out the provisions. Agreeable to his instructions he went and recruited his company, but before he could get back, it being 110 miles from here to the nighest inhabitants, the French came and drove his people off.

In June following when the Indians heard that Coll. Washington with a Detachment of the Virginia troops had reached the great Meadows, the Half-King and Scaruady with about 50 men joined him — notwithstanding the French were in possession of this country with six or seven hundred men; so great was their regard for the English at that time.

After the defeat of Col. Washington, the Indians came to Virginia, where they stayed some time, & then came to my house in Pennsylvania and put themselves under the protection of this Government.

As soon as possible they sent messengers to call down the heads of the Delawares and Shawnese to a meeting at my house, and at the same time they desired the Gover-

nor of this Province, or some Deputy from him, to meet
them there to consult what was best to be done.

The Governor sent Mʳ Wiser the Provincial Interpreter; the Chiefs of those Indians came down and met him
and offered their service, but it was not accepted by Mʳ
Wiser. He in answer told them to sit still, till Governor
Morris arrived, and then he himself wou'd come and let
them know what was to be done. They waited there till
very late in the fall, but received no answer, so set off
for their own country.⁵⁷

This Government continued to maintain the Indians
that lived at my house, till the Spring, when General
Bradock⁵⁸ arrived; they then desired Governor Morris
to let me know they would not maintain them any longer;
at which time Governor Morris desired me to take them
to Fort Cumberland to meet General Bradock; which I
did;— On my arrival at Fort Cumberland General Braddock asked me where the rest of the Indians were. I
told him I did not know, I had brought but fifty men
which was all that was at that time under my care, and
which I had brought there by the directions of Governor
Morris. He replied that Governor Dinwiddie told me
[him] at Alexandria that he had sent for 400 which would
be here before me. I answered I knew nothing of that
but that Captain Montour the Virginia Interpreter was
in camp & could inform His Excellency. On which
Montour was sent for who informed the General that
Mʳ Gist's son was sent off some time agoe for some

⁵⁷ The official report of these affairs is in *Pennsylvania Colonial Records*, vi,
pp. 150-161, 180, 181, 186-191.— Ed.

⁵⁸ On Croghan's relations to Braddock's expedition, see *Pennsylvania
Colonial Records*, vi, pp. 372, 381, 398; *New York Colonial Documents*, vi, p.
973.— Ed.

Cherokee Indians, but whether they would come he could not tell. On which the General asked me whether I could not send for some of the Delawares and Shawnese to Ohio. I told him I could; on which I sent a messenger to Ohio, who returned in eight days and brought with him the Chiefs of the Delawares. The General held a conference the Chiefs in company with those fifty I had brought with me, and made them a handsome present, & behav'd to them as kindly as he possibly could, during their stay, ordering me to let them want for nothing.

The Delawares promised, in Council, to meet the General on the road, as he marched out with a number of their warriors. But whether the former breaches of faith on the side of the English prevented them, or that they choose to see the event of the action between General Braddock and the French, I cannot tell; but they disappointed the General and did not meet him.

Two days after the Delaware Chiefs had left the camp at Fort Cumberland, Mr Gist's son returned from the Southward, where he had been sent by Govr Dinwiddie, but brought no Indians with him.

Soon after, the General was preparing for the march, with no more Indians than I had with me; when Coll. Innis[59] told the General that the women and children of the Indians that were to remain at Fort Cumberland, would be very troublesome, and that the General need

[59] Colonel James Innes was an elderly Scotch officer, who had served under the king's commission in the West Indies, and had settled in North Carolina. He commanded the contingent from that colony that came to the assistance of Virginia in 1754. On the death of Colonel Joshua Fry, Dinwiddie appointed Innes, who was his personal friend, to the position of commander-in-chief of the colonial army, of which Washington was acting commandant. Innes got no further than Fort Cumberland, where he remained as commander of the fort, alternately appealing to his former royal commission, and to his colonial authorization, for authority to maintain his rank.— ED.

not take above eight or nine men out with him, for if he took more he would find them very troublesome on the march and of no service; on which the General ordered me to send back all the men, women and children, to my house in Pennsylvania, except eight or ten, which I should keep as scouts and to hunt; which I accordingly did.

(Indorsed: "Rec^d with Sr Wm Johnson's letter of the 25 June, 1757.")

CROGHAN'S JOURNAL, 1760-61 [60]

(October 21st 1760.— In pursuance to my Instructions
I set of[f] from Fort Pitt to join Major Rogers[61] at Presqu'
Isle[62] in order to proceed with the Detachm[t] of his Majes-
tys Troops under his Command to take possession of
Fort D'Troit.)

25th.— I joined Capt Campbell at Venango who was

[60] The years between the last document (1757) and the commencement of this
journey (October 21, 1760) had been eventful ones for the future of American
history. The French and Indian War, which until the close of 1757 had
resulted only in a series of disasters to the English, was pursued with greater
vigor when a change of administration sent able officers and leaders to America.
The evacuation of Fort Duquesne (1758), the capture of Niagara and Quebec
(1759), and the final capitulation of all Canada at Montreal (1760) gave the
mastery of the continent to the English, and opened the portals of the West.
Croghan was occupied during these momentous years with Indian negotiations
of great importance. As deputy of Sir William Johnson, he endeavored to
hold the Six Nations firm in their alliance, to pacify the frontier tribes, and
finally to announce to the expectant savages the English victory, and their
transfer to British authority. In 1757, he was employed in making peace with
the Susquehanna Indians (*Pennsylvania Colonial · Records*, vii, pp. 517-551,
656-714; *Pennsylvania Archives*, iii, pp. 248, 319; *New York Colonial Documents*, vii, pp. 321-324); and made a journey to Fort Loudoun, in Tennessee
to sound the disposition of the Cherokees — (*Pennsylvania Colonial Records*
vii, pp. 600, 630). His influence was relied upon to pave the way for Forbes's
army (1758), and he was present at the important treaty at Easton, in October
of this year — (*Pennsylvania Archives*, iii, p. 429; *Pennsylvania Colonial
Records*, viii, pp. 175-223; Stone, *Life of Sir William Johnson*, ii, p. 389).
Croghan also accompanied Forbes's expedition, and assisted in pacifying the
Allegheny Indians. The journal in *Pennsylvania Archives*, iii, pp. 560-563,
designated as *Journal of Frederick Post from Pittsburgh, 1758*, is really Croghan's
journal, as a comparison with Post's journal for these dates will reveal. Early
in the next year we find Croghan at Fort Pitt, holding constant conferences
with Western Indians (*Pennsylvania Colonial Records*, viii, pp. 387-391; *Pennsylvania Archives*, iii, pp. 671, 744), where he remained until ordered to join
the expedition sent out under Major Rogers to secure possession of Detroit
and other Western posts, included in the capitulation at Montreal. The diary
of this journey, which we here publish, is reprinted from *Massachusetts Historical Collections*, 4th series, ix, pp. 362-379. Other letters of Croghan's are

on his march to Presqu' Isle with a Detachment of the
Royal Americans to join Major Rogers.[63]

found in the same volume, pp. 246-253, 260, 266, 283-289. These all relate
to Indian affairs, and the information being brought in by his scouts and messengers of conditions in the country lying westward — of the agitation, alarm,
and confusion among the Indian hostiles, who were eager to give in their
allegiance to their conquering English "brothers." This journal of the voyage
to Detroit admirably supplements that of Major Robert Rogers, commandant
of the party which Croghan accompanied, whose account has been the standard
authority. It was published in Dublin, 1770, and several reprints have been
issued, the best of which is that edited by Hough, *Rogers's Journals, 1755-1760*
(Albany, 1883).— ED.

[62] Major Robert Rogers, the noted partisan leader, was born in New Hampshire. On the outbreak of the French and Indian War he raised a company
of scouts known as "Rogers's Rangers," who did great service on the New
York frontier. After receiving the surrender of Detroit and attempting in vain
to reach Mackinac, he was again sent to Detroit to relieve the garrison in
Pontiac's War, after which he proceeded against the Cherokees in the South.
About this time he was retired on half pay, and visitea England, where he
published his journals, and a *Concise Account of North America*. In 1766, he
was assigned to the command of the important post of Mackinac, and there
schemed to betray the fort to the Spaniards. The plot having been discovered,
he was tried in Montreal, but secured an acquittal, when he visited England
a second time, only to be thrown into prison for debt. During the Revolution
he led a body of Loyalists, and having been banished from New Hampshire
retired to England (1780), where he died about 1800.— ED.

[63] Fort Presqu' Isle was built by the French expedition under Marin in
the spring of 1753, on the site of the present city of Erie, Pennsylvania. It
was a post of much importance in maintaining the communication between
Niagara, Detroit, and the Forks of the Ohio. After the fall of Fort Duquesne
at the latter site (1758), a large garrison was collected at Fort Presqu' Isle,
and a movement to re-possess the Ohio country was being organized, when
the capture of Niagara (1759) threw the project into confusion. Johnson sent
out a party to relieve the French officer at this place, and a detachment of the
Royal Americans commanded by Colonel Henry Bouquet advanced from Fort
Pitt and took possession of the stronghold. The fort was captured by Indians
during Pontiac's conspiracy (June 17, 1763), as graphically related by Parkman. After this uprising, a British detachment controlled the place until the
final surrender of the posts to the United States in 1796. Within the same
year, General Anthony Wayne, returning from his fruitful campaign against
the Indians, died in the old blockhouse of the fort. Some remains of the
works are still to be seen at Erie.— ED.

[64] Captain Donald Campbell was a Scotch officer who came to America
with the 62nd regiment in 1756, and was made captain of the Royal Americans

26th.— I halted at Venango as the French Creek was very high, to assist in getting the Pack Horses loaded with Pitch & Blanketts for the Kings service over.[64]

27th.— Left Venango.

30th.— Got to La'Bauf.[65]

in 1759. After accompanying this expedition to Detroit (1760), he was left in command of that post (see letter from Campbell, *Massachusetts Historical Collections*, 4th series, ix, p. 382), and when superseded by Major Gladwin remained as lieutenant-commander. Leaving the fort on an embassy, during the Pontiac uprising (1763), he was treacherously seized, made captive, and cruelly murdered by the Indian hostiles. See Parkman, *Conspiracy of Pontiac* (Boston, 1851), chaps. 11 and 14.— ED.

[64] Marin's expedition (1753), that erected forts Presqu' Isle and Le Bœuf, intended to plant a fort at Venango, at the junction of French Creek with the Allegheny; the first detachment sent out for that purpose was, however, repulsed by the Indians. When Washington visited the place (December, 1753), he found the French flag flying over the house of an English trader, Frazier, who had been driven from the spot. The following year, the French built an out-post on this site, and named it Fort Machault. When Post passed by here in 1758, he found it garrisoned by but six men and a single officer; see *post*. The French abandoned Fort Machault in 1759, and early the following spring the English built Fort Venango, about forty rods nearer the mouth of the creek. At the outbreak of Pontiac's War, the latter fort was commanded by Lieutenant Gordon, and he with all the garrison were captured, tortured, and murdered by Indian foes. No fort was rebuilt at this place until late in the Revolution, when Fort Franklin was erected for the protection of the border, being garrisoned from 1788-96. The present town of Franklin was laid out around the post in 1795.— ED.

[65] The French Fort Le Bœuf (technically, "Fort de la Rivière aux Bœufs") was built by Marin (1753) on a creek of the same name, at the site of the present town of Waterford, the terminus of the road which Marin caused to be constructed south from Presqu' Isle. This was the destination of Washington's expedition in 1753, and here he met the French commandant, Legardeur de St. Pierre. The fort at this place was farmed out to a French officer, who superintended the portage of provisions from Lake Erie to the Ohio. Post found it garrisoned by about thirty soldiers in 1758; see *post*. The following year, after the French had abandoned it, a detachment of the Royal Americans went forward from Fort Pitt to occupy this stronghold; and three years later Ensign Price was beleaguered therein by the Indians, and barely escaped with his life after a brave but futile defense. The Indians destroyed Fort Le Bœuf by fire, and it was never rebuilt. In 1794, another fort with the same name was erected near the old site, and garrisoned until after the War of 1812-15. Subsequently the structure was used as a hotel, until accidentally burned in 1868.— ED.

31ˢᵗ.— Arrived at Presqu-Isle where I delivered Major Rogers his Orders from General Monckton.⁶⁶

November 3ᵈ.— Capᵗ Brewer of the Rangers with a Party of forty Men set of[f] by Land with the Bullocks with whom I sent fifteen Indians of different Nations, to pilot them, with Orders that if they met with any of the Indians of the Western Nations hunting on the Lake Side to tell them to come and meet me.⁶⁷ This Evening we loaded our Boats & lay on the shore that night.

4ᵗʰ.— We set sail at seven o'clock in the morning & at three in the afternoon we got to Siney Sipey or Stoney Creek about ten Leagues from Presqu' Isle where we went ashore in a fine Harbour and encamped.⁶⁸

⁶⁶ General Robert Monckton, a son of the Viscount of Galway, began his military career by service in Flanders (1742). He came to America about 1750, and was stationed at Halifax, being appointed governor of Nova Scotia (1754-56). After being transferred to the Royal Americans (1757), he was at the siege of Louisburg in 1758, and the following year was made second in command for the capture of Quebec. Promoted for gallant services, he was placed in control of the Western department, and had headquarters at Fort Pitt, where Rogers had been detailed to seek him for orders with reference to the latter's Western expedition. General Monckton was military governor of New York City, 1761-63. During that time he made an expedition to the West Indies, and captured Martinique. Returning to England he was made governor of Berwick (1766), and later of Portsmouth, which he represented in Parliament. He refused to take a commission to serve against the Americans in the Revolutionary War.— ED.

⁶⁷ Captain David Brewer joined Rogers's Rangers as ensign in 1756, and three years later was promoted for gallant services on Lake Champlain. He appears to have been one of the most trusted officers of this company. Rogers left him to bring up the troops to Presqu' Isle, while he hastened on to Fort Pitt, at the beginning of the expedition; after the capitulation of Detroit, he sent the larger portion of the Rangers back to Niagara under Brewer's command. See Rogers's *Journal*, pp. 152, 198.— ED.

⁶⁸ The topography of this voyage is a disputed question. Croghan is the only contemporary authority who gives details. Siney Sipey is probably the present Conneaut Creek, about twenty miles from Presqu' Isle. Rogers says "by night we had advanced twenty miles." "Sinissippi" is frequently used for Stoney or Rock Creek; the present Rock River, Illinois, claims that for its Indian title. In 1761, Sir William Johnson describes this place (without

5th.— At seven o'Clock in the Morning we set sail, about 12 we were met by about thirty Ottawas who had an English Flag, they saluted us with a discharge of their fire Arms, we then put ashore shook hands and smoked with them out of their Council Pipe, we drank a dram and then embarked, about two o'Clock arrived at Wajea Sipery or Crooked Creek, went ashore in a good Harbour and encamped, this day went about seven Leagues. After we had encamped I called a meeting of all the Indians and acquainted them of the Reduction of Montreal, and agreeable to the Capitulation we were going to take possession of Fort D'Troit, Misselemakinack, Fort St Joseph's &c. and carry the French Garrisons away Prisoners of War & Garrison the Forts with English Troops, that the French Inhabitants were to remain in possession of their property on their taking the Oath of Fidelity to his Majesty King George, and assured them by a Belt of Wampum that all Nations of Indians should enjoy a free Trade with their Brethren the English and be protected in peaceable possession of their hunting Country as long as they adhered to his Majestys Interest. The Indians in several Speeches made me, expressed their satisfaction at exchanging their Fathers the French for their Brethren the English who they were assured were much better able to supply them with all necessaries, and then begged that we might forget every thing that happened since the commencement of the War, as they were obliged to serve the French from whom they got all their necessitys supplyed, that it was necessity and not choice that made them take part with the French which

naming it) as follows: "Encamped in a very good creek and safe harbor. The creek about fifty yards wide, and pretty deep; two very steep hills at the entrance thereof, and the water of it of a very brown color."— ED.

they confirmed by several Belts and Strings of Wampum.
The principal Man of the Ottawas said on a large Belt
that he had not long to live & said pointing to two Men
''those Men I have appointed to transact the Business
of my Tribe, with them you confirmed the Peace last
year when you came up to Pittsburg, I now recommend
them to you, and I beg you may take notice of them and
pity our women and Children as they are poor and naked,
you are able to do it & by pitying their Necessitys you
will win their Hearts.'' The Speaker then took up the
Pipe of Peace belonging to the Nation and said Brother
to Confirm what we have said to you I give you this
Peace Pipe which is known to all the Nations living in
this Country and when they see it they will know it to be
the Pipe of Peace belonging to our Nation, then [he]
delivered the Pipe.

The principal Man then requested some Powder &
Lead for their young Men to stay there and hunt for the
support of their familys as the Chiefs had agreed to go
with us to D'Troit, and a little Flower which I applyed
to Major Rogers for who chearfully ordered it to me as I
informed him it was necessary & would be for the good
of his Majestys Indian Interest.[69]

[69] Rogers in his *Journal* places this meeting with the Ottawas on the seventh
instead of the fifth of November, and locates it at "Chogage" River (formerly
supposed to be Cuyahoga, but now thought to be Grand River). Croghan's
account is more detailed, and probably written at the time; while Rogers's
was written or revised later. "Wajea Sipery" is probably Ashtabula Creek,
which is sufficiently crooked in its course to make this name appropriate.
This is the traditional meeting for the first time, with Pontiac, the Ottawa
chief. Parkman's well-known account of the haughty bearing and dignified
demands of this great Indian contrast markedly with Croghan's simpler and
more literal account. In truth, it may be doubted whether this chief was
Pontiac at all, as he here speaks of himself as an old man. Rogers's *Journal*
makes no mention of any chief, and alludes but incidentally to meeting the
Ottawa band; but in his *Concise Account of North America*, published in

6th.— At seven o'Clock we set sail in Company with
the Indians arrived at a pretty large Creek called Onchuago or fire Creek[70] about twelve Leagues from Crooked
Creek, where we went ashore and incamped, a fine Harbour; here we met seven familys of Ottawa Indians
Hunting.

7th.— We loaded our Boats, sent of[f] the Battoes with
the Provisions and some Whale Boats to attend them,
but before they had got two Miles they were obliged
to return the Wind springing up so high that no Boat
could live on the Lake. Continued our encampment
here the whole day.

8th 9th & 10th.— We continued here the Wind so high
could not put out of the Harbour here the Indians gave
us great quantitys of Bears & Elks Meat, very fat.

11th.— About One o'Clock P.M. set sail, a great swell
in the Lake, at Eight o'Clock got into a little Cove went
ashore & encamped on a fine strand, about six Leagues

London (1765), when the exploits of Pontiac were causing much attention,
Rogers represents himself as having encountered that chief on his way to
Detroit, and that the latter asked him how he dared to enter that country without
his (Pontiac's) leave. This was probably a flight of the imagination, conse-
quent upon his representing the Indian chief as the hero of the tragedy in the
verses he was then preparing, known as *Ponteach, or the Savages of America*
(London, 1766). See Parkman, *Conspiracy of Pontiac*, i, p. 165, ii, appendix
B. The plain, unadorned account of Croghan, and the begging attitude of
the Ottawa chief, are probably more in accordance with historical verity than
Parkman's and Rogers's more romantic accounts.— ED.

[70] The creek which Croghan calls "Onchuago" was Grand River, whose
Indian name was "Chaeaga" (Sheauga), and which is thus designated on
Evans's map of 1755, and Hutchins's map of 1778. Whittlesey, *Early History
of Cleveland* (Cleveland, 1867), thus identifies this stream. Baldwin, in his
"Early Maps of Ohio and the West," Western Reserve Historical Society
Tracts, No. 25, thinks it is the Conneaut Creek; but that would be too far east
to correspond with this description, and the present Geauga County takes its
title from the Indian name of Grand River.— ED.

from fire Creek, where Mr Braam with his party had been some time encamped.[71]

12th.— At half an hour after Eight A.M. set sail, very Calm, about 10 came on a great squawl, the Waves run Mountains high, about half an hour after twelve we got into Gichawaga Creek where is a fine Harbour, some of the Battoes were forced a shore on the Strand and received considerable damage, some of the flower wet and the Ammunition Boat allmost staved to Pieces, here we found several Indians of the Ottawa Nation hunting, who received us very kindly they being old Acquaintances of mine, here we overtook Capt Brewer of the Rangers with his party who set of by Land with some Cattle, this day came about four Leagues.[72]

13th.— We lay by to mend our Boats.

14th.— The Wind blew so hard we could not set of[f]. This day we were allarmed by one of the Rangers who reported he saw about Twenty French within a Mile of our encampment on which I sent out a party of Indians and Major Rogers a party of Rangers, both partys returned without discovering any thing, but the Tracts of two Indians who went out a hunting that Morning.

15th.— Fine Weather   we set sail and at twelve o'Clock

---

[71] Lieutenant Dietrich Brehm (Braam) was a German engineer who came to America in 1756 with the 32nd regiment (later the 60th or Royal Americans). Little is known of his military career, save that in the line of promotion he was captain in 1774, and major in 1783.— ED.

[72] Probably "Gichawaga" was Cuyahoga River, the site of the city of Cleveland, and a well-known rendezvous of the Ottawa Indians, who had a village some miles up its banks. Rogers speaks of it as Elk River, which by some geographers is placed east of Cuyahoga River; but Rogers's list of distances, allowing for much tacking, would indicate that the expedition had by this time certainly come as far beyond Grand River as Cuyahoga.— ED.

came to Sinquene Thipe or Stony Creek[73] where we met
a Wayondott Indian named Togasoady, and his family
a hunting. He informed me he was fifteen days from
D'Troit, that before he left that the French had Accounts
of the reduction of Montreal & that they expected an
English Army from Niagara to D'Troit every day; that
M. Balletre,[74] would not believe that the Governor of
Montreal had Capitulated for D'Troit; that he had no
more than fifty soldiers in the Fort; that the Inhabitants
and Indians who were at home were very much afraid
of being plundered by our Soldiers, and he requested
that no outrage might be committed by our soldiers on
the Indian settlements, as the chief of the Indians were
out a hunting. I assured them that there should be no
plundering. This afternoon we came to Nechey Thepy
or two Creeks,[75] about Nine Leagues from Gichawga,

[73] Stony Creek was the present Rocky River, about five miles west of Cleveland. Near this spot a part of Bradstreet's fleet was wrecked in 1764. See Western Reserve Historical Society *Tracts*, No. 13.— ED.

[74] Marie François Picoté, Sieur de Bellestre, was born in 1719, and when about ten years of age emigrated with his father to Detroit. Entering the army, he held a number of commands — in Acadia (1745-46), and at the Western posts, especially at St. Josephs, where he had much influence over the Indians. In the Huron revolt (1748), his bravery was especially commended. During the French and Indian War he led his Indian allies on various raids — one to Carolina in 1756, where he received a slight wound; and again in New York against the German Flats (1757). Bellestre was present at Niagara about the time it was attacked; but Pouchot detailed him to retire with the detachments from forts Presqu' Isle and Machault to Detroit, and he was commanding at this post when summoned to surrender to Major Rogers. After the capitulation of Detroit, he returned to Canada, and became a partisan of the British power, captured St. John, and defended Chambly against the Americans in 1775-76. He was made a member of the first legislative council of the province.— ED.

[75] The encampment for the night of November 15 seems to have been made between two small creeks that flow into the lake near together, in Dover Township, Cuyahoga County.— ED

high banks all the way & most part of it a perpendicular Rock about 60 feet high.

16th.— a storm so that we could [not] stir.

17th.— The Wind continued very high, stayed here this day, set of[f] the Cattle with an escort of Souldiers and Indians.

18th.— Set Sail came to Oulame Thepy or Vermillion Creek a narrow Channel about Eight foot Water a large Harbour when in, about four o'Clock came to Notowacy Thepy a fine Creek running through a Meadow about Eighteen foot Water, this day came about seven Leagues;[76] here I met three Indians who informed me that the Deputys I sent from Fort Pitt had passed by their hunting Cabin Eight days agoe on their way to D'Troit in order to deliver the Messages I sent by them to the several Indian Nations.

19th.— Several Indians came down the Creek to our encampment and made us a present of dryed Meat, set of[f], came to the little Lake just as the Cattle set over from thence, set of[f] from here came to a Creek which runs through a marchy Meadow, here we encamped, came this day about six Leagues.[77]

20th.— Mr. Braam set of[f] to D'Troit with a Flag of Truce and took with him Mr Gamblin a French Gentleman an Inhabitant of D'Troit.[78] This day about One

[76] Vermillion Creek or River retains its name. The river where the expedition encamped ("Notowacy Thepy") was probably that now known as the Huron River, in Erie County, Ohio. Rogers's *Journal* mentions these rivers without giving names.— ED.

[77] Rogers names the lake here mentioned, as Sandusky. It is difficult to tell from this description whether or not the flotilla entered the inner Sandusky Bay. Probably the encampment for the nineteenth was on the site of the present city of Sandusky, at Mill or Pipe Creek.— ED.

[78] Médard Gamelin was the son of a French surgeon, and nephew of that Sieur de la Jémerais who accompanied La Vérendrye on his Western explora-

o'Clock we met a Canoe of Wayandott Indians who informed us that the Deputys I sent to y* several Nations living about Fort D'Troit, from Fort Pitt had got there and collected the principal Men of the several Nations together and delivered their Messages which were well received by the Indians, and that a Deputation of the Indians were appointed to come with my Deputys to meet us at that place which was the Carrying place from Sandusky into the Lake, we put into the Creek called Crambary Creek, went a shore & encamped to wait the arrival of those Deputys; we sent over the Carrying place to two Indian Villages which are within two Miles of each other to invite the Indians to come & meet the Deputys at our Camp.[19]   This day came four Leagues.

21st.— Towards Evening some of the Indians from the two Villages came to our Camp; just after dark a Canoe came in sight who immediately saluted us with three discharges of their fire Arms, which was returned from our Camp, on their arrival we found them to be the Deputys sent from the Nations living about D'Troit with the Deputys I had sent from Fort Pitt, as soon as they landed the Deputys I had sent introduced them to Maj[r] Rogers, Cap[t] Campbell and myself & said they had delivered their Messages [to] the several Nations

tions, and died (1735) in the wilderness west of Lake Superior.   Gamelin was born two years before this event.   Emigrating to Detroit, he employed himself in raising and training a militia company composed of the habitants, which he led to the relief of Niagara (1759).   There he was captured and kept a prisoner until released by the orders of General Amherst in order to accompany Rogers's expedition, and pacify the settlers at Detroit.   He took the oath of allegiance and remained in that city after its capitulation to the British, dying there about 1778.— Ed.

[19] The present Cranberry Creek is east of Sandusky.   The creek which Croghan mentions was some small tributary of Portage River (the Carrying-place), or directly beyond it.   Rogers says they went "to the mouth of a river in breadth 300 feet," which is evidently Portage River.— Ed.

and that the Indians which came with them were come
to return Answers which we should hear in the Morning & they hoped their answers would be to our expec-
tations   after drinking a dram round we dismissed them
& gave them Provisions.

· 22ᵈ.— About 9 o'Clock the Indians met in Council,
though several of their People were in Liquor, & made
several speeches on strings and one Belt of Wampum all
to the following purport.

BRETHREN: We your Brethren of the several Nations
living in this Country received your Messages well and
return you thanks for sending us word of what has happened and your coming to remove the French Garrison
out of our Country and putting one there of our Brethren
the English; your Conduct in sending us timely notice
of it is a Confirmation of your sincerity & upright intentions towards us and we are sent here to meet you & bid
you welcome to our Country.

Brethren all our principal Men are met on this side
the French Garrison to shake hands with you in Friendship & have determined in Council to abandon the
French Interest and receive our Brethren the English as
our true Friends & establish a lasting Peace with you &
we expect you will support us and supply us with a fire &
open Trade for the Cloathing of our Women and Children.   Then they delivered two strings of Wampum to
the Six Nations and Delawares returning them thanks for
sending Messages to them with the Deputys I had sent
& desired those strings might be delivered to them in
Council.   Then the Speaker spoke on a Belt & said
Brethren the Chief of our young People are gone out a
hunting and our Women have put up their Effects &
Corn for the maintainance of their Children in the Houses

about the French Fort and we know that all Warriors
plunder when they go on those Occasions, we desire by
this Belt that you will give orders that none of our Houses
may be plundered as we are a poor People and cannot
supply our Losses of that kind.   Then I acquainted
them of the Reduction of all Canada and the terms of the
Capitulation & when I met their Chiefs I would tell
them on what terms the Peace was confirmed between
all Nations of Indians and us.   Then Major Rogers gave
them a string by which he took all the Indians present by
the hand & lead them to D'Troit where he would have
a Conference with them and deliver them some speeches
sent by him to them from General Amherst.[80] At 10
o'Clock we embarked sailed about five Leagues and encamp[d] on a Beach.

23[d].— We embarked sailed about three Leagues and
an half to Ceeder point where is a large Bay, here was
a large encampment of Indians Wayondotts and Ottawas
who insisted on our staying there that day as it was raining
and a large Bay to cross which Major Rogers agreed to.[81]

[80] Rogers's *Journal* (p. 191), gives his own speech. He indicates in his
account that the Indians were preparing to resist the English advance; but
Croghan does not mention any such suspicions.

General Jeffrey Amherst was an English soldier of much distinction, who
after serving a campaign in Flanders and Germany, was commissioned by
Pitt to take charge of the military operations in America (1758). His first
success was the capture of Louisburg, followed by the campaign of 1759, when
he reduced Ticonderoga and Crown Point, and moved upon Montreal, which
capitulated the following year. He was immediately made governor-general
of the British in North America, received the thanks of Parliament, and was
presented with the order of the Bath. It was in obedience to his orders that
Rogers undertook this westward expedition. Amherst's later career was a
succession of honors, emoluments, and high appointments in the British army.
He opposed the cause of the colonies during the American Revolution. Late
in life he was field-marshal of the British army, dying (1797) at his estate in
Kent, as Baron Amherst of Montreal.— ED.

[81] Cedar Point is at the southeastern entrance of Maumee Bay. Rogers's
Journal for November 23 says that an Ottawa sachem came into their camp;
possibly this was Pontiac.— ED.

24th.— We set of[f] at Eight o'Clock across the Bay in which is an Island   the day was so foggy that the Drum was obliged to beat all day to keep the Boats together, this day we went about Eight Leagues.   Where we encamped there came to us five Indian familys.

. 25th.— The Indians desired Major Rogers would order the Boats into a Cove as it was likely to be bad Weather & lay by that day & they would send some men to where their Chiefs were collected to hear News which was agreed to.[82]

. 26th.— The Wind blew so hard that we could not put out of the Cove, the Messengers the Indians sent returned and informed us that the French were very angry with the Indian Nations for meeting us and threatned to burn their Towns; that the Commanding Officer would not let us come to D'Troit till he received his Orders from the Governor of Canada and the Capitulation to which we answered the Indians that they might depend on it, that if any damage was done them by the French that we would see the damage repaired.

27th.— In the Morning a Cannoe with two Interpreters and four French came to our Camp with Letters from Monsieur Balletré.   We decamped and came into the mouth of the River where we met the Chief of the Wayondotts, Ottawas & Putawatimes who bid us welcome to their Country and joined us, we went up the River about 6 miles where we met a French Officer who hoisted a Flag of Truce and beat a parley   here we encamped on an Island and sent for the French Officer who delivered his Messages.

---

[82] From the distances given in Rogers's *Journal* it would appear that the expedition encamped the twenty-fifth and twenty-sixth in the entrance of Swan Creek, Monroe County, Michigan, a short distance north of Stony Point.— ED.

28th.— Capt. Campbell was sent of[f] with a Flag of Truce to give M. Balletré his orders to give up the Place soon after we set of[f] up the River and encamped at an Indian Village, at Night Capt. Campbell joined us and informed us that Monsieur Balletré behaved very politely on seeing M. Vaudreuils[**] Orders & desired we would proceed the next day and take possession of the Fort & Country.

29th.— We set of[f] and arrived about twelve o'Clock at the place where we landed and sent and relieved the Garrison.

30th.— Part of the Militia lay down their Arms and took the Oath of Fidelity.

December 1st.— The rest of the Militia layed down their Arms and took the Oath of Fidelity.

2[d].— Lieu[t] Holms was sent of[f] with M. Balletré and the French Garrison with whom I sent 15 English Prisoners which I got from the Indians.

3[d].— In the Morning the principal Indians of 3 different Nations came to my Lodgings & made the following Speech on a Belt of Wampum.

BRETHREN:— You have now taken possession of this Country, While the French lived here they kept a smith to mend our Guns and Hatchets and a Doctor to attend

---

[**] Pierre François Rigault, Chevalier de Cavagnal, Marquis de Vaudreuil, was Canadian born, and entered the military service at an early age. In 1728 he was in the present Wisconsin on an expedition against the Fox Indians; some years later, he was governor at Trois Rivières, and in 1743 was sent to command in Louisiana, where he remained nine years, until appointed governor of New France, just before the outbreak of the French and Indian War. As the last French governor of Canada, his term of service was embittered by quarrels with the French generals, and disasters to French arms. After his capitulation at Montreal, he went to France, only to be arrested, thrown into the Bastile, and tried for malfeasance in office. He succeeded in securing an acquittal (1763); but, broken by disappointments and enmities, died the following year.— ED.

our People when sick, we expect you will do the same
and as no doubt you have something to say to us from
the English General and Sir William Johnson we would
be glad [to know] how soon you would go on business as
this is our hunting season.

Fort D'Troit December 4th 1760. We met the Wayondotts, Putawatimes and Ottawas[84] in the Council House,
with several of the principal Men of the Ohio Indians
who accompanied his Majestys Forces there when the
following speeches were made to them.

BRETHREN CHIEFS & WARRIORS OF THE SEVERAL
NATIONS NOW PRESENT: You have been made acquainted with the success of his Majestys Arms under the Command of his Excellency General Amherst and the Reduction of all Canada & now you are Eye Witnesses to the
surrender of this place agreeable to the Capitulation as I
sent you word before the arrival of his Majestys Troops;
you see now your Fathers are become British Subjects,
you are therefore desired to look on them as such & not
to think them a separate People; and as long as you ad-
here to his Majestys Interest and behave yoursel[ves]
well to all his subjects as faithfull allies, you may depend
on having a free open Trade with your Brethren the
English & be protected by his Majesty King George now
your Father & my Master.— A Belt.

BRETHREN: At a Conference held with several Chiefs &
Deputys of your several Nations at Pittsburg this Summer, you told me that all our Prisoners which have been
taken since the War, yet remaining in your possession

---

[84] The Potawotami Indians are an Algonquian tribe, being fir₁ encountered
by French explorers on the borders of Green Bay; but later, they had villages
at Detroit, St. Josephs River (southeast Michigan), and Milwaukee. They
were devoted to the French interests, and easily attracted to the vicinity of
the French posts. For the Wyandots (Hurons) and Ottawas, see *ante.*— ED.

were then set at Liberty to return home if they pleased, now I have received by Major Rogers the Commanding Officer here, General Amherst and Sir William Johnson's Orders to demand due performance of your promise & desire that you may forthwith deliver them up as that is the only way you can convince us of your sincerity and future intentions of living in Friendship with all his Majestys Subjects in the several British Colonies in America.— A belt.

BRETHREN: On Condition of your performance of what has been said to you I by this Belt renew and brighten the Ancient Chain of Friendship between his Majestys Subjects, the Six United Nations and our Brethren of the several Western Nations to the Sun setting and wish it may continue as long as the Sun and Moon give light.— A belt.

BRETHREN: As my orders are to return to Pittsburg I now recommend Capt. Campbel to you as he is appointed by his Majestys Commander in Chief to be Governour of this place, with him you must transact the publick business and you may depend he will do you all the service in his power and see that justice is done you in Trade.— A belt.

BRETHREN CHIEFS AND WARRIORS: As the Ancient Friendship that long subsisted between our Ancestors is now renewed I was[h] the Blood of[f] the Earth, that has been shed since the present War, that you may smell the sweet scent of the Springing Herbs & bury the War Hatchet in the Bottomless Pitt.— A belt.

BRETHREN: I know your Warriors have all a martial spirit & must be employed at War & if they want diversion after the fatigue of hunting there is your natural Enemies the Cherookees with whom you have been long at War, there your Warriors will find diversion & there they may go, they have no other place to go, as all Nations else are become the subjects of Great Britain.— A belt.

BRETHREN: As I command this Garrison for his Majesty King George I must acquaint you that all the Settlers living in this Country are my Master's subjects therefore I take this opportunity to desire you our Brethren of the several Nations not to take any of their Effects from them by force, nor kill or steal any of their Cattle, as I shall look on any insult of that kind as if done to me, as they are under my protection.   I desire you will encourage your young Men to hunt and bring their Meat to me for which they shall be paid in Powder and Lead.—A belt.

Major Rogers acquainted the Indians that he was going to Misselemaknach to relieve that Garrison and desired some of their young Men to go with him, whom he would pay for their Services and that he was sending an Officer to S$^{t.}$ Josephs and the Waweoughtannes[ss] to relieve their Post & bring of[f] the French Garrisons & desired they

[ss] The French fort of St. Josephs was established early in the eighteenth century, on the right bank of the river of that name, about a mile from the present city of Niles, Michigan. Its commandant was the "farmer" of the post — that is, he was entitled to what profits he could win from the Indian trade, and paid his own expenses. After the British took possession of this fort, it was garrisoned by a small detachment of the Royal Americans. When Pontiac's War broke out, but fourteen soldiers were at the place, with Ensign Schlosser in command. The fort was captured and eleven of the garrison killed, the rest being carried prisoners to Detroit. During the Revolution, Fort St. Josephs was three times taken from the British — twice by parties from the Illinois led by French traders (in 1777, and again in 1778); and in 1781, a Spanish expedition set out from St. Louis to capture the stronghold, and take possession of this region for Spain. See Mason, *Chapters from Illinois History* (Chicago, 1901). The United States failed to garrison St. Josephs when the British forts were surrendered in 1796, and built instead (1804) Fort Dearborn at Chicago.

Ouiatonon (Waweoughtannes) was situated at the head of navigation on the Wabash River, not far from the present city of Lafayette, Indiana. The French founded this post about 1719, among a tribe of the same name (called would send some of their young Men with him who should likewise be paid for their services.— A belt.

Then we acquainted them by a string that as they had requested a Smith to mend their Guns as usual & the Doctor to attend their sick that it was granted till the Generals pleasure was known.— A string.

December the 4ᵗʰ.— A Principal Man of the Wayondotts spoke and said Brethren we have heard and considered what you said to us yesterday and are met this day to return you an answer agreeable to our promise.

The Wayondott Speaker addressed his speech to Major Rogers, Capt Campbel and myself.

BRETHREN: We have heard what you said to us yesterday, we are like a lost People, as we have lost many of our principal Men, & we hope you will excuse us if we should make any Mistakes, but we assure you our Hearts are good towards our Brethren the English   when your General and Sir William Johnson took all Canada they ordered you to send us Word, we received your Messages & we see, by your removing the French in the manner you have from here, that what you said to us by your Messengers is true.   Brethren be it so, and continue as you have begun for the good of us all.   All the Indians in this Country are Allies to each other and as one People, what you have said to us is very agreeable & we hope you will continue to strengthen the Ancient Chain of Friendship.—A belt.

Weas by the English); and kept an officer stationed there until its surrender to the English party sent out by Rogers (1761). The small garrison under command of Lieutenant Jenkins was captured at the outbreak of Pontiac's conspiracy; but through the intervention of French traders their lives were spared, while the fort was destroyed by burning, and never rebuilt. See Craig, "Ouiatonon," Indiana Historical Society *Collections* (Indianapolis, 1886), v, ii. See also Croghan's description when he passed here five years later, *post.*— ED.

You desired us yesterday to perform our promise & deliver up your Prisoners, it is very true we did promise to deliver them up, and have since delivered up many, what would you have us do there is very few here at present they are all yours & you shall have them as soon as possible tho' we do not choose to force them that have a mind to live with us.— A belt.

BRETHREN: Yesterday you renewed and brightened the Ancient Chain of Friendship between our Ancestors the Six Nations & you. Brethren I am glad to hear that you our Brethren the English and the Six Nations have renewed and strengthened the Ancient Chain of Friendship subsisting between us, & we assure you that if ever it be broke it will be on your side, and it is in your power as you are an able People to preserve it, for while this Friendship is preserved we shall be a strong Body of People, and do not let a small matter make a difference between us.— A belt.

BRETHREN: Yesterday you desired us to be strong and preserve the Chain of Friendship free from rust, Brethren look on this Friendship Belt where we have the Six Nations and you by the hand; this Belt was delivered us by our Brethren the English & Six Nations when first you came over the great Water, that we might go & pass to Trade where we pleased & you likewise with us, this Belt we preserve that our Children unborn may know.

BRETHREN: We heard what you said yesterday it was all good but we expected two things more, first that you would have put it out of the power of the Evil Spirit to hurt the Chain of Friendship, and secondly that you would have settled the prices of goods that we might have them cheaper from you than we had from the

French as you have often told us. Brethren you have renewed the Old Friendship yesterday, the Ancient Chain is now become bright, it is new to our young Men, and Brethren we now take a faster hold of it than ever we had & hope it may be preserved free from rust to our posterity.— A belt [of] 9 rows.

BRETHREN: This Belt is from our Warriors in behalf of our Women & Children and they desire of us to request of you to be strong & see that they have goods cheap from your Traders & not be oppressed as they have been by the French.[86]— A belt [of] 7 rows.

BRETHREN:—Shewing two Medals those we had from you as a token that we might remember our Friendship whenever we should meet in the Woods and smoke under the Tree of Peace, we preserved your token and hope you remember your promise, it was then said that this Country was given by God to the Indians & that you would preserve it for our joint use where we first met under a shade as there were no Houses in those times.

The same speaker addressing himself to the six Nations.

BRETHREN: I am very glad to hear what our Brethren the English have said to us, and I now send this string by you, and take the Chiefs of the six Nations by the hand to come here to Council next spring.

Brother addressing himself to me

You have been employed by the King and Sir William Johnson amongst many Nations of Indians in settling this Peace, now you are sent here where our Council fire is,

---

[86] The speculation and corruption of the French officers at the Western posts, was notorious. Bellestre was not free from suspicions of taking advantage of his official position to exploit the Indian trade. See Farmer, *History of Detroit and Michigan* (Detroit, 1884), p. 766.— ED.

the Smoke of which ascends to the Skies   you are going
away and all Nations to the Sun sitting are to meet here
to see their Brethren the English in possession of this
place and we desire that you may stay here till that Council, that you may take your Master Word of what is to
be transacted here.— A belt.

BRETHREN: By this String we request you will consider it will be difficult for us to understand each other.
It would be agreeable to us if you would continue our old
Interpreter as he understands our Language well.— A
string.

December the 5ᵗʰ the Principal Man of the Putawatimes
spoke

BRETHREN: Yesterday our Uncles of the Six Nations
spoke to you for us all; do not be surprised at it, they have
more understanding in Council affairs than us, we have
employed them to speak for us all, and Confirm what
they have said by this Belt.— A belt.

BRETHREN: Be strong and bring large quantitys of
goods to supply us & we will bring all our Furs to this
place. We are glad you acquainted us that the Inhabitants of French here are become English subjects, we shall
look on them as such for the future and treat them as our
Brethren.— A belt.

BRETHREN: Our Uncles gave us this String of Wampum and desired us to be strong and hunt for you, we
should be glad [if] you would fix the price to be given
for a Deer of Meat, then insisted strongly that the six
Nation Deputys should press their Chiefs to attend the
General meeting to be held here in the spring by a Belt.

The principal Man of the Ottawas got up and made
two speeches to the same purport as above.

Then I made them the following speech.

BRETHREN: I return you thanks for the several affectionate speeches you made us yesterday. To day it is agreed that he [the interpreter] be continued till General Amherst and Sir William Johnson's pleasure be known; you likewise desired I might stay here till your General Meeting in the Spring, I am not my own Master so you must excuse me till I receive further Orders.— A belt.

Then the Present of Goods was delivered to each Nation in his Majestys Name, for which they returned their hearty thanks.

Then Major Rogers spoke to them.

BRETHREN: I return you thanks for your readiness in joining his Majestys Troops under my Command, on my way here, as I soon set out to execute my orders and relieve the Garrison of Misselemakinach I take this opportunity of taking my leave of you, and you may be assured I will acquaint General Amherst and Sir William Johnson of the kind reception I have met with amongst your Nations and recommend your services.— A belt.

Then the Council fire was covered up & the Conference ended.

7th.— Mr Butler of the Rangers set of[f] with an officer & party to relieve the Garrison at the Milineys[87] [Miamis]

---

[87] The French fort among the Miamis (English, Twigtwees) was situated on the Maumee River, near the present site of Fort Wayne. The date of its founding is in doubt; but the elder Vincennes was there in 1704, and soon after this frequent mention is made of its commandants. During the revolt of the French Indians (1748), the fort was partially burned. When Céloron passed, the succeeding year, he described it as in a bad condition, and located on an unhealthful site. About this time, the Miamis removed to the Great Miami River, and permitted the English to build a fortified trading house at Pickawillany. But an expedition sent out from Detroit chastised these recalcitrants, and brought them back to their former abode, about Fort Miami — which latter is described (1757) as protected with palisades, on the right bank of the river. The garrison of the Rangers sent out by Rogers from Detroit to secure this post, was later replaced by a small detachment of the Royal

with whom I sent an Interpreter and gave him Wampum and such other things as was necessary for his Journey and Instructions in what manner to speak to the Indians in those parts.

The 8th.— Major Rogers set of[f] for Misselemachinack with whom I sent Cap[t] Montour and four Indians who were well acquainted with the Country and the Indian Nations that Inhabit it.[88]

The 9th & 10th.— Capt Campble assembled all the Inhabitants and read the Act of Parliament to them & setled matters with them to his satisfaction, they agreeing to y[e] billiting of Troops and furnishing fire Wood & Provisions for the Garrison, and indeed every thing in their power for his Majestys service.

The 11th.— In the Evening Capt. Campble finished his Letters when I set off leaving him what Wampum, Silver Truck & Goods I had for the Indian service.

The 16th.— We came to the little Lake called Sandusky which we found froze over so as not to be passable for some days.

The 22[d].— We crossed the little Lake on the Ice which is about 6 Miles over to an Indian Village where we found our Horses which we sent from D'Troit, there

Americans, under command of Lieutenant Robert Holmes, who notified Gladwin of Pontiac's conspiracy, but nevertheless himself fell a victim thereto. See Morris's *Journal, post.* The fort destroyed at this time was not rebuilt. Croghan (1765) speaks of it as ruinous. In the Indian wars of the Northwest, Wayne, perceiving its strategic importance, built at this site the fort named in his honor (1794), whence arose the present city.— ED.

[88] The expedition of Major Rogers to relieve the French at Mackinac, failed because of the lateness of the season, and the consequent ice in Lake Huron. Rogers returned to Detroit December 21, and two days later left for Pittsburg, where he arrived January 23, 1761, after a land march of just one month. The fort at Mackinac was delivered over to an English detachment under command of Captain Balfour of the Royal Americans, September 28, 1761.— ED.

were but five Indians at home all the rest being gone a hunting.

23ᵈ.— We came to Chenunda an Indian Village 6 miles from Sandusky.[89]

24ᵗʰ.— We stayed to hunt up some Horses.

25ᵗʰ.— We came to the Principal Mans hunting Cabin about 16 miles from Chenunda level Road and clear Woods, several Savannahs.

26ᵗʰ.— We came to Mohicken Village, this day, we crossed several small Creeks all branches of Muskingum, level Road, pretty clear Woods about 30 Miles, the Indians were all out a hunting except one family.

27ᵗʰ.— We halted, it rained all day.

28ᵗʰ.— We set of[f], it snowed all day & come to another branch of Muskingum about 9 Miles   good Road where we stayed the 29ᵗʰ for a Cannoe to put us over, the Creek being very high.

30ᵗʰ.— We set of[f] and came to another branch of Muskingum about 11 Miles and the 31ˢᵗ we fell a Tree over the Creek and carryed over our Baggage and encamped about one Mile up a Run.

January the 1ˢᵗ.— We travelled about 16 Miles clear woods & level Road to a place called the Sugar Cabins.

2ᵈ.— We came about 12 Miles to the Beavers Town clear Woods and good Road.

3ᵈ.— Crossed Muskingum Creek and encamped in a fine bottom on this side the Creek.

4ᵗʰ.— Set of[f] and travelled about 20 Miles up a branch of Muskingum good Road.

---

[89] The place here mentioned was a Wyandot town shown on Hutchins's map (1778). Probably this was the village of the chief Nicholas, founded in 1747 during his revolt from the French. See Weiser's *Journal, ante*.— ED.

5th.— Travelled about 18 Miles and crossed a branch of little Beaver Creek clear Woods & good Road.

6th.— Travelled about Eighteen Miles and crossed two Branches of little Beaver Creek good Road & Clear Woods.

7th.— Crossed the mouth of big Beaver Creek at an Indian Village and came to Pittsburg about 25 Miles good Road & Clear Woods.[90]

[90] Croghan returned to Pittsburg by the "great trail," a famous Indian thoroughfare leading from the Forks of the Ohio to Detroit. For a description of this route, see Hulbert, *Indian Thoroughfares* (Cleveland, 1902), p. 107; and in more detail his article in Ohio Archæological and Historical Society *Publications* (Columbus, 1899), viii, p. 276.

Mohican John's village was on White Woman's Creek, near the site of Reedsburg, Ohio. Beaver's Town was at the junction of the Tuscarawas and the Big Sandy, the antecedent of the present Bolivar; for the town at the mouth of Big Beaver Creek, see Weiser's *Journal, ante.*— ED.

CROGHAN'S JOURNAL, 1765 [91]

May 15th, 1765.— I set off from fort Pitt with two batteaux, and encamped at Chartier's Island, in the Ohio, three miles below Fort Pitt.[92]

16th.— Being joined by the deputies of the Senecas, Shawnesse, and Delawares, that were to accompany me,

[91] The manuscript of the journal that we here reprint came into the possession of George William Featherstonhaugh, a noted English geologist who came to the United States in the early nineteenth century and edited a geological magazine in Philadelphia. He first published the document therein (*The Monthly Journal of American Geology*), in the number for December, 1831. It appeared again in a pamphlet, published at Burlington, N. J. (no date); and Mann Butler thought it of sufficient consequence to be introduced into the appendix to his *History of Kentucky* (Cincinnati and Louisville, 2nd ed., 1836). Another version of this journey (which we may call the official version), also written by Croghan, was sent by Sir William Johnson to the lords of trade, and is published in *New York Colonial Documents*, vii, pp. 779-788. Hildreth published a variant of the second (official) version "from an original MS. among Colonel Morgan's papers," in his *Pioneer-History of the Ohio Valley* (Cincinnati, 1848). The two versions supplement each other. The first was evidently written for some persons interested in lands in the Western country — their fertility, products, and general aspects; therefore Croghan herein confines himself to general topographical description, and omits his journey towards the Illinois, his meeting with Pontiac, and all Indian negotiations. The official report, on the other hand, abbreviates greatly the account of the journey and the appearance of the country, and concerns itself with Indian affairs and historical events. We have in the present publication combined the two journals, indicating in foot-notes the important variations; but the bulk of the narrative is a reprint of the Featherstonhaugh-Butler version.

With regard to the circumstances under which the official journal was transcribed, Johnson makes the following explanation in his letter to the board of trade (*New York Colonial Documents*, vii, p. 775): "I have selected the principal parts [of this journal] which I now inclose to your Lordships, the whole of his Journal is long and not yet collected because after he was made Prisoner, & lost his Baggage &ca. he was necessitated to write it on Scraps of Paper procured with difficulty at *Post Vincent*, and that in a disguised Character to prevent its being understood by the French in case through any disaster he might be again plundered."

The importance of this journal for the study of Western history has frequently been noted. Parkman used it extensively in his *Conspiracy of Pontiac*.

we set off at seven o'clock in the morning, and at ten
o'clock arrived at the Logs Town, an old settlement of
the Shawnesse, about seventeen miles from Fort Pitt,
where we put ashore, and viewed the remains of that
village, which was situated on a high bank, on the south
side of the Ohio river, a fine fertile country round it.   At
11 o'clock we re-embarked and proceeded down the Ohio
to the mouth of Big Beaver Creek, about ten miles below
the Logs Town: this creek empties itself between two
fine rich bottoms, a mile wide on each side from the banks
of the river to the highlands.   About a mile below the
mouth of Beaver Creek we passed an old settlement of the
Delawares, where the French, in 1756, built a town for
that nation.   On the north side of the river some of the
stone chimneys are yet remaining; here the highlands
come close to the banks and continue so for about five
miles.   After which we passed several spacious bottoms
on each side of the river, and came to Little Beaver
Creek, about fifteen miles below Big Beaver Creek.   A
number of small rivulets fall into the river on each side.
From thence we sailed to Yellow Creek,[88] being about

Winsor in his *Critical and Narrative History of America*, v, p. 704, *note*, first
pointed out in some detail the differences between the two versions. He errs,
however, in confusing the letters Croghan wrote from Vincennes and Ouiatonon.
Many secondary authorities also wrongly aver that Croghan on this journey
went as far as Fort Chartres.— ED.

[82] Croghan arrived at Fort Pitt, February 28, 1765, and from then until his
departure was constantly occupied with Indian transactions in preparation for
his journey. See *Pennsylvania Colonial Records*, ix, pp. 250-264; also Withers's
Early History of Western Pennsylvania, app., pp. 166-179.— ED.

[88] Little Beaver Creek (near the western border of Pennsylvania) and Yellow
Creek (in Ohio) were much frequented by Indians. On the former, Half King
had a hunting cabin. Logan, the noted Mingo chief, lived at the mouth of
the latter. Opposite, upon the Virginia shore, occurred the massacre of Logan's
family (April 30, 1774), which was one of the opening events of Lord Dunmore's War. See Withers's *Chronicles of Border Warfare* (Thwaites's ed.,
Cincinnati, 1895), p. 150, *notes*.— ED.

fifteen miles from the last mentioned creek; here and
there the hills come close to the banks of the river on each
side, but where there are bottoms, they are very large,
and well watered; numbers of small rivulets running
through them, falling into the Ohio on both sides. We
encamped on the river bank, and found a great part of the
trees in the bottom are covered with grape vines. This
day we passed by eleven islands, one of which being about
seven miles long. For the most part of the way we made
this day, the banks of the river are high and steep. The
course of the Ohio from Fort Pitt to the mouth of Beaver
Creek inclines to the north-west; from thence to the two
creeks partly due west.

17th.— At 6 o'clock in the morning we embarked: and
were delighted with the prospect of a fine open country
on each side of the river as we passed down. We came
to a place called the Two Creeks, about fifteen miles from
Yellow Creek, where we put to shore; here the Senecas
have a village on a high bank, on the north side of the
river; the chief of this village offered me his service to go
with me to the Illinois, which I could not refuse for fear
of giving him offence, although I had a sufficient number
of deputies with me already.[94] From thence we proceeded down the river, passed many large, rich, and fine
bottoms; the highlands being at a considerable distance

---

[94] The village here described was Mingo Town on Mingo bottom, situated
at the present Mingo Junction, Ohio. It is not to be confused with the Mingo
bottom opposite the mouth of Yellow Creek. The former town was prominent
as a rendezvous for border war-parties in the Revolutionary period. From this
point, started the rabble that massacred the Moravian Indians in 1782. Colonel
Crawford set out from here, in May of the same year, on his ill-fated expedition
against the Sandusky Indians. See Withers's *Chronicles*, chap. 13.

Possibly the chief who joined Croghan at this point was Logan, since
the former had known him in his earlier home on the Susquehanna, near
Sunbury.— ED.

from the river banks, till we came to the Buffalo Creek,
being about ten miles below the Seneca village; and from
Buffalo Creek, we proceeded down the river to Fat Meat
Creek, about thirty miles.[95] The face of the country
appears much like what we met with before; large, rich, and
well watered bottoms, then succeeded by the hills pinch-
ing close on the river; these bottoms, on the north side,
appear rather low, and consequently subject to inundations, in the spring of the year, when there never fail to be
high freshes in the Ohio, owing to the melting of the snows.
This day we passed by ten fine islands, though the greatest
part of them are small. They lay much higher out of
the water than the main land, and of course less subject
to be flooded by the freshes. At night we encamped near
an Indian village. The general course of the river from the
Two Creeks to Fat Meat Creek inclines to the southwest.

18th.— At 6 o'clock, A.M. we set off in our batteaux;
the country on both sides of the river appears delightful;
the hills are several miles from the river banks, and consequently the bottoms large; the soil, timber, and banks
of the river, much like those we have before described;
about fifty miles below Fat Meat Creek, we enter the
long reach, where the river runs a straight course for
twenty miles, and makes a delightful prospect; the banks
continue high; the country on both sides, level, rich, and
well watered. At the lower end of the reach we encamped.[96] This day we passed nine islands, some of
which are large, and lie high out of the water.

---

[95] Buffalo Creek is in Brooke County, West Virginia, with the town of Wells-
burg located at its mouth. The first settlers arrived about 1769. Fat Meat
Creek is not identified; from the distances given, it might be Big Grave Creek,
in Marshall County, West Virginia, or Pipe Creek, nearly opposite, in Belmont
County, Ohio.— ED.

[96] The "Long Reach" lies between Fishing Creek and the Muskingum,
sixteen and a half miles in a nearly straight line to the southwest.— ED.

19th.— We decamped at six in the morning, and sailed
to a place called the Three Islands, being about fifteen
miles from our last encampment; here the highlands come
close to the river banks, and the bottoms for the most
part — till we come to the Muskingum (or Elk)[97] river —
are but narrow: this river empties itself into the Ohio
about fifteen miles below the Three Islands; the banks of
the river continue steep, and the country is level, for
several miles back from the river. The course of the
river from Fat Meat Creek to Elk River, is about south-
west and by south. We proceeded down the river about
fifteen miles, to the mouth of Little Conhawa River, with
little or no alteration in the face of the country; here we
encamped in a fine rich bottom, after having passed
fourteen islands, some of them large, and mostly lying
high out of the water.[98] Here buffaloes, bears, turkeys,
with all other kinds of wild game are extremely plenty.

[97] The French called the Muskingum Yanangué-kouan — the river of the
Tobacco (Petun-Huron) Indians. Céloron (1749) left at the mouth of this
river, one of his plates, which was found in 1798, and is now in possession of
the American Antiquarian Society, at Worcester, Massachusetts. Croghan
had frequently been on the Muskingum, where as early as 1750, he had a trading house. The inhabitants at that time appear to have been Wyandots; but
after the French and Indian War the Delawares retreated thither, and built
their towns on the upper Muskingum. Later, the Moravian missionaries
removed their converts thither, and erected upon the banks of this river their
towns, Salem, Schönbrunn, and Gnadenbütten. In 1785, Fort Harmar was
placed at its mouth; and thither, three years later, came the famous colony of
New England Revolutionary soldiers, under the leadership of Rufus Putnam,
which founded Marietta.— ED.

[98] The Little Kanawha was the terminus of the exploring expedition of
George Rogers Clark and Jones in 1772. They reported unfavorably in regard
to the lands; but settlers soon began to occupy them, and they were a part of
the grant given to Trent, Croghan, and others at the treaty of Fort Stanwix
(1768) as a reparation for their losses in the previous wars. About the time
of Croghan's visit, Captain Bull, a well-known Delaware Indian of New York,
removed to the Little Kanawha, and in 1772 his village, Bulltown, was the
scene of a revolting massacre of friendly Indians by brutal white borderers.— ED.

A good hunter, without much fatigue to himself, could here supply daily one hundred men with meat. The course of the Ohio, from Elk River to Little Conhawa, is about south.

20th.— At six in the morning we embarked in our boats, and proceeded down to the mouth of Hochocken or Bottle River,[90] where we were obliged to encamp, having a strong head wind against us. We made but twenty miles this day, and passed by five very fine islands, the country the whole way being rich and level, with high and steep banks to the rivers. From here I despatched an Indian to the Plains of Scioto, with a letter to the French traders from the Illinois residing there, amongst the Shawnesse, requiring them to come and join me at the mouth of Scioto, in order to proceed with me to their own country, and take the oaths of allegiance to his Britannic Majesty, as they were now become his subjects, and had no right to trade there without license. At the same time I sent messages to the Shawnesse Indians to oblige the French to come to me in case of refusal.

21st.— We embarked at half past 8 o'clock in the morning, and sailed to a place called the Big Bend, about thirty-five miles below Bottle River. The course of the Ohio, from Little Conhawa River to Big Bend, is about south-west by south. The country hereabouts abounds

---

[90] Hockhocking is the local Indian name for a bottle-shaped gourd, to which they likened the course of this river. Its chief historical event is connected with Lord Dunmore's War. Nine years after this voyage of Croghan, Dunmore descended the Ohio with his flotilla, and disembarking at the river with his army of regulars and frontiersmen — Clark, Cresap, Kenton, and Girty among the number — marched overland to the Scioto, leaving Fort Gower here to guard his rear. Signs of the earthwork of this fortification are still visible. At this place, on the return journey, the Virginia officers of the army drew up resolutions of sympathy with the Continental Congress then in session at Philadelphia.— ED.

with buffalo, bears, deer, and all sorts of wild game, in such plenty, that we killed out of our boats as much as we wanted. We proceeded down the river to the Buffalo Bottom, about ten miles from the beginning of the Big Bend, where we encamped. The country on both sides of the river, much the same as we passed the day before. This day we passed nine islands, all lying high out of the water.

22d.— At half an hour past 5 o'clock, set off and sailed to a place, called Alum Hill, so called from the great quantity of that mineral found there by the Indians; this place lies about ten miles from Buffalo Bottom;[100] thence we sailed to the mouth of Great Conhawa River,[101] being ten miles from the Alum Hill. The course of the river, from the Great Bend to this place, is mostly west; from hence we proceeded down to Little Guyondott River, where we encamped, about thirty miles from Great Conhawa; the country still fine and level; the bank of the river high, with abundance of creeks and rivulets falling into it. This day we passed six fine islands. In the evening one of our Indians discovered three Cherokees near our encampment, which obliged our Indians to keep

[100] The "Big Bend" of the river is that now known as Pomeroy's Bend, from the Ohio town at its upper point. Alum Hill was probably West Columbia, Mason County, West Virginia. See Lewis, *History of West Virginia* (Philadelphia, 1889), p. 109.— ED.

[101] The Kanawha takes its name from a tribe of Indians who formerly lived in its valley, but they were destroyed by the Iroquois in the early eighteenth century. Céloron called it the Chinondaista, and at its mouth buried a plate which is now in the museum of the Virginia Historical Society, at Richmond. Gist surveyed here for the Ohio Company in 1752; later, Washington owned ten thousand acres in the vicinity, and visited the spot in 1774. That same year, the battle of Point Pleasant was fought at the mouth of the Kanawha by Colonel Andrew Lewis's division of Lord Dunmore's army; and the succeeding year, Fort Randolph was built to protect the frontiers. Daniel Boone retired hither from Kentucky, and lived in this neighborhood four years (1791-95), before migrating to Missouri.— ED.

out a good guard the first part of the night. Our party being pretty strong, I imagine the Cherokees were afraid to attack us, and so ran off.

23d.— Decamped about five in the morning, and arrived at Big Guyondott, twenty miles from our last encampment: the country as of yesterday; from hence we proceeded down to Sandy River being twenty miles further; thence to the mouth of Scioto, about forty miles from the last mentioned river. The general course of the river from Great Conhawa to this place inclines to the south-west. The soil rich, the country level, and the banks of the river high. The soil on the banks of Scioto, for a vast distance up the country, is prodigious rich, the bottoms very wide, and in the spring of the year, many of them are flooded, so that the river appears to be two or three miles wide. Bears, deer, turkeys, and most sorts of wild game, are very plenty on the banks of this river. On the Ohio, just below the mouth of Scioto, on a high bank, near forty feet, formerly stood the Shawnesse town, called the Lower Town, which was all carried away, except three or four houses, by a great flood in the Scioto. I was in the town at the time, though the banks of the Ohio were so high, the water was nine feet on the top, which obliged the whole town to take to their canoes, and move with their effects to the hills. The Shawnesse afterwards built their town on the opposite side of the river, which, during the French war, they abandoned, for fear of the Virginians, and removed to the plains on Scioto. The Ohio is about one hundred yards wider here than at Fort Pitt, which is but a small augumentation, considering the great number of rivers and creeks, that fall into it during the course of four hundred and twenty miles; and as it deepens but very little, I imagine the water sinks, though there is no visible appearance of it. In general all the lands on the Scioto River, as well as the bottoms on Ohio, are too rich for any thing but hemp, flax, or Indian corn.[102]

24th, 25th, and 26th.— Stayed at the mouth of Scioto, waiting for the Shawnesse and French traders, who arrived here on the evening of the 26th, in consequence of the message I sent them from Hochocken, or Bottle Creek.[103]

27th.— The Indians requested me to stay this day, which I could not refuse.

28th.— We set off: passing down the Ohio, the country on both sides the river level; the banks continue high. This day we came sixty miles; passed no islands. The river being wider and deeper, we drove all night.

29th.— We came to the little Miame River, having proceeded sixty miles last night.

---

[102] The word Scioto probably signified "deer," although it is said by David Jones to mean "hairy" river, from the multitude of deer's hairs which floated down the stream. The valley of the Scioto is famous in Western annals. During the second half of the eighteenth century it was the chief seat of the Shawnees whose lower, or "Shannoah," town has been frequently mentioned in the Indian transactions which we have printed. The Shawnees, on their withdrawal up the valley, built the Chillicothe towns, where Pontiac's conspiracy was largely fomented. These were the starting point of many raids against the Kentucky and West Virginia settlements. From these villages Mrs. Ingles and Mrs. Dennis made their celebrated escapes in 1755 and 1763 respectively. During all the long series of wars closing with Wayne's victory in 1794, the intractable Shawnees were among the most dreaded of the Indian enemy.— Ed.

[103] The result of this message in regard to the French traders, is thus given in the official version of the journal:

"26th. Several of the Shawanese came there & brought with them 7 French Traders which they delivered to me, those being all that resided in their Villages, & told me there was just six more living with the Delawares, that on their return to their Towns they would go to the Delawares & get them to send those French Traders home, & told me they were determined to do everything in their power to convince me of their sincerity & good disposition to preserve a peace."— Ed.

30th.— We passed the Great Miame River, about thirty miles from the little river of that name, *and in the evening arrived at the place where the Elephants' bones are found,* where we encamped, intending to take a view of the place next morning. This day we came about seventy miles. The country on both sides level, and rich bottoms well watered.

31st.— *Early in the morning we went to the great Lick, where those bones are only found, about four miles from the river, on the south-east side. In our way we passed through a fine timbered clear wood; we came into a large road which the Buffaloes have beaten, spacious enough for two waggons to go abreast, and leading straight into the Lick.* It appears that there are vast quantities of these bones lying five or six feet under ground, which we discovered in the bank, at the edge of the Lick. We found here two tusks above six feet long; we carried one, with some other bones, to our boats, and set off.[104] This day we proceeded down the river about eighty miles, through a country much the same as already described, since we passed the Scioto. In this day's journey we passed the mouth of the River Kentucky, or Holsten's River.[105]

[104] Big Bone Lick, in Boone County, Kentucky, was visited by the French in the early eighteenth century. It was a landmark for early Kentucky hunters, who describe it in terms similar to those used by Croghan. At the beginning of the nineteenth century, scientists took much interest in the remains of the mammoth (or mastodon) — the "elephant's bones" described by Croghan. Thomas Jefferson and several members of the American Philosophical Society, at Philadelphia, attempted to secure a complete skeleton of this extinct giant; and a number of fossils from the lick were also sent to Europe. Dr. Goforth of Cincinnati undertook an exploration to the lick at his own expense (1803), but was later robbed of the result. The store of huge bones is not yet entirely exhausted, specimens being yet occasionally excavated — the present writer having examined some there in 1894.— ED.

[105] It is a curious mistake on Croghan's part to designate the Kentucky as the Holston River. The latter is a branch of the Tennessee, flowing through

June 1st.— We arrived within a mile of the Falls of
Ohio, where we encamped, after coming about fifty
miles this day.

2d.— Early in the morning we embarked, and passed
the Falls. The river being very low we were obliged to
lighten our boats, and pass on the north side of a little
island, which lays in the middle of the river. In general,
what is called the Fall here, is no more than rapids; and
in the least fresh, a batteau of any size may come and go
on each side without any risk.[106] This day we proceeded
sixty miles, in the course of which we passed Pidgeon
River. The country pretty high on each side of the River
Ohio.

3d.— In the forepart of this day's course, we passed
high lands; about mid-day we came to a fine, flat, and
level country, called by the Indians the Low Lands; no
hills to be seen. We came about eighty miles this day,
and encamped.

4th.— We came to a place called the Five Islands; these
islands are very long, and succeed one another in a chain;
the country still flat and level, the soil exceedingly rich,
and well watered. The highlands are at least fifty miles

the mountains of Tennessee, North Carolina, and Virginia. Its valley was
early settled by Croghan's friends, Scotch-Irish from Pennsylvania. It is
probable that, as the Kentucky's waters come from that direction, he had a
confused idea of the topography.— ED.

[106] One of the earliest descriptions of the Falls of the Ohio. Gist was
ordered to explore as far as there in 1750, but did not reach the goal. Findlay
was there in 1753. Gordon gives an account similar to Croghan's in 1766.
Ensign Butricke made more of an adventure in passing these falls — see *Historical Magazine*, viii, p. 259. An attempt at a settlement was made by John
Connolly (1773); but the beginnings of the present city of Louisville are due
to the pioneers who accompanied George Rogers Clark thither in 1778, and
made their first home on Corn Island. For the early history of Louisville,
see Durrett, *Centenary of Louisville*, Filson Club *Publications*, No. 8 (Louisville, 1893).— ED.

from the banks of the Ohio. In this day's course we passed about ninety miles, the current being very strong.

5th.— Having passed the Five Islands, we came to a place called the Owl River. Came about forty miles this day. The country the same as yesterday.

6th.— We arrived at the mouth of the Ouabache,[107] where we found a breast-work erected, supposed to be done by the Indians. The mouth of this river is about two hundred yards wide, and in its course runs through one of the finest countries in the world, the lands being exceedingly rich, and well watered; here hemp might be raised in immense quantities. All the bottoms, and almost the whole country abounds with great plenty of the white and red mulberry tree. These trees are to be found in great plenty, in all places between the mouth of Scioto and the Ouabache: the soil of the latter affords this tree in plenty as far as Ouicatonon, and some few on the Miame River. Several large fine islands lie in the Ohio, opposite the mouth of the Ouabache, the banks of which are high, and consequently free from inundations; hence we proceeded down the river about six miles to encamp, as I judged some Indians were sent to way-lay us, and came to a place called the Old Shawnesse Village,

---

[107] Colonel Reuben T. Durrett, of Louisville, thinks Croghan "must have meant Salt River when he spoke of passing Pigeon River during his first day's journey after leaving the Falls of the Ohio." The Owl River he identifies with Highland Creek in Kentucky, between the mouths of the Green and Wabash rivers.

The Wabash River was early considered by the French as one of the most important highways between Canada and Louisiana. Marquette designates it on his map as the Ouabouskiguo, which later Frenchmen corrupted into Ouabache. The name was also applied to that portion of the Ohio below the mouth of the Wabash; but James Logan in 1718 noted the distinction. See Winsor, *Mississippi Basin*, p. 17. Croghan was probably the first Englishman who had penetrated thus far into the former French territory, except Fraser, who had preceded him to the Illinois.— ED.

some of that nation having formerly lived there.[108]   In this day's proceedings we came about seventy-six miles. The general course of the river, from Scioto to this place, is south-west.

7th.— We stayed here and despatched two Indians to the Illinois by land, with letters to Lord Frazer, an English officer, who had been sent there from Fort Pitt, and Monsieur St. Ange,[109] the French commanding officer at Fort Chartres, and some speeches to the Indians there, letting them know of my arrival here; that peace was made between us and the Six Nations, Delawares, and Shawnesse, and of my having a number of deputies of those nations along with me, to conclude matters with them also on my arrival there.   This day one of my men went into the woods and lost himself.[110]

8th.— At day-break we were attacked by a party of Indians, consisting of eighty warriors of the Kiccapoos

[108] The Shawnees had formerly dwelt west and south of their habitations on the Scioto. The Cumberland River was known on early maps as the "Shawana River;" and in 1718, they were located in the direction of Carolina. Their migration east and north took place about 1730. The present Illinois town at this site, is still called Shawneetown.— ED.

[109] Being able to speak French, Lieutenant Alexander Fraser of the 78th infantry had been detailed to accompany Croghan. He went in advance of the latter, and reached the Illinois, where he found himself in such danger that he escaped to Mobile in disguise. See Parkman, *Conspiracy of Pontiac*, ii, pp. 276, 284-286.

Captain Louis St. Ange de Bellerive, was the son of a French officer who came to Louisiana early in the eighteenth century, and commanded in the Illinois country in 1722 and again in 1733. St. Ange had himself seen much pioneer service, having been placed in charge of a fort on the Missouri (1736), and having succeeded Vincennes at the post bearing the latter's name. St. Ange remained at Vincennes until summoned by De Villiers, commandant at Fort Chartres, to supersede him there, and spare him the mortification of a surrender to the English. After yielding Fort Chartres to Captain Sterling (October, 1765), St. Ange retired to St. Louis, where he acted as commandant (after 1766, in the Spanish service) until his death in 1774.— ED.

[110] This man was in reality captured. See Parkman, *Conspiracy of Pontiac*, ii, p. 289, *note*.— ED.

and Musquattimes,[111] who killed two of my men and three
Indians, wounded myself and all the rest of my party,
except two white men and one Indian; then made myself
and all the white men prisoners, plundering us of every
thing we had.   A deputy of the Shawnesse who was shot
through the thigh, having concealed himself in the woods
for a few minutes after he was wounded — not knowing
but they were Southern Indians, who are always at war
with the northward Indians — after discovering what
nation they were, came up to them and made a very bold
speech, telling them that the whole northward Indians
would join in taking revenge for the insult and murder
of their people; this alarmed those savages very much,
who began excusing themselves, saying their fathers, the
French, had spirited them up, telling them that the Indians
were coming with a body of southern Indians to take
their country from them, and enslave them; that it was
this that induced them to commit this outrage.   After
dividing the plunder, (they left great part of the heaviest
effects behind, not being able to carry them,) they set off
with us to their village at Ouattonon, in a great hurry,
being in dread of pursuit from a large party of Indians
they suspected were coming after me.   Our course was
through a thick woody country, crossing a great many
swamps, morasses, and beaver ponds.   We traveled this
day about forty-two miles.

[111] The Kickapoos and Mascoutins were allied Algonquian tribes whc were
first encountered in Wisconsin; but being of roving habits they ranged all the
prairie lands between the Wisconsin and Wabash rivers. In 1712, they were
about the Maumee and at Detroit. Charlevoix describes them (1721) as living
near Chicago. Being concerned in the Fox wars, they fled across the Mississippi; and again, about the middle of the eighteenth century, were with the
Miamis on the Wabash, where they had a town near Fort Ouiatonon. They
were always somewhat intractable and difficult to restrain. The remnant of
these tribes live on reservations in Kansas and Oklahoma.— ED.

9th.— An hour before day we set out on our march; passed through thick woods, some highlands, and small savannahs, badly watered. Traveled this day about thirty miles.

10th.— We set out very early in the morning, and marched through a high country, extremely well timbered, for three hours; then came to a branch of the Ouabache, which we crossed.[112] The remainder of this day we traveled through fine rich bottoms, overgrown with reeds, which make the best pasture in the world, the young reeds being preferable to sheaf oats. Here is great plenty of wild game of all kinds. Came this day about twenty-eight, or thirty miles.

11th.— At day-break we set off, making our way through a thin woodland, interspersed with savannahs. I suffered extremely by reason of the excessive heat of the weather, and scarcity of water; the little springs and runs being dried up. Traveled this day about thirty miles.

12th.— We passed through some large savannahs, and clear woods; in the afternoon we came to the Ouabache; then marched along it through a prodigious rich bottom, overgrown with reeds and wild hemp; all this bottom is well watered, and an exceeding fine hunting ground. Came this day about thirty miles.

13th.— About an hour before day we set out; traveled through such bottoms as of yesterday, and through some large meadows, where no trees, for several miles together, are to be seen. Buffaloes, deer, and bears are here in great plenty. We traveled about twenty-six miles this day.

[112] This branch of the Wabash is now called the Little Wabash River. The party must have taken a very circuitous route, else Croghan greatly overestimates the distances. Vincennes is about seventy-five miles from the point where they were made prisoners.— ED.

14th.— The country we traveled through this day, appears the same as described yesterday, excepting this afternoon's journey through woodland, to cut off a bend of the river. Came about twenty-seven miles this day.

15th.— We set out very early, and about one o'clock came to the Ouabache, within six or seven miles of Port Vincent.[118] On my arrival there, I found a village of about eighty or ninety French families settled on the east side of this river, being one of the finest situations that can be found. The country is level and clear, and the soil very rich, producing wheat and tobacco. I think the latter preferable to that of Maryland or Virginia. The French inhabitants hereabouts, are an idle, lazy people, a parcel of renegadoes from Canada, and are much worse than the Indians. They took a secret pleasure at our misfortunes, and the moment we arrived, they came to the Indians, exchanging trifles for their valuable plunder. As the savages took from me a considerable quantity of

[118] The date of the founding of Vincennes (Post or Port Vincent) has been varyingly assigned from 1702 to 1735; but Dunn, in his *Indiana* (Boston and New York, 1888), p. 54, shows quite conclusively that François Margane, Sieur de Vincennes, went thither at the request of Governor Perier of Louisiana in 1727, and founded a fort to counteract the designs of the English against the French trade. The French colony was not begun until 1735, and the next year the commandant Vincennes was captured and burnt by the Chickasaws, while engaged in an expedition against their country. Louis St. Ange succeeded to the position of commandant at Vincennes, which he continued to hold until 1764, when summoned to the Illinois. He left two soldiers in charge at Vincennes, of whom and their companions Croghan gives this unfavorable account. No English officer appeared to take command at Vincennes until 1777; meanwhile General Gage had endeavored to expel the French inhabitants therefrom (1772-73). It is not surprising, therefore, that they received the Americans under George Rogers Clark (1778), with cordiality; or that after Hamilton's re-capture of the place, they were unwilling to aid the English in maintaining the post against Clark's surprise (February, 1779), which resulted in the capture of Hamilton and all the British garrison. After this event, Vincennes became part of the Illinois government, until the organization of a Northwest Territory in 1787.— Ed.

gold and silver in specie, the French traders extorted ten half johannes[114] from them for one pound of vermilion. Here is likewise an Indian village of the Pyankeshaws,[115] who were much displeased with the party that took me, telling them that ''our and your chiefs are gone to make peace, and you have begun a war, for which our women and children will have reason to cry.'' From this post the Indians permitted me to write to the commander, at Fort Chartres, but would not suffer me to write to any body else, (this I apprehend was a precaution of the French, lest their villany should be perceived too soon,) although the Indians had given me permission to write to Sir William Johnson and Fort Pitt on our march, before we arrived at this place. But immediately after our arrival they had a private council with the French, in which the Indians urged, (as they afterwards informed me,) that as the French had engaged them in so bad an affair, which was likely to bring a war on their nation, they now expected a proof of their promise and assistance. Then delivered the French a scalp and part of the plunder, and wanted to deliver some presents to the Pyankeshaws, but they refused to accept of any, and declared they would not be concerned in the affair. This last information I got from the Pyankeshaws, as I had been well acquainted with them several years before this time.

Port Vincent is a place of great consequence for trade, being a fine hunting country all along the Ouabache, and too far for the Indians, which reside hereabouts, to go

---

[114] A johannies was a Portuguese coin current in America about this time, worth nearly nine dollars. The Indians, therefore, paid over forty dollars for their pound of vermillion.— ED.

[115] The Piankeshaws were a tribe of the Miamis, who had been settled near Vincennes as long as they had been known to the whites.— ED.

either to the Illinois, or elsewhere, to fetch their necessaries.

16th.— We were obliged to stay here to get some little apparel made up for us, and to buy some horses for our journey to Ouicatonon, promising payment at Detroit, for we could not procure horses from the French for hire; though we were greatly fatigued, and our spirits much exhausted in our late march, they would lend us no assistance.

17th.— At mid-day we set out; traveling the first five miles through a fine thick wood. We traveled eighteen miles this day, and encamped in a large, beautiful, well watered meadow.

18th and 19th.— We traveled through a prodigious large meadow, called the Pyankeshaw's Hunting Ground: here is no wood to be seen, and the country appears like an ocean: the ground is exceedingly rich, and partly overgrown with wild hemp; the land well watered, and full of buffalo, deer, bears, and all kinds of wild game.

20th and 21st.— We passed through some very large meadows, part of which belong to the Pyankeshaws on Vermilion River; the country and soil much the same as that we traveled over for these three days past, wild hemp grows here in abundance; the game very plenty: at any time, in half an hour we could kill as much as we wanted.

22nd.— We passed through part of the same meadow as mentioned yesterday; then came to a high woodland, and arrived at Vermilion River, so called from a fine red earth found here by the Indians, with which they. paint themselves. About half a mile from the place where we crossed this river, there is a village of Pyankeshaws, distinguished by the addition of the name of the river. We then traveled about three hours, through a clear high woody country, but a deep and rich soil; then came to a meadow, where we encamped.

23d.— Early in the morning we set out through a fine meadow, then some clear woods; in the afternoon came into a very large bottom on the Ouabache, within six miles of Ouicatanon; here I met several chiefs of the Kickapoos and Musquattimes, who spoke to their young men who had taken us, and reprimanded them severely for what they had done to me, after which they returned with us to their village, and delivered us all to their chiefs.

The distance from port Vincent to Ouicatanon is two hundred and ten miles. This place is situated on the Ouabache. About fourteen French families are living in the fort, which stands on the north side of the river. The Kickapoos and the Musquattimes, whose warriors had taken us, live nigh the fort, on the same side of the river, where they have two villages; and the Ouicatanons have a village on the south side of the river. At our arrival at this post, several of the Wawcottonans, (or Ouicatonans) with whom I had been formerly acquainted, came to visit me, and seemed greatly concerned at what had happened. They went immediately to the Kickapoos and Musquattimes, and charged them to take the greatest care of us, till their chiefs should arrive from the Illinois, where they were gone to meet me some time ago, and who were entirely ignorant of this affair, and said the French had spirited up this party to go and strike us.

The French have a great influence over these Indians, and never fail in telling them many lies to the prejudice of his majesty's interest, by making the English nation odious and hateful to them. I had the greatest difficulties in removing these prejudices. As these Indians are a weak, foolish, and credulous people, they are easily imposed on by a designing people, who have led them hitherto as they pleased. The French told them that as the southern Indians had for two years past made war on them, it must have been at the instigation of the English, who are a bad people. However I have been fortunate enough to remove their prejudice, and, in a great measure, their suspicions against the English. The country hereabouts is exceedingly pleasant, being open and clear for many miles; the soil very rich and well watered; all plants have a quick vegetation, and the climate very temperate through the winter. This post has always been a very considerable trading place. The great plenty of furs taken in this country, induced the French to establish this post, which was the first on the Ouabache, and by a very advantageous trade they have been richly recompensed for their labor.

On the south side of the Ouabache runs a big bank, in which are several fine coal mines, and behind this bank, is a very large meadow, clear for several miles. It is surprising what false information we have had respecting this country: some mention these spacious and beautiful meadows as large and barren savannahs. I apprehend it has been the artifice of the French to keep us ignorant of the country. These meadows bear fine wild grass, and wild hemp ten or twelve feet high, which, if properly manufactured, would prove as good, and answer all the purposes of the hemp we cultivate.[116]

July 1st— A Frenchman arrived from the Illinois with a Pipe and Speech from thence to the Kickapoos &

[116] The entries from July 1 to 18, inclusive, are here inserted from the second (or official) version in the *New York Colonial Documents*, vii, pp. 781, 782; hiatuses therein, are supplied from the Hildreth version. See note 91, *ante*, p. 126.— ED.

Musquattamies, to have me Burnt, this Speech was said
to be sent from a Shawanese Indⁿ who resides at the
Ilinois, & has been during the War, & is much attached
to the French interest.   As soon as this Speech was delivered to the Indians by the French, the Indians informed
me of it in Council, & expressed their great concern for
what had already happened, & told me they then sett me
& my people at liberty, & assured me they despised the
message sent them, and would return the Pipe & Belt to
their Fathers the French, and enquire into the reason of
such a message being sent them by one of his messengers,
& desired me to stay with them 'till the Deputies of the
Six Nations, Shawanese & Delawares arrived with Pondiac at Ouiatonon in order to settle matters, to wᵇ I
consented.

From 4ᵗʰ to the 8ᵗʰ— I had several Conferences with
the Wawiotonans, Pyankeeshas, Kickapoos & Musquatamies in which Conferences I was lucky enough to
reconcile those Nations to his Majesties Interest & obtain
their Consent and Approbation to take Possession of any
Posts in their country which the French formerly possessed
& an offer of their service should any Nation oppose our
taking possession of it, all which they confirmed by four
large Pipes.

11ᵗʰ— Mʳ Maisonville[117] arrived with an Interpreter &

[117] François Rivard dit Maisonville was a member of one of the first families
to settle Detroit. He entered the British service at Fort Pitt as an interpreter,
accompanying Lieutenant Fraser to the Illinois in that capacity. In 1774,
Maisonville was Indian agent on the Wabash with a salary of £100 a year.
When George Rogers Clark invaded the Illinois country (1778), Maisonville
carried the first intelligence of this incursion to Detroit. The next year General
Hamilton employed him on his advance against Vincennes; but on Clark's
approach he was captured, while on a scouting party, and cruelly treated by
some of the American partisans. He made one of the party sent to Virginia
as captives, and the following year committed suicide in prison.— ED.

a message to the Indians to bring me & my party to the Ilinois, till then I had no answer from M^r St. Ange to the letter I wrote him of the 16th June, as I wanted to go to the Ilinois, I desired the Chiefs to prepare themselves & set off with me as soon as possible.

12th— I wrote to General Gage[118] & Sir William Johnson, to Col° Campbell at Detroit, & Major Murray at Fort Pitt & Major Firmer at Mobiel or on his way to the Mississipi,[119] & acquainted [them with] every thing that had happened since my departure from Ft. Pitt.

July 13th— The Chiefs of the Twightwees came to me from the Miamis and renewed their Antient Friendship with His Majesty & all his Subjects in America & confirmed it with a Pipe.

18th— I set off for the Ilinois with the Chiefs of all those Nations when by the way we met with Pondiac together with the Deputies of the Six Nations, Delawares & Shawanese, which accompanied Mr Frazier & myself down the Ohio & also Deputies with speeches from the

---

[118] General Thomas Gage was at this time British commander-in-chief in America, with headquarters at New York. Having come to America with Braddock, he served on this continent for twenty years, in numerous important offices. After the surrender of Montreal he was made governor of that city and province, until in 1763 he superseded Amherst as commander-in-chief, in which capacity he served until the outbreak of the Revolution. His part in the initial battles of that conflict about Boston, where he commanded, is a matter of general history. After his recall to England his subsequent career was uneventful. He died as Viscount Gage in 1787.— Ed.

[119] Major William Murray of the 42nd infantry succeeded Colonel Henry Bouquet as commandant at Fort Pitt, in the spring of 1765.

Major Robert Farmer was sent to receive the surrender of Mobile in 1763. For a description by Aubry, the retiring French governor of Louisiana, of Farmer's character and manner, see Claiborne, *History of Mississippi* (Jackson, 1880), p. 104. Late in this year that Croghan wrote (1765), Farmer ascended the Mississippi with a detachment of the 34th infantry, and took over the command of the Illinois from Major Sterling, being in turn relieved (1767) by Colonel Edward Cole. Farmer died or retired from the army in 1768.— Ed.

four Nations living in the Ilinois Country to me & the
Six Nations, Delawares & Shawanese, on which we
return'd to Ouiatonon and there held another conference,
in which I settled all matters with the Ilinois Indians —
Pondiac & they agreeing to every thing the other Nations
had done, all which they confirmed by Pipes & Belts,
but told me the French had informed them that the English intended to take their Country from them, & give
it to the Cherokees to settle on, & that if ever they suffered the English to take possession of their Country
they would make slaves of them, that this was the reason
of their Opposing the Englifh hitherto from taking possession of *Fort Chartres* & induced them to tell Mr. La
Gutrie & Mr Sinnott[120] that they would not let the English come into their Country. But being informed since
Mr Sinnott had retired by the Deputies of the Six Nations, Delawares & Shawanese, that every difference
subsisting between them & the English was now settled, they were willing to comply as the other Nations
their Brethren had done and desired that their Father the
King of England might not look upon his taking possession of the Forts which the French had formerly possest
as a title for his subjects to possess their Country, as they
never had sold any part of it to the French, & that I
might rest satisfied that whenever the English came to
take possession they would receive them with open arms.

July 25th.[121]— We set out from this place (after set-

---

[120] La Guthrie was the interpreter sent with Lieutenant Fraser. Sinnott
was a deputy-agent sent out by Stuart, agent for the Southern department to
attempt conciliation in the Illinois. His stores had been plundered, and he
himself having escaped with difficulty from Fort Chartres, sought refuge at
New Orleans. See *New York Colonial Documents*, vii, pp. 765, 776.— ED.

[121] We here again resume the first (Featherstonhaugh-Butler) version of the
journal, which continues through August 17.— ED.

tling all matters happily with the natives) for the Miames, and traveled the whole way through a fine rich bottom, overgrown with wild hemp, alongside the Ouabache, till we came to Eel River, where we arrived the 27th. About six miles up this river is a small village of the Twightwee, situated on a very delightful spot of ground on the bank of the river. The Eel River heads near St. Joseph's, and runs nearly parallel to the Miames, and at some few miles distance from it, through a fine, pleasant country, and after a course of about one hundred and eighty miles empties itself into the Ouabache.

28th, 29th, 30th and 31st.— We traveled still along side the Eel River, passing through fine clear woods, and some good meadows, though not so large as those we passed some days before. The country is more overgrown with woods, the soil is sufficiently rich, and well watered with springs.

August 1st.— We arrived at the carrying place between the River Miames and the Ouabache, which is about nine miles long in dry seasons, but not above half that length in freshes. The head of the Ouabache is about forty miles from this place, and after a course of about seven hundred and sixty miles from the head spring, through one of the finest countries in the world, it empties itself into the Ohio. The navigation from hence to Ouicatanon, is very difficult in low water, on account of many rapids and rifts; but in freshes, which generally happen in the spring and fall, batteaux or canoes will pass, without difficulty, from here to Ouicatanon in three days, which is about two hundred and forty miles, and by land about two hundred and ten miles.' From Ouicatanon to Port Vincent, and thence to the Ohio, batteaux and canoes may go at any season of the year. Throughout the whole

course of the Ouabache the banks are pretty high, and in the river are a great many islands. Many shrubs and trees are found here unknown to us.

Within a mile of the Twightwee village, I was met by the chiefs of that nation, who received us very kindly. The most part of these Indians knew me, and conducted me to their village, where they immediately hoisted an English flag that I had formerly given them at Fort Pitt. The next day they held a council, after which they gave me up all the English prisoners they had, then made several speeches, in all which they expressed the great pleasure it gave them, to see the unhappy differences which embroiled the several nations in a war with their brethren, the English, were now so near a happy conclusion, and that peace was established in their country.

The Twightwee village is situated on both sides of a river, called St. Joseph's. This river, where it falls into the Miame river, about a quarter of a mile from this place, is one hundred yards wide, on the east side of which stands a stockade fort, somewhat ruinous.

The Indian village consists of about forty or fifty cabins, besides nine or ten French houses, a runaway colony from Detroit, during the late Indian war; they were concerned in it, and being afraid of punishment, came to this post, where ever since they have spirited up the Indians against the English. All the French residing here are a lazy, indolent people, fond of breeding mischief, and spiriting up the Indians against the English, and should by no means be suffered to remain here. The country is pleasant, the soil rich and well watered. After several conferences with these Indians, and their delivering me up all the English prisoners they had, — [blank space in MS.]

On the 6th of August we set out for Detroit, down the
Miames river in a canoe. This river heads about ten
miles from hence. The river is not navigable till you
come where the river St. Joseph joins it, and makes a
considerably large stream. Nevertheless we found a
great deal of difficulty in getting our canoe over shoals,
as the waters at this season were very low. The banks
of the river are high, and the country overgrown with
lofty timber of various kinds; the land is level, and the
woods clear. About ninety miles from the Miames or
Twightwee, we came to where a large river, that heads
in a large lick, falls into the Miame river; this they call
the Forks.[122] The Ottawas claim this country, and hunt
here, where game is very plenty. From hence we proceeded to the Ottawa village. This nation formerly lived
at Detroit, but is now settled here, on account of the
richness of the country, where game is always to be found
in plenty. Here we were obliged to get out of our canoes,
and drag them eighteen miles, on account of the rifts
which interrupt the navigation.[123] At the end of these
rifts, we came to a village of the Wyondotts, who received
us very kindly and from thence we proceeded to the
mouth of the river, where it falls into Lake Erie. From
the Miames to the lake is computed one hundred and
eighty miles, and from the entrance of the river into the
lake to Detroit, is sixty miles; that is, forty-two miles up

[122] This is the Auglaize River. On the site called the Forks, Wayne built
Fort Defiance during his campaign against the Indians (1794).—ED.

[123] The rapids of the Maumee were famous in the later Indian wars. There,
in 1794, the British built Fort Miami, almost within the reach of whose guns
Wayne fought the battle of Fallen Timbers. Fort Meigs was the American
stockade built here during the War of 1812-15; and this vicinity was the scene
of operations during all the Western campaigns ending with Perry's victory on
Lake Erie, and the re-taking of Detroit.— ED.

the lake, and eighteen miles up the Detroit river to the garrison of that name. The land on the lake side is low and flat. We passed several large rivers and bays, and on the 16th of August, in the afternoon, we arrived at Detroit river. The country here is much higher than on the lake side; the river is about nine hundred yards wide, and the current runs very strong. There are several fine and large islands in this river, one of which is nine miles long; its banks high, and the soil very good.

17th.— In the morning we arrived at the fort, which is a large stockade, inclosing about eighty houses, it stands close on the north side of the river, on a high bank, commands a very pleasant prospect for nine miles above, and nine miles below the fort; the country is thick settled with French, their plantations are generally laid out about three or four acres in breadth on the river, and eighty acres in depth; the soil is good, producing plenty of grain. All the people here are generally poor wretches, and consist of three or four hundred French families, a lazy, idle people, depending chiefly on the savages for their subsistence; though the land, with little labor, produces plenty of grain, they scarcely raise as much as will supply their wants, in imitation of the Indians, whose manners and customs they have entirely adopted, and cannot subsist without them. The men, women, and children speak the Indian tongue perfectly well. In the last Indian war the most part of the French were concerned in it, (although the whole settlement had taken the oath of allegiance to his Britannic Majesty) they have, therefore, great reason to be thankful to the English clemency in not bringing them to deserved punishment. Before the late Indian war there resided three nations of Indians at this place: the Putawatimes, whose

village was on the west side of the river, about one mile
below the fort; the Ottawas, on the east side, about three
miles above the Fort; and the Wyondotts, whose village
lies on the east side, about two miles below the fort.
The former two nations have removed to a considerable
distance, and the latter still remain where they were, and
are remarkable for their good sense and hospitality.
They have a particular attachment to the Roman Catholic
religion, the French, by their priests, having taken uncom-
mon pains to instruct them.

During my stay here, I held frequent conferences with
the different nations of Indians assembled at this place,
with whom I settled matters to their general satisfaction.

August 17th [124]— I arrived at Detroit where I found
several small Tribes of Ottawas, Puttewatamies &
Chipwas waiting in Consequence of Col° Bradstreets
Invitation to see him.[125] Here I met M^r *DeCouagne* and

[124] All that follows, until the conclusion of the Indian speeches, is inserted
from the second (official) version of the journals, found in the *New York Colonial Documents*, vii, pp. 781-787.— ED.

[125] Although English born, Colonel John Bradstreet lived all his mature life
in America, and distinguished himself for his military services in the later
French wars. He was in the campaign against Louisburg (1745), and was
promoted for gallantry, and given the governorship of St. John's, Newfound-
land. The outbreak of the French and Indian War found him at Oswego,
where with great bravery he drove the French back from an attack on a convoy
(1756). On the organization of the Royal Americans, Bradstreet became
lieutenant-colonel, and served with Abercrombie at Ticonderoga (1758). His
most renowned exploit was the capture, the same year, of Fort Frontenac,
which severed the connection between Canada and its Western dependencies.
After the close of the war, Bradstreet received a colonelcy. When the news
of Pontiac's uprising reached the East, he was detailed to make an expedition
into the Indian territory by way of Lake Erie. His confidence in Indian promises proved too great; he made peace with the very tribes who went murdering
and scalping along the frontiers as soon as his army had passed. Bradstreet
was made a major-general in 1772; but two years later, died in the city of New
York. The Indians whom Croghan found at Detroit were small bands from
the north and west, who had not received Bradstreet's message, in time to.
attend before that officer's departure from Detroit.— ED.

Wabecomicat with a Deputation of Indians from Niagara,
with Messages from Sir William Johnson to Pondiac &
those Western Nations.[126]

23ᵈ— Colo Campbell[127] & I had a Meeting with the
Twightwees, Wawiotonans, Pyankeshas, Kickapoos and
Musquattamies, when they produced the several Belts
sent them by Col° Bradstreet, in consequence of which
Invitation they came here.

Then they spoake to the Six Nations Delawares &
Shawanese on several Belts & Pipes, beging in the most
abject manner that they would forgive them for the ill
conduct of their Young Men, to take Pity on their Women
& Children & grant yᵐ peace.

They then spoake to the Col° & me on several Pipes &
Belts Expressing their great satisfaction at a firm and lasting Peace settled between their Bretheren the English, &
the several Indian Nations in this Country, that they saw
the heavy Clouds that hung over their heads for some
time past were now dispersed, and that the Sun shone
clear & bright, & that as their Father the King of England had conquered the French in that [this] Country &
taken into his Friendship all the Indian Nations, they
hoped for the future they would be a happy people, &
that they should always have reason to call the English
their Fathers & beged we would take pity on their

[126] In the Hildreth version these names are spelled "Duquanee" and "Waobecomica." The former was a Detroit habitant Dequindre, who had brought
messages from the Illinois to Pontiac during the siege of Detroit. Waobecomica
was a Missassaga chief, well-affected toward the English, whom Johnson had
sent in the spring of 1765 with messages to Pontiac. See *New York Colonial
Documents,* vii, p. 747.— ED.

[127] This was Lieutenant-colonel Alexander Campbell, formerly commander
of the 95th regiment, who succeeded Major Gladwin in command of Detroit
(1764). He is not to be confused with Captain Donald Campbell, the earlier
commandant, who was killed by the Indians during Pontiac's conspiracy.— ED.

Women & Children, & make up the difference subsisting between them and the Shawanese, Delawares & Six
Nations, and said as they were come here in consequence of
Col° Bradstreet's Invitation, & that he had not met them
they hoped their Fathers would pity their necessity &
give them a little clothing, and a little rum to drink on the
road, as they had come a great way to see their Fathers.
Then the Wyondats spoake to the Shawanese, & all the
Western Nations on severall Belts & strings, by which
they exhorted the several Nations to behave themselves
well to their Fathers the English, who had now taken
them under their Protection, that if they did, they would
be a happy People, that if they did not listen to the Councils of their Fathers, they must take the Consequences,
having assured them that all Nations to the Sun rising
had taken fast hold of their Fathers the English by the
hand, & would follow their Advice, & do every thing they
desired them, & never would let slip the Chain of Friendship now so happily renewed.

August 24th— We had another Meeting with the
Several Nations, when the Wawiotonans, Twightwees,
Pyankeshas, Kickapoos & Musquatamies made several
speeches to Col° Campbell & me, in presence of all the
other Nations, when they promised to become the Children of the King of Great Britain & farther acknowledged
that they had at Ouiatonon before they came there [here]
given up the Soverignty of their Country to me for His
Majesty, & promised to support his subjects in taking
possession of all the Posts given up by the French their
former Fathers, to the English, now their present Fathers,
all which they confirmed with a Belt.

25th— We had another meeting with the same Indians,
when Col° Campbell & I made them several speeches in

answer to theirs of the 23 & 24th then delivered them a
Road Belt in the name of Sir William Johnson Baronet,
to open a Road from the rising to the setting of the Sun
which we charged them to keep open through their
Country & cautioned them to stop their Ears against the
Storys or idle reports of evil minded People & continue
to promote the good Works of Peace, all which they promised to do in a most sincere manner.

26th—Col° Campbell & I made those Nations some
presents, when after taking leave of us, they sett off for
their own Country well satisfied.

27th—We had a Meeting with Pondiac & all the
Ottawa Tribes, Chipwaes & Puttewatamies wth the
Hurons of this Place & the chiefs of those settled at
Sandusky & the Miamis River, when we made them the
following Speeches.

CHILDREN PONDIAC & ALL OUR CHILDREN THE OTTA-
WAS, PUTTEWATAMIES, CHIPWAYS & WYONDATTS: We
are very glad to see so many of our Children here present
at your Antient Council Fire, which has been neglected
for some time past, since those high winds has arose &
raised some heavy clouds over your Country, I now by
this Belt dress up your Antient Fire & throw some dry
wood upon it, that the blaze may ascend to the Clouds so
that all Nations may see it, & know that you live in
Peace & Tranquility with your Fathers the English.— A
Belt.

By this Belt I disperse all the black clouds from over
your heads, that the Sun may shine clear on your Women
and Children, that those unborn may enjoy the blessings
of this General Peace, now so happily settled between
your Fathers the English & you & all your younger
Bretheren to the Sun setting.— A Belt.

Children: By this Belt I gather up all the Bones of your deceased friends, & bury them deep in the ground, that the herbs & sweet flowers of the earth may grow over them, that we may not see them any more.— A Belt.

Children: with this Belt I take the Hatchet out of your Hands & I pluck up a large tree & bury it deep, so that it may never be found any more, & I plant the tree of Peace, where all our children may sit under & smoak in Peace with their Fathers.— A Belt.

Children: We have made a Road from the Sun rising to the Sun setting, I desire that you will preserve that Road good and pleasant to Travel upon, that we may all share the blessings of this happy Union. I am sorry to see our Children dispersed thro' the Woods, I therefore desire you will return to your Antient Settlements & take care of your Council Fire which I have now dressed up, & promote the good work of Peace.— A Belt.

After which Wapicomica delivered his Messages from Sir William Johnson to Pondiac & the rest of the several Chiefs.

Aug. 28th— We had a Meeting with Pondiac & the several Nations when Pondiac made the following Speeches.

FATHER: We have all smoaked out of the Pipe of Peace its your Childrens Pipe & as the War is all over, & the Great Spirit and Giver of Light who has made the Earth & every thing therein, has brought us all together this day for our mutual good to promote the good Works of Peace, I declare to all Nations that I had settled my Peace with you before I came here, & now deliver my Pipe to be sent to *Sir William Johnson* that he may know I have made Peace, & taken the King of England for my Father, in presence of all the Nations now assembled, & whenever any of those Nations go to visit him, they may smoak out of it with him in Peace. Fathers we are oblidged to you for lighting up our old Council Fire for us, & desiring us to return to it, but we are now settled on the Miamis River, not far from hence, whenever you want us you will find us there ready to wait on you, the reason I choose to stay where we are now settled, is, that we love liquor, and did we live here as formerly, our People would be always drunk, which might occasion some quarrels between the Soldiers & them, this Father is all the reason I have for not returning to our old Settlements, & that we live so nigh this place, that when we want to drink, we can easily come for it.— Gave a large Pipe with a Belt of Wampum tied to it.

FATHER: Be strong and take pity on us your Children as our former Father did, 'tis just the Hunting Season of our children, our Fathers the French formerly used to credit his Children for powder & lead to hunt with, I request in behalf of all the Nations present that you will speak to the Traders now here to do the same, my Father, once more I request you will take pity on us & tell your Traders to give your Children credit for a little powder & lead, as the support of our Family's depend upon it, we have told you where we live, that whenever you want us & let us know it, we will come directly to you.— A Belt.

FATHER: You stoped up the Rum Barrel when we came here, 'till the Business of this Meeting[138] was over,

---

[138] There were present at this treaty about thirty chiefs and five hundred warriors. A list of the tribes is given, and the names of the chiefs. This was the last public transaction in which Pondiac was engaged with the English. The year following, in a council with the Indians on the Illinois, this noted chief was stabbed to the heart, by an Indian who had long followed him for that purpose.— HILDRETH.

Comment by Ed.— Hildreth is mistaken in calling this the last public transaction of Pontiac. He was at Oswego and treated with Johnson in the spring of 1766. See *New York Colonial Documents*, vii, pp. 854-867.

as it is now finished, we request you may open the barrel
that your Children may drink & be merry.

August 29ᵗʰ— A Deputation of several Nations sett
out from Detroit for the Ilinois Country with several
Messages from me & the Wyondats, Six Nations, Delawares, Shawanese & other Nations, in answer to theirs
delivered me at Ouiatonon.

30ᵗʰ— The Chiefs of the several Nations who are settled on the Ouabache returned to Detroit from the River
Roche, where they had been encamped, & informed
Col° Campbell & me, they were now going off for their
own Country, & that nothing gave them greater pleasure,
than to see that all the Western Nations & Tribes had
agreed to a general Peace, & that they should be glad [to
know] how soon their Fathers the English, would take
possession of the Posts in their Country, formerly possessed by their late Fathers the French, to open a
Trade for them, & if this could not be done this Fall,
they desired that some Traders might be sent to their
Villages to supply them for the Winter, or else they
would be oblidged to go to the Ilinois and apply to their
old Fathers the French for such necessarys as they might
want.

They then spoke on a Belt & said Fathers, every thing
is now settled, & we have agreed to your taking possession
of the posts in our Country. we have been informed,
that the English where ever they settle, make the Country their own, & you tell us that when you conquered the
French they gave you this Country.— That no difference
may happen hereafter, we tell you now the French never
conquered us neither did they purchase a foot of our
Country, nor have they a right to give it to you, we gave
them liberty to settle for which they always rewarded us,

& treated us with great Civility while they had it in their power, but as they are become now your people, if you expect to keep these Posts, we will expect to have proper returns from you.— A Belt.

Sept[br] 2[d] — The chiefs of the Wyondatts or Huron, came to me & said they had spoke last Summer to Sir Will[m] Johnson at Niagara about the lands, on which the French had settled near Detroit belonging to them, & desired I would mention again to him. they never had sold it to the French, & expected their new Fathers the English would do them justice, as the French were become one People with us.— A Belt.

4th — Pondiac with several chiefs of the Ottawas, Chippawaes & Potowatamies likewise complained that the French had settled part of their country, which they never had sold to them, & hoped their Fathers the English would take it into Consideration, & see that a proper satisfaction was made to them. That their Country was very large, & they were willing to give up such part of it, as was necessary for their Fathers the English, to carry on Trade at, provided they were paid for it, & a sufficient part of the Country left them to hunt on.— A Belt.

6th — The *Sagina* Indians came here,[129] & made a speech on a Belt of Wampum expressing their satisfaction on hearing that a general Peace was made with all the Western Nations & with Pondiac, they desired a little Powder, Lead & a few knives to enable them to

---

[129] The Saginaw Indians were a notoriously turbulent band of Chippewas, who had a village on Saginaw Bay. They had assisted in the siege of Detroit; and going to Mackinac to secure recruits to continue their resistance, they attempted to kill the trader Alexander Henry. See Bain (ed.), Henry's *Travels and Adventures* (Boston, 1901), pp. 148-152, an admirably-edited work, containing much valuable information.— ED.

hunt on their way home, & a little rum to drink their new Fathers health.— A Belt.

9th — *Altewaky* and *Chamindiway* Chiefs of a Band of Ottawas from Sandusky with 20 Men came here and informed me that their late conduct had been peaceable, that on hearing there was a great Meeting of all Nations at this place, they came to hear what would be done, & on their way here they had been informed that a General Peace was settled with all Nations to the Sun setting, & they now came to assure us of their attachment to the English Interest, & beged for some Powder, Lead, some Blankets and a little rum to help them to return to their town.   A String.

Septbr 11th — Col° Campbell & I gave the above parties some presents & a little rum & sent them away well satisfied.

12th — The Grand Sautois[130] came with his band and spoke as follows.

FATHER: You sent me a Belt from the Miamis, & as soon as I received it, I set off to meet you here, on my way I heard what had past between you & the several Tribes that met you here, you have had pity on them, & I beg in behalf of myself & the people of Chicago that you will have pity on us also. 'tis true we have been Fools, & have listened to evil reports, & the whistling of bad birds, we red people, are a very jealous and foolish people, & Father amongst you White People, there are bad people also, that tell us lyes & deceive us, which has

---

[130] According to Parkman, Le Grand Sauteur was Pontiac's chief coadjutor among the northern Indians in his attack on the English. His Indian name was Minavavana, and he was considered the author of the plot against Mackinac. This has been since attributed to Match-e-ke-wis, a younger Indian; but Le Grand Sauteur remained an inveterate enemy of the English, and was at length stabbed by an English trader. See Henry, *Travels*, pp. 42-47.— ED.

been the occasion of what has past, I need not say much
on this head, I am now convinced, that I have been
wrong for some years past, but there are people who
have behaved worse than I & my people, they were pardoned last year at this place, I hope we may meet with
the same, that our Women & Children may enjoy the
blessings of peace as the rest of our Bretheren the red
people, & you shall be convinced by our future conduct
that we will behave as well as any Tribe of Ind* in this
Country.— A Belt.

He then said that the St. Joseph Indians would have
come along with him, but the English Prisoner which
their Fathers want from them, was some distance off a
hunting, & as soon as they could get him in, they would
deliver him up and desire forgiveness.

14th — I had a private meeting with the grand Sautois
when he told me he was well disposed for peace last Fall,
but was then sent for to the Ilinois, where he met with
Pondiac, & that then their Fathers the French told
them, if they would be strong to keep the English out of
possession of that Country but this Summer, That the
King of France would send over an Army next Spring, to
assist his Children the Indians, and that the King of
Spain would likewise send troops to help them to keep
the English out of their Country, that the English were a
bad people, & had a design to cut off all the Indian
Nations in this Country, & to bring the Southern Indians
to live & settle there, this account made all the Indians
very uneasy in their minds, & after holding a Council
amongst themselves, they all determined to oppose the
English, & not to suffer them to take Possession of the
Ilinois, that for his part he behaved as ill as the rest to
the English Officers that came there in the Spring, but

since he had been better informed of the goodness of the
English, & convinced the French had told lyes for the
love of their Beaver, he was now determined with all his
people to become faithfull to their new Fathers the English, & pay no regard to any stories the French should
tell him for the future.

Sepr 15th — Col° Campbell & I had a meeting with
the Grand Sautois, at which we informed him of every
thing that had past with the several Nations & Tribes &
told him that we accepted him and his people in Friendship, & would forgive them as we had the rest of the
Tribes, & forget what was past provided their future
conduct should convince us of their sincerity, after which
we gave them some presents, for which he returned
thanks & departed very well satisfied.

19th — I received a letter by express from Col° Reed
acquainting me of Capt Sterlings setting out from Fort
Pitt, with 100 men of the 42^d Reg^t to take possession of
Fort Chartres in the Ilinois Country

20th — I sent of[f] Huron Andrew Express to Capt
Sterling[181] at the Ilinois, & with messages to the several

[181] Sir Thomas Stirling, Bart., obtained his company in July, 1757, in the
42d, or Royal Highland, regiment, which accompanied Abercromby in 1758,
and Amherst in 1759 in their respective expeditions on Lakes George and
Champlain; was afterwards detailed to assist at the siege of Niagara, and
accompanied Amherst from Oswego to Montreal in 1760. *Knox.* Captain
Stirling was appointed a Major in 1770, and Lieutenant-colonel of the 42d in
September, 1771. He was in command of his regiment in the engagement on
Staten Island, and in the battle of Brooklyn Heights, in 1776; was afterwards
at the storming of Fort Washington and accompanied the expedition against
Philadelphia. He became Colonel in the army in 1779, and was Brigadier,
under Sir Henry Clinton, in the expedition against Charleston, S. C., in 1780.
Beatson. He succeeded Lieutenant-general Frazer as Colonel of the 71st High-
landers, in February, 1782, and in November following, became Major-general.
He went on the retired list in 1783, when his regiment was disbanded. In 1796
he was appointed Lieutenant-general; was created a Baronet some time after,
and became a General in the army on the first of January, 1801. He died in
1808. *Army Lists.*— E. B. O'CALLAGHAN.

Nations in that Country & those on the Ouabache, to acquaint them of Cap[t] Starling's departure from Fort Pitt for the Ilinois Country.

25th — The Chiefs of the S[t] Joseph Indians arrived and addressed themselves to Col[o] Campbell & me as follows,

FATHERS: We are come here to see you, altho' we are not acquainted with you, we had a Father formerly, with whom we were very well acquainted, & never differed with him, you have conquered him some time ago, & when you came here first notwithstanding your hands were all bloody, you took hold of us by the hands, & used us well, & we thought we should be happy with our Fathers, but soon an unlucky difference happened, which threw us all in confusion, where this arose we don't know but we assure you, we were the last that entered into this Quarrel, the Ind[a] from this place solicited us often to join them, but we would not listen to them, at last they got the better of our foolish young Warriors, but we never agreed to it, we knew it would answer no end, & often told our Warriors they were fools, if they succeeded in killing the few English in this Country, they could not kill them all because we knew you to be a great People.

Fathers: you have after all that has happened, received all the several Tribes in this Country for your Children, we from St. Joseph's seem to be the last of your Children that come to you, we are no more than Wild Creatures to you Fathers in understanding therefore we request you'l forgive the past follies of our young people & receive us for your Children since you have thrown down our former Father on his back, we have been wandering in the dark like blind people, now you have dispersed all this darkness which hung over the heads of the several Tribes, & have accepted them for your Children, we hope you will let us partake with them of the light, that our Women & Children may enjoy Peace, & we beg you'l forget all that is past, by this belt we remove all evil thoughts from your hearts.— A Belt.

Fathers, When we formerly came to visit our late Fathers the French they always sent us home joyfull, & we hope you will have pity on our Women & Young Men who are in great Want of necessarys, & not let us return home to our Villages ashamed.

Col° Campbell & I made them the following answer.

CHILDREN: I have heard with attention what you have said, & am glad to hear that you have delivered up the Prisoners at Michillimakinac, agreeable to my desire, as the other Prisoner who I always thought belonged to your Nation does not, but the man who has him resides now in your Country, I must desire you'l do every thing in your Power to get him brought to me, nothing will give me greater pleasure than to promote the good Works of Peace, & make my Children the Indians happy as long as their own Conduct shall deserve it. I did not know what to think of your conduct for some time past, but to convince you of my sincere desire to promote Peace, I receive you as Children as I have done the other Nations, & hope your future Conduct may be such, as will convince me of your sincerity.— A Belt.

Children: Sometimes bad people take the liberty of stragling into your Country, I desire if you meet any such people to bring them immediately here, likewise I desire that none of your Young Men may steal any Horses out of this settlement as they have done formerly, we shall see always strict justice done to you, & expect the same from you, on that your own happiness depends, & as long as you continue to merit our friendship by good actions in promoting Peace & Tranquility between your Young People & His Majesties Subjects, you may expect to be received here with open arms, & to convince you further of my sincerity, I give you some cloaths, powder, lead, vermillion & 2 cags of rum for your young People, that you may return home without shame as you desired.

Children, I take this oppertunity to tell you that your Fathers the English are gone down the Ohio from Fort Pitt to take possession the Ilinois, & desire you may acquaint all your people of it on your return home, & likewise desire you will stop your Ears against the Whistling of bad birds, & mind nothing else but your Hunting to support your Familys, that your Women & Children may enjoy the Blessing of Peace.— A Belt.

September 26th.[122]— Set out from Detroit for Niagara; passed Lake Erie along the north shore in a birch canoe, and arrived the 8th of October at Niagara. The navigation of the lake is dangerous for batteaux or canoes, by reason the lake is very shallow for a considerable distance from the shore. The bank, for several miles, high and steep, and affords a harbor for a single batteau. The lands in general, between Detroit and Niagara, are high, and the soil good, with several fine rivers falling into the lake. The distance from Detroit to Niagara is computed three hundred miles.

[122] The entry for September 26, and the list of tribes following, are taken from the Featherstonhaugh-Butler edition of the journal.— ED.

A List of the different Nations and Tribes of Indians in the Northern District of North America, with the number of their fighting Men.

Names of the Tribes.	Nos.	Their Dwelling Ground.	Their Hunting Grounds.
Mohocks, a	160	Mobock River.	Between that and Lake George.
Oneidas, b	300	East side of Oneida Lake, & on the head waters of the east branch of Susquehannah.	In the country where they live.
Tuscaroras, b	200	Between the Oneidas and Onandagoes.	Between Oneida Lake & Lake Ontario.
Onandagoes, b	260	Near the Onandaga Lake.	Between Onandago L. & mouth of Seneca River, near Oswego.
Cayugas, b	200	On two small Lakes, called the Cayugas, on the north branch of Susquehannah.	Where they reside.
Senecas, b	1,000	Seneca Country, on the waters of Susquehannah, the waters of Lake Ontario, and on the heads of Ohio River.	Their chief hunting country thereabouts.
Aughquagas, c	150	East branch of Susquehannah River, and on Aughquaga.	Where they live.
Nanticokes, c	100 }	Utsanango, Chagmett, Oswego, and on the east branch of Susquehannah.	Do.
Mohickons, c	100 }		
Conoys, c	30 }		
Monsays, c	150 }	At Diahogo, and other villages up the north branch of Susquehannah.	Do.
Sapoones, c	30 }		
Delawares, c	150 }		

a These are the oldest Tribe of the Confederacy of the Six Nations.
b Connected with New York, part of the Confederacy with New York.
c Connected with, and depending on the Five Nations.

Names of the Tribes.	Nos.	Their Dwelling Ground.	Their Hunting Grounds.
Delawares, d	600	Between the Ohio & Lake Erie, on the branches of Beaver Creek, Muskingum and Guyehugo.	Where they live.
Shawnesse, d	300	On Scioto & branch of Muskingum.	Do.
Mohickone, d	300	In villages near Sandusky.	Do.
Goghnawages, d			On the head banks of Scioto.
Twightwees, e	250	Miame River, near Fort Miame.	On the ground where they live.
Wayoughtanies, f	300 }	On the branches of Ouabache, near Fort Ouitanon.	Between Ouitanon & the Miames.
Pyankeshas, f	300 }		
Shockays, f	200 }		
Huskhuskeys, g	300 }	Near the French settlements, in the Illinois Country.	
Illinois, g	300 }		
Wayondotts, h	250	Near Fort Detroit.	About Lake Erie.
Ottawas, h	400		
Putawatimes, h	200 }		
Chipawas, i	200	On Saganna Creek, which empties into Lake Huron.	Thereabouts.
Ottawas,			
Chippawas, j	400 }	Near Michilimachinac.	On the north side of Lake Huron.
Ottawas, j	260 }		

d Dependent on the Six Nations, and connected with Pennsylvania.
e Connected with Pennsylvania.
f Connected with the Twightwees.
g These two Nations the English had never any trade, or connection with.
h Connected formerly with the French.
i Connected with the Indians about Detroit, and dependant on the commanding officer.
j Always connected with the French.

Names of the Tribes.	Nos.	Their Dwelling Ground.	Their Hunting Grounds.
Chipawas, *k	400	Near the entrance of Lake Superior, and not far from Fort St. Mary's.	Thereabouts.
Chepawas, k Mynonamies, k Shockeys, k	550	Near Fort Labay on the Lake Michigan.	Thereabouts.
Putawatimes, k	150	Near Fort St. Joseph's.	Thereabouts.
Ottawas, k Kicapoos, l	150		
Outtagamies, l Musquatans, l Miscotins, l	4,000	On Lake Michigan and between it and the Mississippi.	Where they respectively reside.
Outtamacks, l Musquaykeys, l Oswegatches, h	100	Settled at Swagatchy in Canada, on the River St. Lawrence.	Thereabouts.
Connesedagoes, k Coghnewagoes, k	300	Near Montreal.	
Orondocks, k	100		
Abonakies, k	150	Settled near Trois Rivers.	
Alagonkins, k	100		
La Suil, *	10,1000	South-west of Lake Superior.	

k Connected with the French.

* There are several villages of Chipawas settled along the bank of Lake Superior, but as I have no knowledge of that country, cannot ascertain their numbers.

l Never connected in any trade or otherwise with the English.

* These are a nation of Indians settled south-west of Lake Superior, called by the French La Sue, who, by the best account that I could ever get from the French and Indians, are computed ten thousand fighting men. They spread over a large tract of country, and have forty odd villages; in which country are several other tribes of Indians, who are tributaries to the La Sues, none of whom except a very few, have ever known the use of fire-arms: as yet but two villages. I suppose the French don't choose to risk a trade among such a powerful body of people, at so vast a distance.

CROGHAN TO SIR WILLIAM JOHNSON [188]

SIR: In the scituation I was in at Ouiatonon, with great numbers of Indians about me, & no Necessaries such as Paper & Ink, I had it not in my power to take down all the speeches made by the Indian Nations, nor what I said to them, in so particular a manner as I could wish, but hope the heads of it as I have taken down will meet with your approbation.

In the Course of this Tour through the Ind" Countrys I made it my study to converse in private with Pondiac, & several of the Chiefs of the different Nations, as often as oppertunity served, in order to find out the sentiments they have of the French & English, Pondiac is a shrewd sensible Indian of few words, & commands more respect amongst those Nations, than any Indian I ever saw could do amongst his own Tribe. He and all his principal men of those Nations seem at present to be convinced that the French had a view of interest in stirring up the late difference between his Majesties Subjects & them & call it a Bever War, for neither Pondiac nor any of the Indians which I met with, ever pretended to deny but the French were at the bottom of the whole, & constantly supplyed them with every necessary they wanted, as far as in their power, every where through that Country & notwithstanding they are at present convinced, that it was for their own Interest, yet it has not changed the Indians affections to them, they have been bred up together like Children in that Country, & the French have always

[188] This letter is reprinted from *New York Colonial Documents*, vii, pp. 787, 788. It was evidently written after Croghan's return from the West, and accompanied the official version of his journal, which Johnson sent to England November 16, 1765. See *New York Colonial Documents*, vii, p. 775.— ED.

adopted the Indians customs & manners, treated them civily & supplyed their wants generously, by which means they gained the hearts of the Indians & commanded their services, & enjoyed the benefit of a very large Furr Trade, as they well knew if they had not taken this measure they could not enjoy any of those Advantages. The French have in a manner taught the Indians in that Country to hate the English, by representing them in the worst light they could on all occasion, in particular they have made the Indians there believe lately, that the English would take their Country from them & bring the *Cherokees* there to settle & to enslave them, which report they easily gave credit to, as the Southern Ind⁸ had lately commenced war against them. I had great difficulty in removing this suspicion and convincing them of the falsity of this report, which I flatter myself I have done in a great measure, yet it will require some time, a very even Conduct in those that are to reside in their Country, before we can expect to rival the French in their affection, all Indians are jealous & from their high notion of liberty hate power, those Nations are jealous and prejudiced against us, so that the greatest care will be necessary to convince them of our honest Intention by our Actions. The French sold them goods much dearer than the English Traders do at present, in that point we have the advantage of the French, but they made that up in large presents to them for their services, which they wanted to support their Interest in the Country, & tho' we want none of their services, yet they will expect favours, & if refused look on it in a bad light, & very likely think it done to distress them for some particular Advantages we want to gain over them. they are by no means so sensible a People as the Six Nations or other Tribes this way, & the French have learned them for their own advantage a bad custom, for by all I could learn, they seldom made them any general presents, but as it were fed them with Necessaries just as they wanted them Tribe by Tribe, & never sent them away empty, which will make it difficult & troublesome to the Gentlemen that are to command in their Country for some time, to please them & preserve Peace, as they are a rash inconsiderate People and don't look on themselves under any obligations to us, but rather think we are obliged to them for letting us reside in their Country.   As far as I can judge of their Sentiments by the several Conversations I have had with them, they will expect some satisfaction made them by Us, for any Posts that should be established in their Country for Trade.   But you will be informed better by themselves next Spring, as Pondiac & some Chiefs of every Nation in that Country intend to pay you a visit. The several Nations on the Ouiabache, & towards the *Ilinois*, *St. Josephs*, *Chicago*, *Labaye*, *Sagina* & other places have applyed for Traders to be sent to their settlements, but as it is not in the power of any Officer to permit Traders to go from Detroit or *Michillimackinac*, either English or French, I am of opinion the Ind⁸ will be supplied this year chiefly from the *Ilinois*, which is all French property & if Trading Posts are not established at proper Places in that Country soon the French will carry the best part of the Trade over the *Missisipi* which they are determined to do if they can, for I have been well informed that the French are preparing to build a strong trading Fort on the other side Missisipi, about 60 miles above *Fort Chartres*,[124] and have this

---

[124] Fort Chartres was originally built as a stockade post in 1720; but in 1756 was rebuilt in stone, and became the most important French fortification in the

Summer in a private manner transported 26 pieces of small canon up the River for that purpose.

G. CROGHAN.

November, 1765.

West. It was an irregular quadrangle, with houses, magazines, barracks, etc., defended with cannon.— See Pittman, *Settlements on the Mississippi* (London, 1770), pp. 45, 46. After its surrender by the French, the English garrisoned the stronghold until 1772, when the river's erosion made it untenable. For the present state of the ruins, see Mason, *Chapters from Illinois History*, pp. 241-249.

The French trading post sixty miles above Fort Chartres, on the western bank of the river, was the beginning of the present city of St. Louis, which was founded in April, 1764, by Pierre Laclède. Upon the surrender of the Illinois to the English, St. Ange, with the garrison and many French families, removed to this new post, in the expectation of living under French authority. To their chagrin the place was surrendered to the Spanish the following year.— ED.

III

TWO JOURNALS OF WESTERN TOURS, BY CHARLES FRED-
ERICK POST: ONE, TO THE NEIGHBORHOOD OF FORT
DUQUESNE (JULY–SEPTEMBER, 1758); THE OTHER, TO
THE OHIO (OCTOBER, 1758–JANUARY, 1759)

SOURCE: Proud's *History of Pennsylvania* (Philadelphia, 1798),
ii, appendix.

INTRODUCTORY NOTE

Christian Frederick Post, author of the following journals, was a simple, uneducated missionary of the Moravian Church. His chief qualifications for the perilous journeys herein detailed, were his intimate acquaintance with Indian life and character, the belief of the tribesmen in his truthfulness and honesty, and his own steadfast courage and trust in the protection of a higher power. Born in Polish Prussia in 1710, Post early came under the influence of the Moravians, whose remarkable missionary movement was just beginning to germinate.

The first attempt of this church to christianize the American Indians in Georgia having failed because of Spanish hostility, the Moravian disciples removed to Pennsylvania (1739), and were granted land on which to establish their colony at Bethlehem. Thither in 1742 came Post, eager to join in evangelizing the Indians; for which purpose he was sent the following year to assist Henry Rauch in his mission to the Mohegans and Wampanoags. This mission had been established about 1740, Count Zinzendorf, the great Moravian bishop, having visited its site at Shekomeko (Pine Plains, Dutchess County, New York) and baptized three Indians as its first fruits. The work spread to the neighboring Indian villages of Connecticut, and Post was assigned to a circuit in Sharon Township, Litchfield County, consisting of the villages of Pachgatgoch and Wechquadnach. Here, in his zeal for the service, he married a converted Indian woman (1743), and endeared himself to all the tribe.

But persecutions began to assail the humble brethren and their converts; they were accused of being papists, arrested and haled before local magistrates, by whom they were no sooner released than a mob of those whose gain in pampering to Indian vices was endangered by Moravian success, set upon them and rendered their lives and those of their new converts intolerable. Post, who had been on a journey to the Iroquois country (1745), was arrested at Albany and sent to New York, where he was imprisoned for seven weeks on a trumped-up charge of abetting Indian raids.

The situation made retreat necessary; therefore, in 1746, the Shekomeko and Connecticut settlements were broken up, and the Christian Indians with their missionaries moved in detachments to Pennsylvania, where, after kindly entertainment at Bethlehem, a town called Gnadenhütten (huts of Grace), was built for them, at Weisport, Carbon County. It was during their stay at Bethlehem that Rachel, Post's Indian wife, died (1747), and there two years later he married a Delaware convert, Agnes, who lived only until 1751.

Meanwhile, Post was employed as missionary assistant, going to Shamokin in 1747 to aid the missionary blacksmith established there, to clear and plant more ground. Again in 1749, he revisited the scene of his early labors, and helped David Bruce to re-establish a mission among the remnant left at Pachgatgoch. Two years later he was summoned to a more distant field on the dismal shores of Labrador, where a company of four Moravian brethren were sent to begin a mission to the Eskimos. An untoward accident rendered this project futile; the

major part of the crew of the vessel which had transported them having been lost, the captain impressed the
missionaries to carry his ship back to England.

Thereupon Post again sought his home in Pennsylvania, dwelling principally at Bethlehem, until called
upon by the Pennsylvania authorities to assist in public
affairs. There is no certain information of his introduction to the managers of Indian matters in Pennsylvania;
but several Christian Indians from his flock had been
utilized as interpreters, and the Friendly Association of
Quakers, which was assuming so large a rôle in treating
with the natives, was well-inclined toward the Moravian
brothers.

The first mention of Post in the public records is in
connection with a message which he was employed to
carry (June, 1758) in conjunction with Charles Thomson to Teedyuscung at Wyoming.[1] On his return to
the settlements, he was immediately commissioned to
go back to Wyoming with a message from the Cherokee
auxiliaries, who had come to join the army of Forbes,
and whose presence caused consternation among Pennsylvania's savage allies. With but five days' respite, Post
again started on a journey beset with perils on every side,
through the wilderness of Northern Pennsylvania.[2] At
Teedyuscung's cabin he met two Indians from the Ohio,
who declared that their tribes were sorry they had gone to
war against the English; they had often wished that messengers from the government would come to them, for
then they should long before have abandoned war.

On the receipt of this important information, the council

---

[1] *Pennsylvania Colonial Records*, viii, p. 132; *Pennsylvania Archives*, iii, pp.
412-422.

[2] Journal of this journey in *Pennsylvania Colonial Records*, viii, pp. 142-145.

at Philadelphia debated to what use it might be put in furthering the plans for Forbes's advance. "Post was desired to accompany the Indians, and he readily consented to go."[3]

Antiquarians and historians have alike admired the sublime courage of the man, and the heroic patriotism which made him capable of advancing into the heart of a hostile territory, into the very hands of a cruel and treacherous foe. But aside from Post's supreme religious faith, he had a shrewd knowledge of Indian customs, and knew that in the character of an ambassador requested by the Western tribes, his mission would be a source of protection. Therefore, even under the very walls of Fort Duquesne, he trusted not in vain to Indian good faith.

The results of this embassy were most gratifying. The report of his mission coming during the important negotiations at Easton, aided in securing the Indian neutrality which made the advance of Forbes so much less hazardous than that of Braddock.

But the work was only begun; and to complete it Post's renewed co-operation was necessary. This time he was not to venture alone. Two militia officers, Captain John Bull and Lieutenant William Hays, volunteered for the service,[4] and having joined Post at Reading, all proceeded with Indian companions in their van, to overtake the army and reach the Ohio in advance of the column.

Their mission was not in time to save the Indian ferocity at Grant's defeat; but it contributed to assure the French that aid from the neighboring Indians was dubious, and that in retreat lay their only safety.

[3] *Pennsylvania Colonial Records*, viii, p. 147.

[4] *Pennsylvania Archives*, iii, pp. 556, 557.

Through the simple narrative of Indian speeches and replies, one feels the intensity of the strain: the French captain "looked as pale as death;" "we hanged out the English flag, in spite of the French, on which our prisoners folded their hands, in hopes that their redemption was nigh." Then the news came "which gave us the pleasure to hear, that the English had the field, and that the French had demolished and burnt the place entirely and went off."

Of Post's later life and its vicissitudes, we get but scattered glimpses. ˉ For the two years succeeding these adventurous journeys, he served the Pennsylvania authorities as messenger and interpreter, at the same time begging to be allowed to go and preach to the newly-appeased Indians on the Ohio. The last official act of Governor Denny was the affixing of his signature to a passport for Post, of whose loyalty, integrity and prudence he testifies to have had good experience.[5]

This desire to begin a mission to the Western Indians was consummated in 1761, when Post proceeded alone to the Muskingum and built the first white man's house within the present limits of Ohio. The following spring, he applied to the Moravian brethren for an assistant; whereupon John Heckewelder was assigned to this service, and in his *Narrative* describes their courteous reception by Bouquet at Fort Pitt, the restless conditions among the Delawares and Shawnees, and the warnings against the storm of fire and blood which was so soon to break over the frontier. Heckewelder retreated in due season; Post barely saved himself by a sudden flight.

---

[5] *Pennsylvania Colonial Records*, viii, pp. 341, 419, 463, 466, 469, 491; *Pennsylvania Archives*, iii, pp. 581, 582, 689, 702, 703.

In 1764, the ecclesiastical authorities saw fit to send this intrepid missionary to the Mosquito Coast, where he stayed two years, making a second visit in 1767. Toward the close of his life he retired from the Moravian sect, and entered the Protestant Episcopal Church. His death occurred at Germantown in 1785.

The journal of the first tour to the Ohio Indians (July 15 – September 22, 1758), was printed in the appendix to *An Enquiry into the Causes of the Alienation of the Delaware and Shawanese Indians from the British Interest* (London, 1759; reprinted Philadelphia, 1867). This book was published anonymously, but was known to be the work of Charles Thomson, a prominent Philadelphia Quaker, later secretary of the Continental Congress. Thomson gives a brief preface to Post's journal, and the matter in the notes thereof is evidently by his hand; it is probable that the notes to the second journal are also by him. The first journal was reprinted by Proud, *History of Pennsylvania* (Philadelphia, 1798), ii, appendix, pp. 65-95, from which edition our reprint has been made. Craig also published this in *The Olden Time*, i, pp. 99-125, following almost verbatim the edition of Thomson and Proud. Rupp, *Early History of Western Pennsylvania* (Pittsburg and Harrisburg, 1846), appendix, pp. 75-98, gives the same journal. The *Pennsylvania Archives*, iii, pp. 520-544, also contains this journal, evidently taken from the same manuscript, with but slight variations in the spelling of proper names.

Heckewelder, *Narrative of the Mission of the United Brethren* (Philadelphia, 1820), pp. 55, 56, says: "To enumerate all the hardships, difficulties and dangers, Frederick Post had been subjected to on these journies, especially on the first, in the summer of the year 1758, is at this time both impossible and needless. Suffice it to say, that what *he* intended the public should know, was published in the year after, in England, under the title of 'Christian Frederick Post's Journal from Philadelphia to the Ohio,' &c. His *original* manuscript journal, however, which had for some time been placed in the hands of the writer of this narrative, was far more interesting, and evinced that few men would be found able to undergo the fatigues of a journey, bearing so hard on the constitution, or a mind to sustain such trials of adversity — at least not with that calmness with which Mr. Post endured it.''

The diary of the second journey of Christian Frederick Post to the Ohio, October 25, 1758 – January 8, 1759, was first printed in London, 1759, for J. Wilkie; see Field, *An Essay towards an Indian Bibliography* (New York, 1873), p. 315. Proud, *History of Pennsylvania*, ii, appendix, pp. 96-132, also reprints Post's second journal, and from this our reprint is made. It appears also in *The Olden Time*, i, pp. 144-177; and in Rupp, *Early History of Western Pennsylvania*, appendix, pp. 99-126. The extract from a journal in the *Pennsylvania Archives*, iii, pp. 560-563, entitled "Journal of Fredcrick Post from Pittsburg, 1758," is in reality that of Croghan's — see *ante*, p. 100. For an example of the form and spelling of the original manuscripts of these journals before they were rigorously edited, see letter of Post's in *Pennsylvania Archives*, iii, pp. 742-744. The following is a sample extract therefrom:

To his honnour da Governor of Pansylvanea:

Broder, I cam to Machochlaung, wa mane Indeans luve, I cald dam all togader, and I told dam wat we bous had agread on wan we sa one anoder last, and wat you

ar sorre for and have so mouts at hart, and dasayrt me
to mack it avere war noun avere war, and dasayrd dam
to be strong and sea dat your flasch and blod may be
rastord to you; now br'r, you know dat it is aur agrea-
mand, dat as soun as I hoar any ting, I geave yu daracktly
notys of, and as I am as jat closs bay you, so I sand daes
prasonars to you which da daleverat to me, and I geave
dam to Papunnahanck to dalever dam to you; br. I do
not sand daes poepel daun, da have had damself a long
dasayr to go daun to sea dar br. da Englesch, so I tot it
proper to sand dam along; I hop you will rajoys to sea
dam and be kaynd to dam, and allso to dam poepel dat
bryng dam daun; wan I am farder from you and I schall
meat wit som, I schall bryng dam maysalf daun wan I
com along; br. you know aur worck is grat, and will tack
a long taym befor we coan com back, I salud all da
schandel pepel, and dasayr you to be strong.
    Ye 20 Day of May, 1760, rot at Machochloschung.

    Ordinarily, the modern historical student very properly
deprecates any tampering with original manuscripts; but
an examination of the foregoing inclines one not only to
forgive but to thank the early editors for having translated
Post's jargon into understandable English.

                                                    R. G. T.

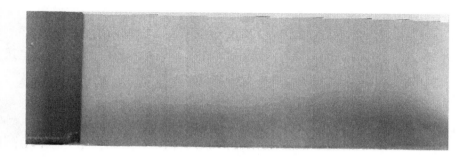

THE JOURNAL OF CHRISTIAN FREDERICK POST, FROM PHILADELPHIA TO THE OHIO, ON A MESSAGE FROM THE GOVERNMENT OF PENNSYLVANIA TO THE DELAWARE, SHAWNESE, AND MINGO INDIANS, SETTLED THERE.

July the 15th, 1758.— This day I received orders from his honour, the Governor, to fet out on my intended journey, and proceeded as far as *German Town*, where I found all the *Indians* drunk.[6] *Willamegicken* returned to *Philadelphia*, for a horfe, that was promifed him.[7]

16th.— This day I waited for the faid *Willamegicken* till near noon, and when he came, being very drunk, he could proceed no further, fo that I left him, and went to *Bethlehem.*[8]

17th.— I arrived at *Bethlehem*, and prepared for my journey.

---

[6] All Indians are exceffive fond of rum, and will be drunk whenever they can get it.— [CHARLES THOMSON ?]

[7] Willamegicken (Wellemeghikink), known to the whites as James, was a prominent brave of the Allegheny Delawares, who had been employed as a messenger between them and the Susquehanna tribes of the same race. He had agreed to accompany Post on this journey, for which the Pennsylvania Council had voted to supply him with a horse. *Pennsylvania Archives*, iii, p. 415; *Pennsylvania Colonial Records*, viii, p. 148.— ED.

[8] Bethlehem is a Moravian town built in 1741-42, after the retreat of these people from Georgia. Count Zinzendorf organized the congregation at this place, and named the settlement (1742). For the first twenty years a community system prevailed among the inhabitants, called the "Economy." Portions of the buildings erected under that régime are still standing. See "Moravians and their Festival," in *Outlook*, August 1, 1903. In 1752, the brethren built a large stone house for the accommodation of Indian visitors, and those who escaped the massacre of 1755 were domiciled there when Post passed through.— ED.

18th.— I read over both the laſt treaties, that at
Eaſton, and that at *Philadelphia*, and made myſelf
acquainted with the particulars of each.[9]

19th.— With much difficulty I perſuaded the *Indians*
to leave *Bethlehem*, and travelled this day no further
than *Hayes's* having a hard ſhower of rain.

20th.— Arrived at fort *Allen.*[10]

21ſt.— I called my company together, to know if we
ſhould proceed. They complained they were ſick, and
muſt reſt that day. This day, I think, *Teedyuſcung*[11]

<hr>

[9] These two treaties were made with Teedyuscung: the first at Easton in
July and August, 1757, whereby the neutrality of the Susquehanna Indians and
the Six Nations was secured (*Pennsylvania Colonial Records*, vii, pp. 649-714);
the second at Philadelphia in April, 1758 (see *Id.*, viii, pp. 29-56, 87-97.— ED.

[10] After Braddock's defeat, the ravaging of the frontiers both west and north
of the settled portions of Pennsylvania became so serious that the colonial
government appointed a commission, headed by Franklin, to take means to
protect the settlers, and defend the territory. Franklin proceeded into Northumberland County, and made arrangements to fortify the point on the Lehigh
where Weisport, Carbon County, now stands. But before the stockade was
completed a body of Indians fell upon and seriously defeated a party of militia
from the neighboring Irish settlements, led by Captain Hayes (January, 1756).
The works were pushed rapidly after this setback, and the fort was named in
honor of William Allen, chief-justice of the province. This post was garrisoned
until after Pontiac's War, and probably throughout the Revolution. See
Franklin's *Writings* (New York, 1887), ii, pp. 449-454.— ED.

[11] Teedyuscung, one of the most famous of Delaware chiefs, was born in
Trenton about 1705. When nearly fifty years old, he was chosen chief of the
Susquehanna Delawares, and being shrewd and cunning played a game of
diplomacy between the Iroquois, the Ohio Indians, and the authorities of
Pennsylvania, by which he managed largely to enhance his own importance,
and to free the Delawares from their submission to the Six Nations. His
headquarters were in the Wyoming Valley, whence he descended to the Moravian
settlements, and even to Easton and Philadelphia, to secure supplies from the
Pennsylvania authorities. In 1756 a truce was patched up with this chief at
Easton, after he had bitterly complained of the "Walking Purchase" of 1737,
and the white settlements on the Juniata. His loyalty to the English was
doubtful and wavering, and his opposition to Post's journey was probably due
to fears that his own importance as a medium between the Ohio Indians and
the English would be diminished by the former's success. His cabin at Wyom-

laid many obftacles in my way, and was very much
againſt my proceeding: he faid, he was afraid I ſhould
never return; and that the Indians would kill me. About
dinner time two *Indians* arrived from *Wyoming*,[13] with
an account that *Teedyujcung's* ſon, *Hans Jacob*, was
returned, and brought news from the *French* and *Allegheny Indians*. *Teedyujcung* then called a Council, and
propoſed that I ſhould only go to *Wyoming*, and return,
with the meſſage his ſon had brought, to *Philadelphia*.
I made anſwer, that it was too late, that he ſhould have
propoſed that in *Philadelphia*; for that the writings containing my orders were ſo drawn, as obliged me to go,
though I ſhould loſe my life.

22d.— I deſired my companions to prepare to ſet out,
upon which *Teedyujcung* called them all together in the
fort, and proteſted againſt my going. His reaſons were,
that he was afraid the *Indians* would kill me, or the
French get me; and if that ſhould be the caſe he ſhould
be very ſorry, and did not know what he ſhould do. I

---

ing having treacherously been set on fire, during one of his drunken sleeps,
Teedyuscung was burned to death in 1763. The Iroquois, who were the guilty
party, threw the obloquy upon the Connecticut settlement, whereupon Teedyuscung's followers murdered all the band.— ED.

[13] Wyoming Valley was the bone of contention between the Connecticut
and Pennsylvania colonies, each claiming that it was within their charter
limits. The Connecticut agents succeeded in securing an Indian title at the
Albany conference (1754); but their first settlement being effaced by an Indian
massacre (see preceding note), their next body of emigrants did not proceed
thither until 1769. Meanwhile, on the strength of the Indian purchase at
Fort Stanwix (1768) the Pennsylvanians had occupied the valley; and a border
warfare began, which lasted until the Revolution. The massacre of 1778, by
the Tories and British Indians, is a matter of general history.

The Indians of the valley were of many tribes — Oneidas, Delawares,
Shawnees, Munseys, Nanticokes, etc. The Moravian Christian Indians
settled at Wyoming in 1752. After the murder of Teedyuscung they fled, but
returned to found the town of Wyalusing (1765), where the missionary Zeis-
berger lived with them until their removal, three years later to the Ohio.— ED.

gave for anfwer, ''that I did not know what to think of
their conduct. It is plain, faid I, that the *French* have a
public road[13] to your towns, yet you will not let your own
flefh and blood, the *Englifh*, come near them; which is
very hard: and if that be the cafe, the *French* muft be
your mafters.'' I added, that, if I died in the undertaking, it would be as much for the *Indians* as the *Englifh*, and that I hoped my journey would be of this
advantage, that it would be the means of faving the lives
of many hundreds of the *Indians*: therefore, I was refolved
to go forward, taking my life in my hand, as one ready to
part with it for their good. Immediately after I had
fpoken thus, three rofe up and offered to go with me the
neareft way; and we concluded to go through the inhabitants, under the Blue mountains to fort *Augufta*, on
Sufquahanna; where we arrived the 25th.[14]

It gave me great pain to obferve many plantations deferted and laid wafte; and I could not but reflect on the
diftrefs, the poor owners muft be drove to, who once
lived in plenty; and I prayed the Lord to reftore peace
and profperity to the diftreffed.

At fort *Augufta* we were entertained very kindly, had
our horfes fhod, and one being lame, we exchanged for

---

[13] An *Indian* expreffion meaning free admiffion.—[C. T. ?]

[14] Post, after leaving Fort Allen, passed through the present Carbon County,
crossed the headwaters of the Schuylkill, and traversed Northumberland County
to Fort Augusta. On the massacres in that region see Rupp, *History of Northumberland*, etc., (Lancaster, 1847), pp. 100-116. Fort Augusta, at the forks
of the Susquehanna, was built in 1756, at the request of the Indians settled
there under the chieftainship of Shickalamy. It was not a mere stockade and
blockhouse, but a regular fortification, provided with cannon, and was commanded at first by Colonel Clapham, succeeded by Colonel James Burd. This
stronghold was garrisoned until after the Revolutionary War; but before that
time settlement had begun to spring up about the fort, and the town of Sunbury
was laid out in 1772.— ED.

another. Here we received, by *Indians* from *Diahogo*,[15] the difagreeable news that our army was, as they faid, entirely cut off at *Ticonderoga*,[16] which difcouraged one of my companions, *Lappopetung's* fon, fo much, that he would proceed no further. *Shamokin Daniel* here asked me, if I thought he fhould be fatisfied for his trouble in going with me. I told him every body, that did any fervice for the province, I thought, would be paid.

27th.— They furnifhed us here with every neceffary for our journey, and we fet out with good courage. After we rode about ten miles, we were caught in a hard guft of rain.

28th.— We came to *Wekeeponall*, where the road turns off for *Wyoming*, and flept this night at *Queenafhawakee*.[17]

29th.— We croffed the *Sufquahanna* over the *Big Ifland*. My companions were now very fearful, and this night went a great way out of the road, to fleep without fire, but could not fleep for the mufquetoes and vermin.

30th & 31ft.— We were glad it was day, that we might fet out. We got upon the mountains, and had heavy rains all night. The heavens alone were our covering, and we accepted of all that was poured down from thence.

Auguft 1ft.— We faw three hoops[18] on a bufh; to one

[15] An Indian fettlement towards the heads of Sufquahanna.—[C. T. ?]

[16] The reference is to Abercrombie's defeat and retreat from Fort Ticonderoga in July, 1758.— ED.

[17] The Indian trail followed by Post, paffed up the West Branch of the Susquehanna, through a region which had earlier been thickly sprinkled with Indian towns. The Moravian missionaries had been here as early as 1742, and had been hospitably received by Madame Montour, whose town was at the mouth of Loyalsock Creek, opposite the present village of Montoursville. This was probably Post's "Wekeponall," as the path to Wyoming led northeast from this place. Queenashawakee (Quenslehague) Creek is in Lycoming County, with the town of Linden at its mouth.— ED.

[18] Little hoops on which the *Indians* ftretch and drefs the raw fcalps.—[C. T. ?]

of them there remained fome long white hair. Our horfes left us, I fuppofe, not being fond of the dry food on the mountains: with a good deal of trouble we found them again. We flept this night on the fame mountain.

2d.— We came acrofs feveral places where two poles, painted red, were ftuck in the ground by the *Indians*, to which they tye the prifoners, when they ftop at night, in their return from their incurfions. We arrived this night at *Shinglimuhee*,[19] where was another of the fame pofts. It is a difagreeable and melancholy fight, to fee the means they make ufe of, according to their favage way, to diftrefs others.

3d.— We came to a part of a river called *Tobeco*, over the mountains, a very bad road.

4th.— We loft one of our horfes, and with much difficulty found him, but were detained a whole day on that account.

I had much converfation with *Pifquetumen*;[20] of which I think to inform myfelf further when I get to my journey's end.

5th.— We fet out early this day, and made a good long ftretch, croffing the big river *Tobeco*, and lodged between two mountains. I had the misfortune to lofe my pocket book with three pounds five fhillings,[21] and fundry other

[19] Big Island is at the mouth of Bald Eagle Creek, in Clinton County. From that point the trail led up the creek to a point above Milesburg, Center County, then turned almost due west across Center and Clearfield counties to Clearfield (Shinglimuhee). This was the "Chinklacamoos path," north of the Kittanning trail followed by Weiser in 1748. The word "Chinklacamoos" is said to signify "it almost joins," in allusion to a horseshoe bend at this place. See Meginness, *Otsinachson: A History of the West Branch Valley* (rev. ed., Williamsport, Pa., 1889), p. 272.— ED.

[20] An *Indian* Chief, that travelled with him.— [C. T. ?]

[21] The money of *Pennfylvania*, being paper, is chiefly carried in pocket books.— [C. T. ?]

things. What writings it contained were illegible to any body but myfelf.

6th.— We paffed all the mountains, and the big river, *Wejhawaucks*, and croffed a fine meadow two miles in length, where we flept that night, having nothing to eat.[21]

7th.— We came in fight of fort *Venango*, belonging to the *French*, fituate between two mountains, in a fork of the *Ohio* river. I prayed the Lord to blind them, as he did the enemies of *Lot* and *Elijha*, that I might pafs unknown. When we arrived, the fort being on the other fide of the river, we hallooed, and defired them to fetch us over; which they were afraid to do; but fhewed us a place where we might ford. We flept that night within half gun fhot of the fort.

8th.— This morning I hunted for my horfe, round the fort, within ten yards of it. The Lord heard my prayer, and I paffed unknown till we had mounted our horfes to go off, when two *Frenchmen* came to take leave of the *Indians*, and were much furprifed at feeing me, but faid nothing.

By what I could learn of *Pijquetumen*, and the *Indians*, who went into the fort, the garrifon confifted of only fix men, and an officer blind of one eye.[22] They enquired

---

[21] From Chinklacamoos the Indian trail crossed Clearfield, Jefferson, and Clarion counties, over Little Toby's Creek (Tobeco), the Clarion River (big river Tobeco), and east Sandy Creek (Weshawaucks). That no Indians were met through all th..s region is proof of its deserted condition, its former frequenters having withdrawn to the French sphere of influence.—ED.

[22] The officer commanding Venango at this time was Jean Baptiste Boucher Sieur de Niverville, a noted border ranger and Indian raider. Born in Montreal in 1716, he early acquired an ascendency over the Abenaki Indians, which was utilized in leading their parties against the English settlements of New England. In King George's War, bands under his command ravaged New Hampshire and Vermont, and penetrated as far as Fort Massachusetts in the Berkshire Hills (1748). During the French and Indian War, he was similarly employed, and after Braddock's defeat, conducted a winter campaign of thirty-

much of the *Indians* concerning the *Englijh*, whether they knew of any party coming to attack them, of which they were apprehenfive.

9th.— Heavy rains all night and day: we flept on fwampy ground.

10th.— We imagined we were near *Kujhkujhkee*; and having travelled three miles, we met three *Frenchmen*, who appeared very fhy of us, but faid nothing more than to enquire, whether we knew of any *Englijh* coming againft fort *Venango*.

After we travelled two miles farther, we met with an *Indian*, and one that I took to be a runagade *Englijh Indian* trader; he fpoke good *Englijh*, was very curious in examining every thing, particularly the filver medal about Pifquitumen's neck. He appeared by his countenance to be guilty. We enquired of them where we were, and found we were loft, and within twenty miles of fort *Duquejne*. We ftruck out of the road to the right, and slept between two mountains; and being deftitute of food, two went to hunt, and others to seek a road, but to no purpofe.

11th.— We went to the place where they had killed two deers, and *Pifquetumen* and I roafted the meat. Two went to hunt for the road, to know which way we fhould go: one came back, and found a road; the other loft himfelf.

12th.— The reft of us hunted for him, but in vain; fo, as we could not find him, we concluded to fet off, leaving fuch marks, that, if he returned, he might know which

three days, in the direction of Fort Cumberland on the Potomac, bringing off numerous English captives. At Lake George in 1757, he led the Abenaki auxiliaries, and was present at the massacre of Fort William Henry. The last that is known of his military exploits is during the siege of Quebec, when he defended dangerous outposts with the aid of savage allies.— ED.

way to follow us; and we left him fome meat. We came
to the river *Conaquonajhon* [Conequenessing Creek],
where was an old *Indian* town. We were then fifteen
miles from *Kujhkujhkee*.

There we ftopt, and fent forward *Pijquetumen* with
four ftrings of *wampum* to apprize the town of our coming,[24] with this meffage:

"Brother,[25] thy brethren are come a great way, and
want to fee thee, at thy fire, to *fmoak that good tobacco*,[26]
which our good grandfathers ufed to fmoak. Turn thy
eyes once more upon that road, by which I came."[27] I
bring thee words of great confequence from the Governor, and people of *Pennfylvania*, and from the king of
England. Now I defire thee to call all the kings and
captains from all the towns, that none may be miffing.
I do not defire that my words may be hid, or fpoken under
cover. I want to fpeak loud, that all the *Indians* may
hear me. I hope thou wilt bring me on the road, and
lead me into the town. I blind the *French*, that they may
not fee me, and ftop their ears, that they may not hear
the great news I bring you.

About noon we met fome *Shawaneje*, that ufed to live at
Wyoming. They knew me, and received me very kindly.
I faluted them, and affured them the government of
Pennfylvania wifhed them well, and wifhed to live in
peace and friendfhip with them. Before we came to the

---

[24] According to the rules of Indian politenefs, you muft never go into a
town without fending a previous meffage to denote your arrival, or, ftanding
at a diftance from the town, and hallooing till fome come out, to conduct you
in. Otherwife you are thought as *rude as white men*.— [C. T. ?]

[25] When the people of a town, or of a nation, are addreffed, the *Indians*
always ufe the fingular number.— [C. T. ?]

[26] *i. e.* To confer in a friendly manner.— [C. T. ?]

[27] *i. e.* Call to mind our ancient friendly intercourfe.— [C. T. ?]

town, two men came to meet us and lead us in. King
Beaver fhewed us a large houfe to lodge in.[28] The people
foon came and fhook hands with us. The number was
about fixty young able men. Soon after king *Beaver*
came and told his people, ''Boys, hearken, we fat here
without ever expecting again to fee our brethren the
Englifh; but now one of them is brought before you,
that you may fee your brethren, the *Englifh*, with your
own eyes; and I wifh you may take it into confideration.''
Afterwards he turned to me and faid,

''Brother, I am very glad to fee you, I never thought
we fhould have had the opportunity to fee one another
more; but now I am very glad, and thank God, who has
brought you to us. It is a great fatisfaction to me.'' I
faid, ''Brother, I rejoice in my heart, I thank God, who
has brought me to you. I bring you joyful news from
the Governor and people of *Pennfylvania*, and from your
children, the Friends:[29] and, as I have words of great
confequence I will lay them before you, when all the kings
and captains are called together from the other towns. I
wifh there may not be a man of them miffing, but that
they may be all here to hear.''

In the evening king Beaver came again, and told me,
they had held a council, and fent out to all their towns,
but it would take five days before they could all come
together. I thanked him for his care. Ten captains
came and faluted me. One faid to the others; ''We
never expected to fee our brethren the *Englifh* again,
but now God has granted us once more to fhake hands

---

[28] Every *Indian* town has a large cabbin for the entertainment of ftrangers
by the public hofpitality.— [C. T. ?]

[29] That is, the *Quakers*, for whom the *Indians* have a particular regard.—
[C. T. ?]

with them, which we will not forget.'' They fat by my fire till midnight.

14th.— The people crowded to my houfe; it was full. We had much talk. *Delaware George*[20] faid, he had not flept all night, fo much had he been engaged on account of my coming. The *French* came, and would fpeak with me. There were then fifteen of them building houfes for the *Indians.* The captain is gone with fifteen to another town. He can fpeak the *Indian* tongue well. The *Indians* fay he is a cunning fox; that they get a great deal of goods from the *French*; and that the French cloath the *Indians* every year, men, women and children, and give them as much powder and lead as they want.

15th.— *Beaver* king was informed, that *Teedyufcung* had faid he had turned the hatchet againft the *French*, by advice of the *Alleghany Indians*; this he blamed, as they had never fent him fuch advice. But being informed it was his own doing, without any perfuafion of the Governor, he was eafy on that head. *Delaware Daniel* prepared a dinner, to which he invited me, and all the kings and captains; and when I came, he faid, ''Brother, we are as glad to fee you among us, as if we dined with the Governor and people in Philadelphia. We have thought a great deal fince you have been here. We never thought fo much before.''[21] I thanked them for their kind reception; I faid, it was fomething great, that God had

---

[20] Delaware George was an important chief of that tribe, who had been a disciple of Post's in his Pennsylvania mission. He maintained friendly relations with the English until after the defeat of Braddock. Although closely associated with King Beaver and Shingas, he seems to have leaned more than they to the English interest.— ED.

[21] That is, we look on your coming as a matter of importance, it engages our attention.— [C. T. ?]

fpared our lives, to fee one another again, in the old brother-like love and friendfhip. There were in all thirteen, who dined together.

In the evening they danced at my fire, firft the men, and then the women, till after midnight.

On the 16th, the king and captains called on me privately. They wanted to hear what *Teedyujcung* had faid of them, and begged me to take out the writings. I read to them what *Teedyujcung* had faid, and told them, as *Teedyujcung* had faid he would fpeak fo loud, that all at *Allegheny*, and beyond fhould hear it, I would conceal nothing from them. They faid, they never fent any fuch advice (as above mentioned), to *Teedyujcung*, nor ever fent a meffage at all to the government,[12] and now the *French* were here, their captain would come to hear, and this would make difturbance. I then told them I would read the reft, and leave out that part, and they might tell the kings and captains of it, when they came togéther.

17th.— Early, this morning they called all the people together to clean the place, where they intended to hold the council, it being in the middle of the town. *Kujh-kujhkee* is divided into four towns, each at a distance from the others; and the whole confifts of about ninety houfes, and two hundred able warriors.

About noon two public meffengers arrived from the *Indians* at fort *Duquejne* and the other towns. They

___

[12] At the Easton treaty in the autumn of 1757, Teedyuscung had promised to "halloo" to all the far Indian tribes, and bring them to an understanding with the English. In January, 1758, he reported to the governor that "all the Indian Nations from the Sun Rise to these beyond the Lakes, as far as the Sun setts, have heard what has passed between you and me, and are pleased with it," and urged him to continue the work of peace. Teedyuscung was evidently enlarging upon his own importance, and to this end giving unwarrantable information.— ED.

brought three large belts and two bundles of ftrings;[38]
there came with them a *French* captain, and fifteen men.
The two meffengers infifted that I fhould go with them
to fort *Duquefne*; that there were *Indians* of eight nations,
who wanted to hear me; that if I brought good news, they
inclined to leave off war, and live in friendfhip with the
Englifh. The above meffengers being *Indian* captains,
were very furly. When I went to fhake hands with one
of them, he gave me his little finger; the other withdrew
his hand entirely; upon which I appeared as ftout as
either, and withdrew my hand as quick as I could.
Their rudenefs to me was taken very ill by the other captains, who treated them in the fame manner in their turn.

I told them my order was to go to the *Indian* towns,
kings and captains, and not to the *French*; that the *Englifh*
were at war with the French, but not with thofe *Indians*,
who withdrew from the *French*, and would be at peace
with the *Englifh*.

King Beaver invited me to his houfe to dinner, and
afterwards he invited the *French* captain, and faid before
the *Frenchman*, that the *Indians* were very proud to fee
one of their brothers, the *Englifh*, among them; at which
the *French* captain appeared low fpirited, and feemed to
eat his dinner with very little appetite.

In the afternoon the *Indian* kings and captains called
me afide, and defired me to read them the writings that
I had. Firft I read part of the *Eafton* treaty to them;

---

[38] Thefe belts and ftrings are made of fhell-beads, called *wampum*. The
wampum ferves, among the *Indians*, as money; of it they alfo make their neck-
laces bracelets, and other ornaments. Belts and ftrings of it are ufed in all
public negotiations; to each belt or ftring there is connected a meffage, fpeech,
or part of a fpeech, to be delivered with a belt by the meffenger, or fpeaker.
Thefe belts alfo ferve for records, being worked with figures, compofed of beads
of different colours, to affift the memory.—[C. T. ?]

but they prefently ftopped me, and would not hear it; I then began with the articles of peace made with the *Indians* there. They ftopped me again, and faid, they had nothing to fay to any treaty, or league, of peace, made at *Eafton*, nor had any thing to do with *Teedyufcung*; that, if I had nothing to fay to them from the government, or Governor, they would have nothing to fay to me; and farther faid, they had hitherto been at war with the *Englifh*, and had never expected to be at peace with them again; and that there were fix of their men now gone to war againft them with other *Indians*; that had there been peace between us, thofe men fhould not have gone to war. I then fhewed them the belts and ftrings from the Governor; and they again told me to lay afide *Teedyufcung*, and the peace made by him; for that they had nothing to do with it.[84] I defired them to fuffer me to produce my papers, and I would read what I had to fay to them.

18th.— *Delaware George* is very active in endeavouring to eftablifh a peace. I believe he is in earneft. Hitherto they have all treated me kindly. .

In the afternoon, all the kings and captains were called together, and fent for me to their council. King Beaver firft addreffed himfelf to the captains; and afterwards fpoke to me, as follows:

"Brother, you have been here now five days by our fire.[85] We have fent to all the kings and captains, defiring them to come to our fire and hear the good news

---

[84] The peace made with *Teedyufcung*, was for the *Delawares*, &c. on *Sufquahanna* only. and did not include the *Indians* on the *Ohio*; they having no deputies at the treaty. But he had promifed to *halloo* to them, that is, fend meffengers to them, and endeavour to draw them into the peace, which he accordingly did.— [C. T. ?]

[85] A fire, in public affairs, fignifies, among the *Indians* a council.— [C. T. ?]

you brought. Yefterday they fent two captains to acquaint us, they were glad to hear our *Englifh* brother was come among us, and were defirous to hear the good news he brought; and fince there are a great many nations that went [want] to fee our brother, they have invited us to their fire, that they may hear us all. Now, brother, we have but one great fire; fo, brother, by this ftring we will take you in our arms, and deliver you into the arms of the other kings, and when we have called all the nations there, we will hear the good news, you have brought.'' Delivers four ftrings.

King *Beaver*, *Shingas*, and *Delaware George*, fpoke as follows:

''Brother, we alone cannot make a peace; it would be of no fignificance; for, as all the *Indians*, from the fun-rife to the funfet, are united in a body, it is neceffary that the whole fhould join in the peace, or it can be no peace; and we can affure you, all the *Indians*, a great way from this, even beyond the lakes, are defirous of, and wifh for a peace with the *Englifh*, and have defired us, as we are the neareft of kin, if we fee the *Englifh* incline a peace, to hold it faft.''

On the 19th, all the people gathered together, men, women, and children; and king *Beaver* defired me to read to them the news I had brought, and told me that all the able men would go with me to the other town. I complied with his defire, and they appeared very much pleafed at every thing, till I came to that part refpecting the prifoners. This they difliked; for, they fay, it appears very odd and unreafonable that we fhould demand prifoners before there is an eftablifhed peace; fuch an unreafonable demand makes us appear as if we wanted brains.

20th.— We fet out from *Kujhkujhkee*, for *Sankonk*; my company confifted of twenty-five horfemen and fifteen foot. We arrived at *Sankonk*, in the afternoon. The people of the town were much difturbed at my coming, and received me in a very rough manner. They furrounded me with drawn knives in their hands, in fuch a manner, that I could hardly get along; running up againft me, with their breafts open, as if they wanted fome pretence to kill me. I faw by their countenances they fought my death. Their faces were quite diftorted with rage, and they went fo far as to fay, I fhould not live long; but fome *Indians*, with whom I was formerly acquainted, coming up, and faluting me in a friendly manner, their behaviour to me was quickly changed.

On the 21ft, they fent Meffengers to Fort *Duquefne*, to let them know I was there, and invited them to their fire. In the afternoon, I read them all my meffage, the *French* captain being prefent; for he ftill continued with us: upon which they were more kind to me. In the evening, fifteen more arrived here from *Kujhkujhkee*. The men here now [were] about one hundred and twenty.

22d.— Arrived about twenty *Shawaneje* and *Mingos*. I read to them the meffage; at which they feemed well pleafed. Then the two kings came to me, and fpoke in the following manner:

"Brother, we, the *Shawaneje* and *Mingos*, have heard your meffage; the meffenger we fent to Fort *Duquefne*, is returned, and tells us, there are eight different nations there, who want to hear your meffage; we will conduct you there, and let both the *Indians* and *French* hear what our brothers, the Englifh, have to fay."

I protefted againft going to Fort *Duquefne*, but all in vain; for they infifted on my going, and faid that I need not fear the *French*, for they would carry me in their bofoms, i. e. engage for my fafety.

23d.— We fet off for Fort *Duquefne*, and went no farther this night than Log's town, where I met with four *Shawaneje*, who lived in *Wyoming* when I did. They received me very kindly, and called the prifoners to fhake hands with me, as their countryman, and gave me leave to go into every houfe to fee them, which was done in no other town befides.

24th.— They called to me, and defired that I would write to the general for them. The jealoufy natural to the *Indians* is not to be defcribed; for though they wanted me to write for them, they were afraid I would, at the fame time, give other information, and this perplexed them.

We continued our journey to the fort; and arrived in fight, on this fide the river, in the afternoon, and all the *Indian* chiefs immediately came over; they called me into the middle, and king *Beaver* prefented me to them, and faid, "Here is our *Englifh* brother, who has brought great news." Two of them rofe up and fignified they were glad to fee me. But an old deaf *Onondago Indian* rofe up and fignified his difpleafure. This *Indian* is much difliked by the others; he had heard nothing yet, that had paffed, he has lived here a great while, and conftantly lives in the fort, and is mightily attached to the *French*; he fpoke as follows, to the *Delawares*:

"I do not know this *Swannock*;[26] it may be that you know him. I, the *Shawaneje*, and our father[27] do not know him. I ftand here (ftamping his foot) as a man

---

[26] *i. e.* This Englifhman.— [C. T. ?]

[27] By father, they exprefs the *French*.— [C. T. ?]

on his own ground;[38] therefore, I, the *Shawaneje* and my father do not like that a *Swannock* come on our ground.''
Then there was filence awhile, till the pipe went round;[39] after that was over, one of the *Delawares* rofe up, and fpoke in oppofition to him that fpoke laft, and delivered himfelf as follows:

''That man fpeaks not as a man; he endeavours to frighten us, by faying this ground is his; he dreams; he and his father have certainly drunk too much liquor; they are drunk; pray let them go to fleep till they are fober. You do not know what your own nation does, at home; how much they have to fay to the *Swannocks.* You are quite rotten. You ftink.[40] You do nothing but fmoke your pipe here. Go to fleep with your father, and when you are fober we will fpeak to you.''

After this the *French* demanded me of the *Indians.* They faid it was a cuftom among the white people when a meffenger came, even if it was the Governor, to blind his eyes, and lead him into the fort, to a prifon, or private room. They, with fome of the *Indians* infifted very much on my being fent into the fort, but to no purpofe; for the other *Indians* faid to the *French*; ''It may be a rule among you, but we have brought him here, that all the *Indians* might fee him, and hear what our brothers the Englifh have to fay; and we will not fuffer him to be blinded and carried into the fort.'' The *French* ftill infifted on my being delivered to them; but the *Indians*

---

[38] By I, he here means, I, the Six Nations, of which the *Onondagoes* are one of the greateft. This was, therefore, a claim of the *Ohio* lands, as belonging to the Six Nations, exclufive of the *Delawares*, whom they formerly called women.— [C. T. ?]

[39] The *Indians* fmoke in their councils.— [C. T. ?]

[40] That is, the fentiments you exprefs, are offenfive to the company.— [C. T. ?]

defired them, to let them hear no more about it; but to
fend them one hundred loaves of bread; for they were
hungry.

25th.— This morning early they fent us over a large
bullock, and all the *Indian* chiefs came over again, and
counfelled a great deal among themfelves; then the
Delaware, that handled the old deaf *Onondago* Indian fo
roughly yefterday, addreffed himfelf to him, in this
manner; ''I hope, to day, you are fober. I am certain
you did not know what you faid yefterday. You endeavoured to frighten us; but know, *we are now men*,
and not fo eafily frightened. You faid fomething yefterday of the *Shawaneje*; fee here what they have fent
you,'' (*prefenting him with a large roll of tobacco.*)

Then the old deaf *Indian* rofe up, and acknowledged
he had been in the wrong; he faid, that he had now
cleaned *himfelf*,[41] and hoped they would forgive him.

Then the Delaware delivered the meffage, that was
fent by the *Shawaneje* which was, ''That they hoped the
Delawares, &c. would be ftrong,[42] in what they were
undertaking; that they were extremely proud to hear
fuch good news from their brothers, the *Englifh*; that
whatever contracts they made with the *Englifh*, the
Shawaneje would agree to; that they were their brothers,
and that they loved them.''

The *French* whifpered to the *Indians*, as I imagined,
to infift on my delivering what I had to fay, on the other
fide of the water. Which they did to no purpofe, for
my company ftill infifted on a hearing on this fide the
water. The *Indians* croffed the river to council with

---

[41] That is, he had changed his offenfive fentiments.—[C. T.?]

[42] That is, that they would act vigoroufly.—[C. T.?]

their Fathers." My company defired to know whether
they would hear me or no.   This afternoon three hundred
Canadians arrived at the fort, and reported that fix
hundred more were foon to follow them, and forty battoes
laden with amunition. Some of my party defired me
not to ftir from the fire; for that the *French* had offered
a great reward for my fcalp, and that there were feveral
parties out on that purpofe. Accordingly I ftuck conftantly as clofe to the fire, as if I had been chained there.

26th.— The Indians, with a great many of the *French*
officers, came over to hear what I had to fay. The
officers brought with them a table, pens, ink and paper.
I fpoke in the middle of them with a free confcience, and
perceived by the look of the *French*, they were not pleafed
with what I faid; the particulars of which were as follows;
I fpoke in the name of the government and people of
Penfilvania.

"Brethren at Allegheny, We have a long time defired
to fee and hear from you; you know the road was quite
ftopt; and we did not know how to come through. We
have fent many meffengers to you; but we did not hear
of you; now we are very glad we have found an opening
to come and fee you, and to fpeak with you, and to hear
your true mind and refolution. We falute you very
heartily." A ftring, No. 1.

"Brethren at Allegheny, Take notice of what I fay.
You know that the bad fpirit has brought fomething
between us, that has kept us at a diftance one from
another; I now, by this belt, take every thing out of the
way, that the bad fpirit has brought between us, and all
the jealoufy and fearfulnefs we had of one another, and
whatever elfe the bad fpirit might have poifoned your

  The *French*, at the fort.—[C. T. ?]

heart and mind with, that nothing of it may be left.
Moreover let us look up to God, and beg for his affiftance, that he may put into our hearts what pleafes him,
and join us clofe in that brotherly love and friendfhip,
which our grandfathers had. We affure you of our love
towards you.'' A belt of eleven rows.

"Brothers at Allegheny, Hearken to what I fay; we
began to hear of you from *Wellemeghihink*, who returned from *Allegheny*. We heard you had but a flight,
confufed account of us; and did not know of the peace,
we made twelve months paft, in *Eafton*. It was then
agreed, that the large belt of peace fhould be fent to you
at *Allegheny*. As thefe our two old friends from *Allegheny*, who are well known to many here, found an opening to come to our council fire, to fee with their own eyes,
to fit with us face to face, to hear with their own ears,
every thing that has been tranfacted between us; it gives
me and all the people of the province great pleafure to
fee them among us. And I affure all my brethren at
Allegheny, that nothing would pleafe me, and all the
people of the province better, than to fee our countrymen
the *Delawares* well fettled among us.'' A belt.

"Hearken, my brethren at *Allegheny*. When we
began to make peace with the *Delawares*, twelve months
ago, in behalf of ten other nations, we opened a road, and
cleared the bufhes from the blood, and gathered all
the bones, on both fides, together; and when we had
brought them together, in one heap, we could find no
place to bury them: we would not bury them as our
grandfathers did. They buried them under ground,
where they may be found again. We prayed to God, that
he would have mercy on us, and take all thefe bones
away from us, and hide them, that they might never be

found any more; and take from both fides all the remembrance of them out of our heart and mind. And we have a firm confidence, that God will be pleafed to take all the bones and hide them from us, that they may never be remembered by us, while we live, nor our children, nor grand children, hereafter. The hatchet was buried on both fides, and large belts of peace exchanged. Since we have cleared every thing from the heart, and taken every thing out of our way; now, my brethren at *Allegheny*, every one that hears me, if you will join with us, in that brotherly love and friendfhip. which our grandfathers had, we affure you, that all paft offences fhall be forgotten, and never more talked of, by us, our children and grand children hereafter. This belt affures you of our fincerity, and honeft and upright heart towards you.'' A belt of feven rows.

"Hearken, brethren at *Allegheny*. I have told you that we really made peace with part of your nation, twelve months paft; I now by this belt open the road from *Allegheny* to our council fire, where your grandfathers kept good councils with us, that all may pafs without moleftation or danger. You muft be fenfible, that unlefs a road be kept open, people at variance can never come together to make up their differences. Meffengers are free in all nations throughout the world, by a particular token. Now, brethren at *Allegheny*, I defire you will join with me in keeping the road open, and let us know in what manner we may come free to you, and what the token fhall be. I join both my hands to yours, and will do all in my power to keep the road open." A belt of feven rows.

"Now, brethren at *Allegheny*, Hear what I fay. Every one that lays hold of this belt of peace, I proclaim

peace to them from the *Englijh* nation, and let you
know that the great king of *England* does not incline to
have war with the *Indians*; but he wants to live in peace
and love with them, if they will lay down the hatchet, and
leave off war againft him.''

''We love you farther, we let you know that the great
king of *England* has fent a great number of warriors into
this country, not to go to war againft the *Indians*, in
their towns, no, not at all; thefe warriors are going againft
the *French*; they are on the march to the *Ohio*, to revenge
the blood they have fhed.   And by this belt I take you
by the hand, and lead you at a diftance from the *French*,
for your own fafety, that your legs may not be ftained
with blood.   Come away on this fide of the mountain,
where we may oftener converfe together, and where
your own flefh and blood lives.   We look upon you as
our countrymen, that fprung out of the fame ground
with us; we think, therefore, that it is our duty to take
care of you, and we in brotherly love advife you to come
away with your whole nation, and as many of your
friends as you can get to follow you.   We do not come
to hurt you, we love you, therefore we do not call you to
war, that you may be flain; what benefit will it be to you
to go to war with your own flefh and blood?   We wifh
you may live without fear or danger with your women
and children.''   The large peace belt.

''Brethren, I have almoft finifhed what I had to fay,
and hope it will be to your fatisfaction; my wifh is, that
we may join clofe together in that old brotherly love and
friendfhip, which our grandfathers had; fo that all
the nations may hear and fee us, and have the benefit
of it; and if you have any uneafinefs, or complaint, in
your heart and mind, do not keep it to yourfelf.   We have

opened the road to the council fire, therefore, my brethren, come and acquaint the Governor with it; you will be readily heard, and full juftice will be done you." A belt.

"Brethren, One thing I muft bring to your remembrance. You know, if any body lofes a little child, or fome body takes it from him, he cannot be eafy, he will think on his child by day and night; fince our flefh and blood is in captivity, in the *Indian* towns, we defire you will rejoice the country's heart, and bring them to me; I fhall ftretch out my arms to receive you kindly." A ftring.

After I had done, I left my belts and ftrings ftill before them. The *Delawares* took them all up, and laid them before the *Mingoes*;" upon which they rofe up, and fpoke as follows:

"*Chau*, What I have heard pleafes me well; I do not know why I go to war againft the *Englifh*. *Noques*, what do you think? You muft be ftrong. I did not begin the war, therefore, I have little to fay; but whatever you agree to, I will do the fame." Then he addreffed himfelf to the *Shawaneje*, and faid, "You brought the hatchet to us from the *French*, and perfuaded us to ftrike our brothers the *Englifh*; you may confider (laying the belts, &c. before them) wherefore you have done this."

The *Shawaneje* acknowledged they received the hatchet from the *French*, who perfuaded them to ftrike the *Englifh*; that they would now fend the belts to all the *Indians*, and in twelve days would meet again.

Prefent at this council, three hundred *French* and *Indians*. They all took leave, and went over again to

" The Six Nations.— [C. T ?]

the fort, but my companions, who were about feventy in
number.

Shamokin Daniel, who came with me, went over to
the fort by himfelf, (which my companions difapproved
of) and counfelled with the Governor; who prefented him
with a laced coat and hat, a blanket, fhirts, ribbons, a
new gun, powder, lead, &c.   When he returned he was
quite changed, and faid, "See here, you fools, what the
French have given me.   I was in *Philadelphia,* and never
received a farthing;" and, directing himfelf to me, he
faid, "The Englifh are fools, and fo are you."   In
fhort, he behaved in a very proud, faucy and imperious
manner.   He further faid, "The *Englijh* never give the
Indians any powder, and that the *French* would have
given him a horfeload, if he would have taken it; fee that
young man there, he was in *Philadelphia* and never got
any thing; I will take him over to the *French*; and get
fome cloathing for him."

Three *Indians* informed me, that as foon as the *French*
got over, they called a council, with their own *Indians,*
among whom there happened accidentally to be a *Delaware* captain, who was privately invited by one of his
acquaintances to hear what the French had to fay; and
when they were affembled, the *French* fpoke, as
follows:

"My children, now we are alone, hearken to what I
have to fay.   I perceive the *Delawares* are wavering;
they incline to the *Englifh,* and will be faithful to us no
longer.   Now all the chiefs are here, and but a handful,
let us cut them off, and then we fhall be troubled with
them no longer."   Then the *Tawaas* [Ottawas] anfwered, "No, we cannot do this thing; for though there
is but a handful here, the *Delawares* are a ftrong people,

and are fpread to a great diftance, and whatever they agree to muft be.''

This afternoon, in council, on the other fide of the river, the *French* infifted that I muft be delivered up to them, and that it was not lawful for me to go away; which occafioned a quarrel between them and the *Indians,* who immediately came away and croffed the river to me; and fome of them let me know thet *Daniel* had received a ftring from the *French,* to leave me there; but it was to no purpofe, for they would not give their confent; and then agreed that I fhould fet off before day the next morning.

27th.— Accordingly, I fet out before day, with fix *Indians,* and took another road, that we might not be feen; the main body told me, they would ftay behind, to know whether the *French* would make an attempt to take me by force; that if they did, they, the *Indians,* would endeavour to prevent their croffing the river, and coming fecretly upon me. Juft as I fet off the *French* fired all their great guns, it being Sunday (I counted nineteen) and concluded they did the fame every Sabbath. We paffed through three *Shawaneje* towns; the *Indians* appeared very proud to fee me return, and we arrived about night at *Sawcunk,* where they were likewife very glad to fee me return. Here I met with the two captains, who treated me fo uncivilly before; they now received me very kindly, and accepted of my hand, and apologized for their former rude behaviour. Their names are *Kuckque-tackton* and *Killbuck.*⁴⁶ They faid,

⁴⁶ Kuckquetackton (Koquethagechton) was the Indian name of the famous Delaware chief Captain White Eyes. About 1776, he succeeded Netawatwes, of whom he had been chief counsellor, as head of the nation Heckewelder first met him at this same town, where Post encountered him in 1772, and says that he strove to keep the neutrality during both Lord Dunmore's War and the

"Brother, we, in behalf of the people of *Sawcunk*, defire that you will hold faft what you have begun, and be ftrong."* We are but little and poor, and therefore cannot do much. You are rich, and muft go on and be ftrong. We have done all in our power towards bringing about a peace: we have had a great quarrel about you with the *French*; but we do not mind them. Do you make hafte, and be ftrong, and let us fee you again." The faid *Killbuck* is a great captain and conjurer; he defired me to mention him to the Governor, and afk him if he would be pleafed to fend him a good faddle by the next meffenger; and that he would do all in his power for the fervice of the Englifh.

28th.— We fet out from *Sawcunk*, in company with twenty, for *Kufhkufhkee*; on the road *Shingas* addreffed himfelf to me, and afked, if I did not think, that, if he came to the Englifh, they would hang him, as they had offered a great reward for his head. He fpoke in a very foft and eafy manner. I told him that was a great while ago, it was all forgotten and wiped clean away; that the

Revolution. Finding that impossible, he joined the American cause (1778), and brought an Indian contingent to the aid of General McIntosh at Fort Laurens; dying, however, before the attack was made on the Sandusky towns. He was always a firm friend of the Moravians, and though of small stature was one of the best and bravest of Delaware chiefs.

There were two chiefs known by the name of Killbuck, the younger of whom was the more famous. His Indian name was Gelelemend, and he was a grandson of the great chief Netawatwes. Born near Lehigh Water Gap in the decade 1730-40, he removed to the Allegheny with the Delawares, and later to the Muskingum, where was a village called Killbuck's Town. Like White Eyes, he was a firm friend of peace and of the whites, and his life was imperilled because of this advocacy. He joined the Moravians, and was baptized as William Henry, about 1788. Later he removed to Pittsburg to secure protection from his enemies, but died at Goshen in 1811. A lineal descendant of Killbuck is at present a Moravian missionary in Alaska.— ED.

* That is, go on fteadily with this good work of eftablifhing a peace.— C. T. ?]

Englifh would receive him very kindly. Then *Daniel* interrupted me, and faid to *Shingas*, "Do not believe him, he tells nothing but idle lying ftories. Wherefore did the *Englijh* hire one thoufand two hundred *Indians*[47] to kill us." I protefted it was falfe; he faid, G–d d–n[48] you for a fool; did you not fee the woman lying [in] the road that was killed by the *Indians*, that the *Englijh* hired? I faid, "Brother do confider how many thoufand *Indians* the *French* have hired to kill the *Englijh*, and how many they have killed along the frontiers." Then *Daniel* faid, "D–n you, why do not you and the *French* fight on the fea? You come here only to cheat the poor *Indians*, and take their land from them." Then *Shingas* told him to be ftill; for he did not know what he faid. We arrived at *Kujhkujhkee* before night, and I informed *Pijquetumen* of *Daniel's* behaviour, at which he appeared forry.

29th.— I dined with *Shingas*; he told me, though the *Englijh* had fet a great price on his head, he had never thought to revenge himfelf, but was always very kind to any prifoners that were brought in;[49] and that he affured the Governor, he would do all in his power to bring about an eftablished peace, and wifhed he could be certain of the *Englijh* being in earneft.

Then feven chiefs prefent faid, when the Governor fends the next meffenger, let him fend two or three white men, at leaft, to confirm the thing, and not fend fuch a man as *Daniel*; they did not underftand him; he always

---

[47] Meaning the *Cherokees.*—[C. T. ?]

[48] Some of the firft *Englijh* fpeech, that the *Indians* learn from the traders, is fwearing.—[C. T. ?]

[49] Heckewelder testifies that Shingas, though a dreaded foe in battle, was never known to treat prifoners cruelly. See his *Indian Nations*, Historical Society of Pennsylvania *Memoirs* (Philadelphia, 1876), xii, pp. 269, 270.—ED.

fpeaks, faid they, as if he was drunk; and if a great many
of them had not known me, they fhould not know what
to think; for every thing I faid he contradicted. I
affured them I would faithfully inform the Governor of
what they faid, and they fhould fee, as meffengers, other
guife *Indians* than *Daniel*, for the time to come; and I
farther informed them, that he was not fent by the Governor, but came on his own accord; and I would endeavour
to prevent his coming back. *Daniel* demanded of me
his pay, and I gave him three dollars; and he took as
much wampum from me as he pleafed, and would not
fuffer me to count it. I imagined there was about two
thoufand.

About night, nine *Tawaas* paft by here, in their way
to the *French* fort.

30th and 31ft.— The *Indians* feafted greatly, during
which time, I feveral times begged of them to confider and
difpatch me.

September 1ft.— *Shingas*, King *Beaver*, *Delaware
George*, and *Pifquetumen*, with feveral other captains faid
to me,

"Brother, We have thought a great deal fince God
has brought you to us; and this is a matter of great confequence, which we cannot readily anfwer; we think on
it, and will anfwer you as foon as we can. Our feaft
hinders us; all our young men, women and children are
glad to fee you; before you came, they all agreed together
to go and join the *French*; but fince they have feen you,
they all draw back; though we have great reafon to
believe you intend to drive us away, and fettle the country;
or elfe, why do you come to fight in the land that God
has given us?"

I faid, we did not intend to take the land from them;

but only to drive the *French* away. They faid, they knew better; for that they were informed fo by our greateſt traders; and fome Juſtices of the Peace had told them the fame, and the *French*, faid they, tell us much the fame thing,—"that the *Engliſh* intend to deſtroy us, and take our lands;" but the land is ours, and not theirs; therefore, we fay, if you will be at peace with us, we will fend the *French* home. It is you that have begun the war, and it is neceſſary that you hold faſt, and be not difcouraged, in the work of peace. We love you more than you love us; for when we take any prifoners from you, we treat them as our own children. We are poor, and yet we clothe them as well as we can, though you fee our children are as naked as at the firſt. By this you may fee that our hearts are better than yours. It is plain that you white people are the caufe of this war; why do not you and the *French* fight in the old country, and on the fea? Why do you come to fight on our land? This makes every body believe, you want to take the land from us by force, and fettle it.[60]

I told them, "Brothers, as for my part, I have not one foot of land, nor do I defire to have any; and if I had any land, I had rather give it to you, than take any from you. Yes, brothers, if I die, you will get a little more land from me; for I ſhall then no longer walk on that ground, which God has made. We told you that you ſhould keep

---

[60] The Indians, having plenty of land, are no niggards of it. They fome-times give large tracts to their friends freely; and when they fell it, they make moſt generous bargains. But fome *fraudulent purchaſes*, in which they were groffly impoſed on, and fome *violent intruſions*, imprudently and wickedly made without purchafe, have rendered them jealous that we intend finally to take all from them by force. We fhould endeavour to recover our credit with them by fair purchafes and honeſt payments; and then there is no doubt but they will readily fell us, at reaſonable rates, as much, from time to time, as we can poſſibly have occaſion for.—[C. T. ?]

nothing in your heart, but bring it before the council fire, and before the Governor, and his council; they will readily hear you; and I promife you, what they anfwer they will ftand to. I further read to you what agreements they made about *Wioming*,[11] and they ftand to them.''

They faid, ''Brother, your heart is good, you fpeak always fincerely; but we know there are always a great number of people that want to get rich; they never have enough; look, we do not want to be rich, and take away that which others have. God has given you the tame creatures; we do not want to take them from you. God has given to us the deer, and other wild creatures, which we muft feed on; and we rejoice in that which fprings out of the ground, and thank God for it. Look now, my brother, the white people think we have no brains in our heads; but that they are great and big, and that makes them make war with us: we are but a little handful to what you are; but remember, when you look for a wild turkey you cannot always find it, it is fo little it hides itfelf under the bufhes: and when you hunt for a rattle-fnake, you cannot find it; and perhaps it will bite you before you fee it. However, fince you are fo great and big, and we fo little, do you ufe your greatnefs and ftrength in compleating this work of peace. This is the firft time that we faw or heard of you, fince the war begun, and we have great reafon to think about it, fince fuch a great body of you comes into our lands.[12] It is told us, that you and the *French* contrived the war, to wafte the *Indians* between you; and that you and the *French* intended to divide the land between you: this was

---

[11] The agreement made with *Teedyufcung*, that he fhould enjoy the *Wioming* lands, and have houfes built there for him and his people.— [C. T. ?]

[12] The army under *General Forbes*.—[C. T. ?]

told us by the chief of the *Indian* traders; and they faid
further, brothers, this is the laft time we fhall come among
you; for the *French* and the *Englijh* intend to kill all the
Indians, and then divide the land among themfelves.

Then they addreffed themfelves to me, and faid,
"Brother, I fuppofe you know fomething about it; or
has the Governor ftopped your mouth, that you cannot
tell us?"

Then I faid, "Brothers, I am very forry to fee you fo
jealous. I am your own flefh and blood, and fooner than
I would tell you any ftory that would be of hurt to you,
or your children, I would fuffer death: and if I did not
know that it was the defire of the Governor, that we
fhould renew our old brotherly love and friendfhip, that
fubfifted between our grandfathers, I would not have
undertaken this journey. I do affure you of mine and
the people's honefty. If the *French* had not been here,
the *Englijh* would not have come; and confider, brothers,
whether, in fuch a cafe, we can always fit ftill."

Then they faid, "It is a thoufand .pities we did not
know this fooner; if we had, it would have been peace
long before now."

Then I faid, "My brothers, I know you have been
wrongly perfuaded by many wicked people; for you muft
know, that there are a great many Papifts in the country,
in *French* intereft, who appear like gentlemen, and have
fent many runaway Irifh papift fervants⁵⁸ among you,
who have put bad notions into your heads, and ftrength-
ened you againft your brothers the *Englijh*.

⁵⁸ The *Indian* traders ufed to buy the tranfported *Irifh*, and other convicts,
as fervants, to be employed in carrying up the goods among the *Indians*. The
ill behaviour of thefe people has always hurt the character of the *Englijh* among
the *Indians*.— [C. T.?]

"Brothers, I beg that you would not believe every idle and falfe ftory, that ill-defigning people may bring to you againft us your brothers. Let us not hearken to what lying and foolifh people may bring to you, againft us your brothers. Let us not hearken to what lying and foolifh people fay, but let us hear what wife and good people fay; they will tell us what is good for us and our children.''

Mem. There are a great number of *Irifh* traders now among the *Indians*, who have always endeavoured to fpirit up the *Indians* againft the *Englifh*; which made fome, that I was acquainted with from their infancy, defire the chiefs to enquire of me, for that they were certain I would fpeak the truth.

Pifquetumen now told me, we could not go to the General, that it was very dangerous, the *French* having fent out feveral fcouts to wait for me on the road. And further, *Pifquetumen* told me, it was a pity the Governor had no ear,[14] to bring him intelligence; that the *French* had three ears, whom they rewarded with great prefents; and fignified, that he and *Shingas* would be ears, at the fervice of his honour, if he pleafed.

2d.— I bade *Shingas* to make hafte and difpatch me, and once more defired to know of them, if it was poffible for them to guide me to the General. Of all which they told me they would confider; and *Shingas* gave me his hand, and faid, ''Brother, the next time you come, I will return with you to *Philadelphia*, and will do all in my power to prevent any body's coming to hurt the *Englifh* more.''

3d.— To-day I found myfelf unwell, and made a little tea, which refrefhed me: had many very pretty difcourfes

---

[14] No fpy among his enemies.— [C. T. ?]

with *George.* In the afternoon they called a council together, and gave me the following anfwer in council; the fpeaker addreffing the Governor and people of *Pennfylvania*:

"Brethren, It is a great many days fince we have feen or heard from you.[44] I now fpeak to you in behalf of all the nations, that have heard you heretofore.

"Brethren, it is the first meffage which we have feen or heard from you. Brethren, you have talked of that peace and friendfhip which we had formerly with you. Brethren, we tell you to be ftrong, and always remember that friendfhip, which we had formerly. Brethren, we defire you would be ftrong, and let us once more hear of our good friendfhip and peace, we had formerly. Brethren, we defire that you make hafte, and let us hear of you again; for, as yet, we have not heard you rightly." Gives a ftring.

"Brethren, hear what I have to fay: look, brethren, we, who have now feen and heard you, we, who are prefent, are part of all the feveral nations, that heard you fome days ago; we fee that you are forry we have not that friendfhip, we formerly had.

"Look, brethren, we at *Allegheny* are likewife forry we have not that friendfhip with you, which we formerly had. Brethren, we long for that peace and friendfhip we had formerly. Brethren, it is good that you defire that friendfhip, that was formerly among our fathers and

---

[44] That is, fince we had a friendly intercourfe with each other. The frequent repetition of the word, *Brethren,* is the effect of their rules of politenefs, which enjoin, in all converfations, a conftant remembrance of the relation fubfifting between the parties, efpecially where that relation implies any affection, or refpect. It is like the perpetual repetitions among us, of *Sir,* or, *Madam,* or, *Your Lordfhip.* In the fame manner the *Indians* at every fentence repeat, *My Father, My Uncle, My Coufin, My Brother, My Friend,* &c.— [C. T. ?]

grandfathers. Brethren, we will tell you, you muſt not let that friendſhip be quite loſt, which was formerly between us.

"Now, brethren, it is three years ſince we dropt that peace and friendſhip, which we formerly had with you. Brethren, it was dropt, and lay buried in the ground, where you and I ſtand, in the middle between us both. Brethren, I ſee you have digged up, and revived, that friendſhip, which was buried in the ground; and now you have it, hold it faſt. Do be ſtrong, brethren, and exert yourſelves, that that friendſhip may be well eſtablished and finiſhed between us. Brethren, if you will be ſtrong, it is in your power to finiſh that peace and friendſhip well. Therefore, brethren, we deſire you to be ſtrong and eſtabliſh it, and make known to all the *Engliſh* this peace and friendſhip, that it may embrace all and cover all. As you are of one nation and colour, in all the *Engliſh* governments, ſo let the peace be the ſame with all. Brethren, when you have finiſhed this peace, which you have begun; when it is known every where amongſt your brethren, and you have every where agreed together on this peace and friendſhip, then you will be pleaſed to ſend the great peace belt to us at *Allegheny*.

"Brethren, when you have ſettled this peace and friendſhip, and finiſhed it well, and you ſend the great peace-belt to me, I will ſend it to all the nations of my colour, they will all join to it, and we all will hold it faſt.

"Brethren, when all the nations join to this friendſhip, then the day will begin to ſhine clear over us. When we hear once more of you, and we join together, then the day will be ſtill, and no wind, or ſtorm, will come over us, to diſturb us.

"Now, brethren, you know our hearts, and what we have to fay; be ftrong; if you do what we have now told you, and in this peace all the nations agree to join. Now, brethren, let the king of *England* know what our mind is as foon as poffibly you can.''[56] Gives a belt of eight rows.

I received the above fpeech and belt from the under-written, who are all captains and counfellors.

BEAVER, KING,	CAPTAIN PETER,
DELAWARE GEORGE,	MACOMAL,
PISQUETUMEN,	POPAUCE,
TASUCAMIN,	WASHAOCAUTAUT,
AWAKANOMIN,	COCHQUACAUKEEHLTON,
CUSHAWMEKWY,	JOHN HICKOMEN, and
KEYHEYNAPALIN,	KILL BUCK.

Delaware George fpoke as follows:

"Look, brothers, we are here of three different nations. I am of the Unami nation:[57] I have heard all the fpeeches that you have made to us with the many other nations.

"Brothers, you did let us know, that every one that takes hold of this peace-belt, you would take them by the hand, and lead them to the council fire, where our grand-fathers kept good councils. So foon as I heard this, I took hold of it.

[56] In this fpeech the *Indians* carefully guard the honour of their nation, by frequently intimating, that the peace is *fought by the Englifh: you have talked of peace: you are forry for the war: you have digged up the peace, that was buried*, &c. Then they declare their readinefs to grant peace, if the Englifh agree to its being general for all the colonies. The *Indian* word, that is tranflated, be ftrong, fo often repeated, is an expreffion they ufe to fpirit up perfons, who have undertaken fome difficult task, as to lift, or move, a great weight, or execute a difficult enterprise; nearly equivalent to our word, *courage! courage!*—[C. T.?]

[57] The three tribes of the Delaware nation — the Unamis, Unalachtgo, and Minfi — were designated by the totems turtle, turkey, and wolf. The chief of the first of these was the head chief of the nation, being chosen and installed with great ceremony and rejoicing. See Heckewelder, *Indian Nations*, pp. 51, 53.— ED.

"Brother, I now let you know that my heart never was parted from you. I am forry that I fhould make friend-fhip with the *French* againft the *Englifh*. I now affure you my heart fticks clofe to the Englifh intereft. One of our great captains, when he heard it, immediately took hold of it as well as myfelf. Now, Brother, I let you know that you fhall foon fee me by your council fire, and then I fhall hear from you myfelf, the plain truth, in every refpect.

"I love that which is good, like as our grandfathers did: they chofe to fpeak the fentiments of their mind: all the *Five Nations* know me, and know that I always fpoke ruth; and fo you fhall find, when I come to your council fire." Gives a ftring.

The above *Delaware George* had in company with him,

CUSHAWMEKWY,   JOHN PETER,
KEHKEHNOPATIN,   STINFEOR.
CAPTAIN PETER,

4th.— Prefent, *Shingas*, King *Beaver*, *Pifquetumen*, and feveral others. I afked what they meant by faying, "*They had not rightly heard me yet.*" They faid,

"Brother, you very well know that you have collected all your young men about the country, which makes a large body;[86] and now they are ftanding *before our doors*;[87] you come with good news and fine fpeeches. Brother, this is what makes us jealous, and we do not know what to think of it: if you had brought the news of peace before your army had begun to march, it would have caufed a great deal more good. We do not fo readily believe you, becaufe a great many great men and traders have told us, long before the war, that you and

---

[86] Meaning General Forbes's army.— [C. T. ?]

[87] *i. e.* Juft ready to enter our country.— [C. T. ?]

the *French* intended to join and cut all the *Indians* off. Thefe were people of your own colour, and your own countrymen; and fome told us to join the *French*; for that they would be our fathers: befides, many runaways have told us the fame ftory; and fome we took prifoners told us how you would ufe us, if you caught us: therefore, brother, I fay, we cannot conclude, at this time, but muft fee and hear you once more.'' And further they faid,

''Now, brother, you are here with us, you are our flefh and blood, fpeak from the bottom of your heart, will not the *French* and *Englijh* join together to cut off the *Indians*? Speak, brother, from your heart, and tell us the truth, and let us know who were the beginners of the war.''

Then I delivered myfelf thus:

''Brothers, I love you from the bottom of my heart. I am extremely forry to fee the jealousy fo deeply rooted in your hearts and minds. I have told you the truth; and yet, if I was to tell it you a hundred times, it feems you would not rightly believe me. My *Indian* brothers, I wifh you would draw your hearts to God, that he may convince you of the truth.

''I do now declare, before God, that the *Englijh* never did, nor never will, join with the French to deftroy you. As far as I know, the *French* are the beginners of this war. Brothers, about twelve years ago, you may remember, they had war with the Englifh, and they both agreed to articles of peace. The *Englijh* gave up *Cape Breton* in *Acadia*, but the *French* never gave up the part of that country, which they had agreed to give up; and, in a very little time, made their *Children* ftrike the *Englijh*. This was the firft caufe of the war. Now, brothers; if any body ftrike you three times, one after another, you ftill fit ftill and confider: they ftrike you again, then, my brothers, you fay, it is time, and you will rife up to defend yourfelves. Now, my brothers, this is exactly the cafe between the *French* and *Englifh*. Confider farther, my brothers, what a great number of our poor back inhabitants have been killed fince the *French* came to the *Ohio*. The French are the caufe of their death, and if they were not there, the *Englifh* would not trouble themfelves to go there. They go no where to war, but where the French are. Thofe wicked people that fet you at variance with the *Englifh*, by telling you many wicked ftories, are papifts in French pay: befides, there are many among us, in the *French* fervice, who appear like gentlemen, and buy Irifh papift fervants, and promife them great rewards to run away to you and ftrengthen you againft the *Englifh*, by making them appear as black as devils.''

This day arrived here two hundred *French* and *Indians*, on their way to fort *Duquefne*. They ftaid all night. In the middle of the night king *Beaver's* daughter died, on which a great many guns were fired in the town.

5th.— It made a general ftop in my journey. The *French* faid to their Children, they fhould catch me privately, or get my fcalp. The commander wanted to examine me, as he was going to *fort Duquefne*. When they told me of it, I faid, as he was going to *fort Duquefne*, he might enquire about me there: I had nothing at all to fay, or do with the *French*: they would tell them every particular they wanted to know in the fort. They all came into the houfe where I was, as if they would fee a new creature.

In the afternoon there came fix *Indians*, and brought three German prifoners, and two fcalps of the *Catabaws*.

As *Daniel* blamed the *Englifh*, that they never paid

him for his trouble, I afked him whether he was pleafed with what I paid him. He faid, no. I faid, ''Brother, you took as much as you pleafed.'' I afked you, whether you was fatisfied; you faid, yes. I told him, I was afhamed to hear him blame the country fo. I told him, ''You fhall have for this journey whatever you defire, when I reach the inhabitants.''

6th.— *Pijquetumen, Tom Hickman* and *Shingas* told me,

''Brother, it is good that you have ftayed fo long with us; we love to fee you, and wifh to fee you here longer; but fince you are fo defirous to go, you may fet off to morrow: *Pijquetumen* has brought you here, and he may carry you home again: you have feen us, and we have talked a great deal together, which we have not done for a long time before. Now, Brother, we love you, but cannot help wondering why the *Englijh* and *French* do not make up with one another, and tell one another not to fight on our land.''

I told them, ''Brother, if the *Englijh* told the *French* fo a thoufand times, they never would go away. Brother, you know fo long as the world has ftood there has not been fuch a war. You know when the French lived on the other fide, the war was there, and here we lived in peace. Confider how many thoufand men are killed, and how many houfes are burned fince the *French* lived here; if they had not been here it would not have been fo; you know we do not blame you; we blame the *French*; they are the caufe of this war; therefore, we do not come to hurt you, but to chaftife the *French*.''

They told me, that at the great council, held at *Onondago*, among the *Five Nations*, before the war began (*Conrad Weijer* was there, and wrote every thing down)

it was faid to the *Indians* at the *Ohio*, that they fhould
let the *French* alone there, and leave it entirely to the
Five Nations; the *Five Nations* would know what to
do with them. Yet foon after two hundred *French* and
Indians came and built *Fort Duquefne.*

King *Beaver* and *Shingas* fpoke to *Pifquetumen.*

"Brother, you told us that the Governor of *Philadelphia* and *Teedyufcung* took this man out of their bofoms,
and put him into your bofom, that you fhould bring him
here; and you have brought him here to us; and we have
feen and heard him; and now we give him into your
bofom, to bring him to the fame place again, before the
Governor; but do not let him quite loofe; we fhall rejoice
when we fhall fee him here again." They defired me to
fpeak to the Governor, in their behalf, as follows:

"Brother, we beg you to remember our oldeft brother,
Pifquetumen, and furnifh him with good cloathes, and
reward him well for his trouble; for we fhall look upon
him when he comes back."

7th.— When we were ready to go, they began to council which courfe we fhould go, to be fafeft; and then they
hunted for the horfes, but could not find them; and fo
we loft that day's journey.

It is a troublefome crofs and heavy yoke to draw this
people: They can punifh and fqueeze a body's heart
to the utmoft. I fufpect the reafon they kept me here fo
long was by inftigation of the *French.* I remember
fomebody told me, the *French* told them to keep me
twelve days longer, for that they were afraid I fhould get
back too foon, and give information to the general. My
heart has been very heavy here, becaufe they kept me
for no purpofe. The Lord knows how they have been
counfelling about my life; but they did not know who

was my protector and deliverer: I believe my Lord has been too ftrong againft them; my enemies have done what lies in their power.

8th.— We prepared for our journey on the morning, and made ourfelves ready. There came fome together and examined me what I had wrote yefterday. I told them, I wondered what need they had to concern themfelves about my writing. They faid, if they knew I had wrote about the prifoners, they would not let me go out of the town. I told them what I writ was my duty to do. "Brothers, I tell you, I am not afraid of you, if there were a thoufand more. I have a good confcience before God and man. I tell you I have wrote nothing about the prifoners. I tell you, Brothers, this is not good; there's a bad fpirit in your heart, which breeds that jealoufy; and it will keep you ever in fear, that you will never get reft. I beg you would pray to God, for grace to refift that wicked fpirit, that breeds fuch wicked jealoufies in you; which is the reafon you have kept me here fo long. How often have I begged of you to difpatch me? I am afhamed to fee you fo jealous; I am not, in the leaft, afraid of you. Have I not brought writings to you? and what, do you think I muft not carry fome home, to the Governor? or, fhall I fhut my mouth, and fay nothing? Look into your hearts, and fee if it would be right or wrong, if any body gives a falutation to their friends, and it is not returned in the fame way. You told me many times how kind you were to the prifoners, and now you are afraid that any of them fhould fpeak to me."[60]

They told me, they had caufe to be afraid; and then

[60] Two of the prisoners mention their pleasure at seeing Post, and the fact that the Indians forbade them to communicate with him. See "Narrative of Marie le Roy and Barbara Leininger," *Pennsylvania Archives*, 2nd series (Harrisburg, 1878), vii, pp. 401-412.— ED.

made a draught, and fhewed me how they were furrounded with war.   Then I told them, if they would be
quiet, and keep at a diftance, they need not fear.   Then
they went away, very much afhamed, one after another.
I told my men, that we muft make hafte and go; accordingly we fet off, in the afternoon, from *Kufhkufhkee*, and
came ten miles.

9th.— We took a little foot-path hardly to be feen.
We left it, and went through thick bufhes, till we came
to a mire, which we did not fee, till we were in it; and
Tom Hickman fell in, and almoft broke his leg.   We had
hard work before we could get the horfe out again.   The
Lord helped me, that I got fafe from my horfe.   I and
Pifquetumen had enough to do to come through.   We
paffed many fuch places: it rained all day; and we got
a double portion of it, becaufe we received all that hung
on the bufhes.   We were as wet as if we were fwimming
all the day; and at night we laid ourfelves down in a
fwampy place to fleep, where we had nothing but the
heavens for our covering.

10th.— We had but little to live on.   *Tom Hickman*
fhot a deer on the road.   Every thing here, upon the
Ohio, is extremely dear, much more fo than in *Pennfylvania*: I gave for one difh of corn four hundred and fixty
wampum.   They told me that the Governor of *fort
Duquefne* kept a ftore of his own, and that all the *Indians*
muft come and buy the goods of him; and when they come
and buy, he tells them, if they will go to war, they fhall
have as much goods as they pleafe.   Before I fet off, I
heard further, that a *French* captain who goes to all the
Indian towns⁶¹ came to *Sacunck*, and faid, ''Children,

---

⁶¹ He was fent to collect the *Indians* together, to attack General Forbes's
army, once more, on their march.— [C. T. ?]

will you not come and help your father againft the *Englijh*?'' They anfwered, ''Why fhould we go to war
againft our brethren? They are now our friends.'' ''O!
Children,'' faid he, ''I hope you do not own them for
friends.'' ''Yes,'' faid they, ''We do; we are their
friends, and we hope they will remain ours.'' ''O!
Children, faid he, you muft not believe what you have
heard, and what has been told you by that man.'' They
faid to him, ''Yes, we do believe him more than we do you:
it was you that fet us againft them; and we will by and by
have peace with them;'' and then he fpoke not a word
more, but returned to the fort. So, I hope, fome good is
done: praifed be the name of the Lord.

11th.— Being Monday, we went over *Antigoc*:[a] we
went down a very fteep hill, and our horfes flipt fo far,
that I expected, every moment, they would fall heels over
head. We found frefh *Indian* tracts on the other fide
of the river. We croffed *Allegheny* river, and went
through the bufhes upon a high hill, and flept upon the
fide of the mountain, without fire, for fear of the enemy.
It was a cold night, and I had but a thin blanket to cover
myfelf.

12th.— We made a little fire, to warm ourfelves in the
morning. Our horfes began to be weary with climbing
up and down thefe fteep mountains. We came this night
to the top of a mountain, where we found a log-houfe.
Here we made a fmall fire, juft to boil ourfelves a little
victuals. The *Indians* were very much afraid, and lay
with their guns and tomhocks on all night. They heard
fomebody run and whifper in the night. I flept very
found, and in the morning they afked me, if I was not

---

[a] The creek, here called ''Antigoc'' was probably Venango or the French
Creek, which the Delawares defignated as Attigé.— ED.

afraid the enemy *Indians* would kill me. I faid, "No, I am not afraid of the *Indians*, nor the devil himfelf: I fear my great Creator, God." "Aye, they faid, you know you will go to a good place when you die, but we do not know that: that makes us afraid."

,13th.— In the afternoon we twice croffed *Chowatin*, and came to *Ponchejtanning*,⁴ an old deferted Indian town, that lies on the fame creek. We went through a bad fwamp, where were very thick fharp thorns, fo that they tore our cloaths and flefh, both hands and face, to a bad degree. We had this kind of road all the day. In the evening we made a fire, and then they heard fomething rufh, in the bufhes, as though they heard fomebody walk. Then we went about three gun-fhot from our fire, and could not find a place to lie down on, for the innumerable rocks; fo that we were obliged to get fmall ftones to fill up the hollow places in the rocks, for our bed; but it was very uneafy; almoft fhirt and fkin grew together. They kept watch one after another all night.

14th.— In the morning, I afked them what made them afraid. They faid, I knew nothing; the *French* had fet a great price on my head; and they knew there was gone out a great fcout to lie in wait for me. We went over great mountains and a very bad road.

15th.— We came to *Sufquehanna*, and croffed it fix times, and came to *Catawawejhink*. where had been an old *Indian* town.⁴⁴ In the evening there came three *Indians*, and faid they faw two *Indian* tracks, which came to the place where we flept, and turned back, as if to

---

⁴ The Indian name of this town, in Jefferson County, on the Mahoning Creek, is usually given as Punxatawny.— ED.

⁴⁴ Probably this was the town called "Calamaweshink" or "Chinklemoose," Clearfield.— ED.

give information of us to a party; fo that we were fure
they followed us.

16th and 17th.— We croffed the mountain.

18th.— Came to the *Big Ifland*, where having nothing
to live on, we were obliged to ftay to hunt.

19th.— We met 20 warriors, who were returning from
the inhabitants, with five prifoners and one fcalp; fix
of them were *Delawares*, the reft *Mingoes*. We fat down
all in one ring together. I informed them where I had
been, and what was done; they afked me to go back a
little, and fo I did, and flept all night with them. I informed them of the particulars of the peace propofed;
they faid, "If they had known fo much before, they
would not have gone to war. Be ftrong; if you make a
good peace, then we will bring all the prifoners back
again." They killed two deer, and gave me one.

20th.— We took leave of each other, and went on our
journey, and arrived the 22d at *fort Augufta*, in the afternoon, very weary and hungry; but greatly rejoiced of our
return from this tedious journey.

There is not a prouder, or more high minded people, in
themfelves, than the Indians. They think themfelves
the wifeft and prudenteft men in the world; and that
they can over-power both the *French* and *Englifh* when
they pleafe. The white people are, in their eyes, nothing
at all. They fay, that through their conjuring craft they
can do what they pleafe, and nothing can withftand them
In their way of fighting they have this method, to fee
that they first fhoot the officers and commanders; and
then, they fay, we fhall be fure to have them. They
alfo fay, that if their conjurers run through the middle
of our people, no bullet can hurt them. They fay too,
that when they have fhot the commanders, the foldiers

will all be confufed, and will not know what to do. They
fay of themfelves, that every one of them is like a king
and captain, and fights for himfelf. By this way they
imagine they can overthrow any body of men, that may
come againft them. They fay, ''The *Englifh* people
are fools; they hold their guns half man high, and then
let them fnap: we take fight and have them at a fhot, and
fo do the *French*; they do not only fhoot with a bullet,
but big fwan fhot.'' They fay, the French load with a
bullet and fix fwan-fhot. They further fay, ''We take
care to have the firft fhot at our enemies, and then they
are half dead before they begin to fight.''

The *Indians* are a people full of jealoufy, and will not
eafily truft any body; and they are very eafily affronted,
and brought into jealoufy; then afterwards they will have
nothing at all to do with thofe they fufpect; and it is
not brought fo eafy out of their minds; they keep it to
their graves, and leave the feed of it in their children and
grand children's minds; fo, if they can, they will revenge
themfelves for every imagined injury. They are a very
diftruftful people. Through their imagination and reafon they think themfelves a thoufand times ftronger than
all other people. *Fort du Quefne* is faid to be under-
mined. The *French* have given out, that, if we over-
power them, and they fhould die, we fhould certainly all
die with them. When I came to the fort, the garrifon, it
was faid, confifted of about one thoufand four hundred
men; and I am told they will now be full. three thoufand
French and *Indians*. They are almoft all *Canadians*,
and will certainly meet the general before he comes to
the fort, in an ambufh. You may depend upon it the
French will make no open field-battle, as in the old
country, but lie in ambufh. The *Canadians* are all

hunters. The *Indians* have agreed to draw back; but
how far we may give credit to their promiſes the Lord
knows. It is the beſt way to be on our guard againſt
them, as they really could with one thouſand overpower
eight thouſand.

Thirty-two nights I lay in the woods; the heavens were
my covering. The dew came ſo hard ſometimes, that
it pinched cloſe to the ſkin. There was nothing that
laid ſo heavy on my heart, as the man that went along
with me. He thwarted me in every thing I ſaid or did;
not that he did it againſt me, but againſt the country, on
whoſe buſineſs I was ſent: I was afraid he would overthrow what I went about. When he was with the *Englijh* he would ſpeak againſt the *French*, and when with
the *French* againſt the *Englijh*. The *Indians* obſerved
that he was a falſe fellow, and deſired me, that I would
not bring him any more, to tranſact any buſineſs between
the *Englijh* and them; and told me, it was through his
means I could not have the liberty to talk with the priſoners.

Praiſe and glory be to the *Lamb*, that has been ſlain,
and brought me through the country of dreadful jealouſy
and miſtruſt, where the prince of this world has his rule
and government over the children of diſobedience.

The Lord has preſerved me through all the dangers and
difficulties, that I have ever been under. He directed
me according to his will, by his holy ſpirit. I had no one
to converſe with but him. He brought me under a
thick, heavy, and dark cloud, into the open air; for which
I adore, praiſe, and worſhip the Lord my God, that I
know has graſped me in his hands, and has forgiven me
for all ſins, and ſent and waſhed my heart with his moſt
precious blood; that I now live not for myſelf, but for him

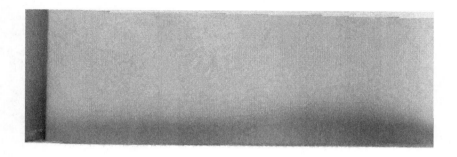

that made me; and to do his holy will is my pleafure. I own that, in the children of light, there dwells another kind of fpirit, than there does in the children of this world; therefore, thefe two fpirits cannot rightly agree in fellowfhip.

CHRISTIAN FREDERICK POST.

THE JOURNAL OF CHRISTIAN FREDERICK POST, ON A MESSAGE FROM THE GOVERNOR OF PENNSYLVANIA, TO THE INDIANS ON THE OHIO, IN THE LATTER PART OF THE SAME YEAR.

October 25th, 1758.— HAVING received the orders of the honourable Governor *Denny*,[46] I fet out from *Eajton* to *Bethlehem,* and arrived there about three o'clock in the afternoon; I was employed moft of the night, in preparing myfelf with neceffaries, &c. for the journey.

26th.— Rofe early, but my horfe being lame, though I travelled all the day, I could not, till after night, reach to an inn, about ten miles from *Reading.*

27th.— I fet out early, and about feven o'clock in the morning came to *Reading,* and there found Captain *Bull,* Mr. *Hays,*[46] and the *Indians* juft mounted, and ready to fet out on their journey; they were heartily glad to fee me; *Pifquetomen* ftretched out his arms, and faid, "Now, Brother, I am glad I have got you in my arms, I will not let you go, I will not let you go again from me, you muft

<hr />

[46] The proprietors of Pennsylvania chose William Denny lieutenant-governor (1756), because they wifhed a "military man with a ready pen." He had been captain in the British army, and his experience in Pennsylvania gave opportunity for military talents. But bound by instructions from his principals, and hampered by the hostility of the provincial assembly, he made no headway in his government. Accused of accepting bribes to betray the proprietors' interests, he was removed in October, 1759. Returning to England, he was given a high position in the army, and died about 1766.— ED.

[46] Captain Bull and Lieutenant Hays were militia officers, the latter of Northampton County, where was an Irish settlement between Bethlehem and Fort Allen, known as "Hays's." Captain John Bull commanded at Fort Allen in the summer of 1758. They both volunteered to undertake this hazardous mission of a visit to the Ohio Indians. For the instructions given them, see *Pennsylvania Archives,* iii, p. 556.— ED.

go with me:" and I likewife faid the fame to him, and
told him, "I will accompany you, if you will go the fame
way as I muft go." And then I called them together, in
Mr. *Weifer's* houfe, and read a letter to them, which I
had received from the Governor, which is as follows, viz.
''To *Pifquetomen* and *Thomas Hickman*, to *Totiniontenna* and *Shickalamy*, and to *Ifaac Still*.**[87]**

"Brethren, Mr. *Frederick Poft* is come exprefs from
the general, who fends his compliments to you, and
defires you would come by the way of his camp, and give
him an opportunity of talking with you.

"By this ftring of wampum I requeft of you to alter
your intended rout by way of *Shamokin*,**[88]** and to go to
the general,**[89]** who will give you a kind reception. It is a

---

[87] Thomas Hickman was an Indian who had taken an English name, and
was much employed by the province of Pennsylvania as an interpreter. A
brutal white man murdered Hickman in the Tuscarora Valley in 1761.

Totiniontenna was a Cayuga chieftain who with Shickalamy was deputed
by the Six Nations to undertake this embassy to the Ohio Indians.

The chief here called Shickalamy was the youngest son, of the famous
Oneida of that name, who dwelt so long at the forks of the Susquehanna, and
was friendly to the whites, especially the Moravians. The elder chief died in
1749, his most famous son being Logan.

Isaac Still was a Moravian Christian Indian, frequently employed as a
messenger and interpreter.— ED.

[88] Shamokin was an Indian town at the forks of the Susquehanna, the
abode of Shickalamy, "vice-king" of the Indians of that region. It was
first visited by the whites in 1728. Weiser built a house at this village by request of the chief, in 1744. Frequent visits of the Moravians led to the establishment here of a blacksmith's shop, and a quasi-mission. Fort Augusta was
built there in 1756; but on the proclamation of war against the Delawares in the
same year, the Indians abandoned the place and destroyed the settlement.— ED.

[89] The general here referred to was John Forbes, a Scotchman who in 1757
was appointed brigadier-general for the war in America. His first service was
at Louisburg. In 1758, he was appointed to organize the expedition against
Fort Duquesne. After the French, on the approach of Forbes's army, had
abandoned that stronghold, the general, suffering from a serious disease, was
carried by slow stages to Philadelphia, where he died in March, 1760. He
was a man of iron purpose, and great strength of character, being popular alike
with his soldiers and Indian allies.— ED.

nigher way, in which you will be better fupplied with
provifions, and can travel with lefs fatigue and more
fafety.   "WILLIAM DENNY.
"*Eafton, October 23d*, 1758."

To which I added, "Brethren, I take you by this
ftring,[70] by the hand, and lift you from this place, and lead
you along to the general."

After which they confulted among themfelves, and foon
refolved to go with me. We fhook hands with each other,
and Mr. Hays immediately fet out with them; after which,
having with fome difficulty procured a frefh horfe, in
the king's fervice, I fet off about noon with captain
Bull; and when we came to *Conrad Weifer's* plantation,
we found *Pifquetomen* lying on the ground very drunk,[71]
which obliged us to ftay there all night; the other *Indians*
were gone eight miles farther on their journey.

28th.— We rofe early, and I fpoke to *Pifquetomen* a
great deal; he was very fick, and could hardly ftir; when
we overtook the reft, we found them in the fame condition; and they feemed difcouraged, from going the way
to the general; and wanted to go through the woods. I
told them, I was forry to fee them wavering, and reminded
them, that when I went to their towns, I was not fent
to the *French*, but when your old men infifted on my
going to them, I followed their advice, and went; and as
the general is, in the king's name, over the provinces, in

---

[70] A ftring of *wampum* beads. Nothing of importance is faid, or propofed
without *wampum*.— [C. T. ?]

[71] The *Indians*, having learned drunkennefs of the white people, do not
reckon it among the vices. They all, without exception, and without fhame,
practice it when they can get ftrong liquor. It does not, among them, hurt the
character of the greateft warrior, the greateft counfellor, or the modefteft
matron. It is not fo much an *offence*, as an *excufe* for other ofences; the in-
juries they do each other in their drink being charged, not upon the man, but
upon the rum.— [C. T. ?]

matters of war and peace, and the *Indians*, at *Allegheny*,[71]
want to know, whether all the *Englijh* governments will
join in the peace with them; the way to obtain full fatisfaction is to go to him, and there you will receive another
great belt to carry home; which I defire you ferioufly to
take into confideration. They then refolved to go to
Harris's ferry, and confider about it as they went; — we
arrived there late in the night.[72]

29th.— In the morning, the two *Cayugas* being moft
defirous of going through the woods, the others continued
irrefolute;[74] upon which I told them, "I wifh you would
go with good courage, and with hearty refolution," and
repeated what I had faid to them yefterday, and reminded
them, as they were meffengers, they fhould confider what
would be the beft for their whole nation; "confult among
yourfelves, and let me know your true mind and determination;" and I informed them, I could not go with
them, unlefs they would go to the general, as I had mef-
fages to deliver him. After which, having confulted
together, *Pejquitomen* came and gave me his hand, and
faid, "Brother, here is my hand, we have all joined to
go with you, and we put ourfelves under your protection
to bring us fafe through, and to fecure us from all danger." We came that night to *Carlijle*[75] and found a

---

[71] The Ohio.— [C. T. ?]

[72] An Indian trader, John Harris, built a log house on the Susquehanna in
1705, and later established an inn and a ferry at the spot called Harris's Ferry,
which was maintained for three-quarters of a century. His son laid out the
present town of Harrisburg.— ED.

[74] They were afraid of going where our people were all in arms, left fome of
the indifcreet foldiers might kill them.— [C. T. ?]

[75] Carlisle, the seat of Cumberland County (erected in 1750), was originally
settled by Scotch-Irish immigrants, who in the decade between 1720 and 1730
formed the "back settlements" of Pennsylvania. The Indian title was ex-
tinguished by a treaty in 1736; but when Fort Lowther was built at this site

fmall houfe without the fort, for the *Indians* to be by themfelves, and hired a woman to drefs their victuals, which pleafed them well.

30th.— Setting out early, we came to *Shippenſburg*,[76] and were lodged in the fort, where the *Indians* had a houfe to themfelves.

31ſt.— Set out early; in our paſſing by *Chambers* Fort,[77] ſome of the *Iriſh* people, knowing ſome of the *Indians*, in a raſh manner exclaimed againſt them, and we had ſome difficulty to get them off clear. At fort *Loudon* we met about ſixteen of the *Cherokees*, who came in a friendly manner to our *Indians*, enquiring for *Bill Sockum*,[78] and ſhewed the pipe[79] they had received from

in 1753, there were but five houses in the place. Later it became the eastern terminus of the Pennsylvania highroad, and the centre of an extensive overland trade.— ED.

[76] The town of Shippensburg was one of the oldest west of the Susquehanna, having been laid out in 1749, by Edward Shippen — later chief-justice of Pennsylvania — on land of which he was proprietor. It was the site of two frontier forts — Franklin, built before Braddock's defeat; and Morris, erected after that disaster. Shippensburg became an important station on the Pennsylvania state road; and until the opening of the nineteenth century was the end of the stage-route from Lancaster westward.— ED.

[77] Chambers's Fort was a private stockade erected (1756) on the Conococheague Creek, by a Scotch-Irishman, Benjamin Chambers, who for some time had had a mill and settlement here. The fort was a large stone building, protected by cannon, and considered one of the strongest defenses in that region. The government attempted to take possession of the guns in 1757, lest they should be captured and turned against the other forts; but the Scotch-Irish settlers stoutly resisted this attempt, and it was abandoned. The present city of Chambersburg occupies the site.— ED.

[78] This should not be confused with the more famous Fort Loudoun, built the same year (1756) in Tennessee as a check upon the Cherokees. The Pennsylvania fort was on the road between Shippensburg and Fort Lyttleton, about a mile east of the present village of Loudon, Franklin County, being erected by Armstrong after Braddock's defeat. This was the scene of the plundering of the Indian goods, dispatched to the Ohio (1765) for Croghan's use on his journey to the Illinois.

The Cherokees were employed by the English as auxiliaries in this campaign. Their presence had caused much concern among the Northern Indians,

the *Shawaneſe*, and gave it, according to their cuſtom,
to ſmoak out of, and ſaid, they hoped they were friends
of the *Engliſh*. They knew me. *Peſquitomen* begged
me to give him ſome *wampum*, that he might ſpeak to
them: I gave him 400 white *wampum*, and he then ſaid
to them:— "We formerly had friendſhip one with another;
we are only meſſengers, and cannot ſay much, but by
theſe ſtrings we let you know we are friends, and we are
about ſettling a peace with the *Engliſh*, and wiſh to be
at peace alſo with you, and all other *Indians*."— And
informed them further, they came from a treaty, which
was held at *Eaſton*, between the *Eight United Nations*
and their confederates, and the *Engliſh*; in which peace
was eſtabliſhed; and ſhewed them the two meſſengers
from the *Five Nations*, who were going, with them, to
make it known to all the *Indians* to the weſtward.   Then
the *Cherokees* anſwered and ſaid; "they ſhould be glad
to know how far the friendſhip was to reach; they, for
themſelves, wiſhed it might reach from the ſun-riſe to
the ſun-ſet; for, as they were in friendſhip with the *Engliſh*, they would be at peace with all their friends, and at
war with their enemies."

Nov. 1.— We reached fort *Littleton*,[80] in company with
the *Cherokees*, and were lodged, in the fort; they, and our

and Poſt had been ſent to Wyoming the previous ſpring, with reaſſuring
meſſages on this account.

   Bill Sock was a Conestoga Indian, employed as a meſſenger to the Six
Nations. He was maſſacred in the Paxton affair (1763). See Heckewelder
Narrative, p. 79.— Ed.

   [79] A calumet pipe; the ſignal of peace.—[C. T. ?]

   [80] Fort Lyttleton was another of the chain of frontier poſts built in 1756
for the protection of the frontiers. It was located at the place called by the
Indian traders "Sugar Cabins," near the present McConnellsburg Fulton
County. A garriſon was maintained at this point until after Pontiac's War,
when it gradually fell into ruins, ſome relics of its occupation being ſtill found
in the locality.— Ed.

Indians, in diftinct places; and they entertained each other with ftories of their warlike adventures.

2d.— *Pejquitomen* faid to me, "you have led us this way, through the fire; if any mifchief fhould befal us, we fhall lay it entirely to you; for we think it was your doing, to bring us this way; you fhould have told us at *Eafton*, if it was neceffary we fhould go to the general."

I told him, "that I had informed the great men, at *Eafton*, that I then thought it would be beft not to let them go from thence, till they had feen the general's letter; and affured them that it was agreeable to the general's pleafure."

3d.— *Pejquitomen* began to argue with captain *Bull* and Mr. *Hays*, upon the fame fubject, as they did with me, when I went to them with my firft meffage; which was, "that they should tell them, whether the general would claim the land as his own, when he fhould drive the *French* away? or, whether the *Englifh* thought to fettle the country? We are always jealous the *Englifh* will take the land from us. Look, brother, what makes you come with fuch a large body of men, and make fuch large roads into our country; we could drive away the *French* ourfelves, without your coming into our country."

Then I defired captain *Bull* and Mr. *Hays* to be careful how they argued with the *Indians*; and be fure to fay nothing, that might affront them; for it may prove to our difadvantage, when we come amongft them. This day we came to *Rays-town*,[81] and with much diffi-

81 Ray's town, so named from its first settler (1751), was the chief rendezvous for Forbes's army in this campaign, where he had the stronghold of Fort Bedford built, and whence he made his final advance against Fort Duquesne. From 1760-63, the fort at this place was commanded by Captain Lewis Ourry of the Royal Americans; and its apparent strength saved it from attack by the

culty got a place to lodge the *Indians* by themfelves, to their fatisfaction.

4th.— We intended to fet out, but our *Indians* told us, the *Cherokees* had defired them to ftay that day, as they intended to hold a council; and they defired us to read over to them the governor's meffage; which we accordingly did. *Pejquitomen*, finding *Jenny Frazer* there, who had been their prifoner, and efcaped, fpoke to her a little rafhly. Our *Indians*, waiting all the day, and the *Cherokees* not fending to them, were dif-pleafed.

5th.— Rofe early, and, it raining fmartly, we afked our *Indians*, if they would go; which they took time to confult about.

The *Cherokees* came and told them, the *Englifh* had killed about thirty of their people, for taking fome horfes, which they refented much; and told our *Indians* they had better go home, than go any farther with us, left they fhould meet with the fame. On hearing this, I told them how I had heard it happened; upon which our *Indians* faid, they had behaved like fools, and brought the mifchief on themfelves.

Pejquitomen, before we went from hence, made it up with *Jenny Frazer*, and they parted good friends; and though it rained hard, we fet out at 10 o'clock, and got to the foot of the *Alleghenny*, and lodged at the firft run of water.

6th.— One of our horfes went back; we hunted a good while for him. Then we fet off, and found one of the

Indians of the conspiracy. Bouquet made it the rendezvous in his advance in 1764. Throughout the Indian wars, Fort Bedford was the most important station between Carlisle and Fort Pitt. The town of Bedford was incorporated in 1766.— ED.

worſt roads that ever was travelled until *Stoney creek*.[82]
Upon the road we overtook a great number of pack
horſes; whereon *Peſquitomen* ſaid, ''Brother, now you
ſee, if you had not come to us before, this road would not
be ſo ſafe as it is; now you ſee, we could have deſtroyed
all this people on the road, and great miſchief would
have been done, if you had not ſtopt, and drawn our
people back.''— We were informed that the general was
not yet gone to fort *Duqueſne*, wherefore *Peſquitomen*
ſaid, he was glad, and expreſſed, ''If I can come to our
towns before the general begins the attack, I know our
people will draw back, and leave the *French*.''— We
lodged this night at *Stoney creek*.

7th.— We aroſe early, and made all the haſte we could
on our journey; we croſſed the large creek, *Rekempalin*;
near *Lawrel hill*. Upon this hill we overtook the artillery,
and came, before ſun ſet, to *Loyal Hanning*.[83] We were
gladly received in the camp by the general, and moſt
of the people. We made our fire near the other *Indian*
camps; which pleaſed our people. Soon after ſome of
the officers came, and ſpoke very raſhly to our *Indians*,
in reſpect to their conduct to our people; at which they
were much diſpleaſed, and anſwered as raſhly, and

[82] Post's testimony as to the condition of the new road cut for the army
west from Fort Bedford is interesting. For an account of the controversy
over the building of this road, see Hulbert, *Old Glade Road* (Cleveland, 1903),
pp. 65-161.

Stony Creek flows northward through the valley between the Allegheny
and Laurel Hill ranges of mountains.— ED.

[83] The creek called "Rekempalin," apparently was Pickings Run in Somer-
set County — not a large creek, but all streams were swollen by unusual rains.

Loyal Hanna was an old Indian town situated on the trail passing west to
Shannopin's Town at the Forks of the Ohio. Upon the advance of Forbes's
army (1758), this was made the last station on the road to Fort Duquesne, and
a fort was built called Ligonier. Before the erection of this fort the station
was known simply as the "Camp on Loyal Hanna."— ED.

faid, ''they did not underftand fuch ufage; for they were
come upon a meffage of peace; if we had a mind to war,
they knew how to help themfelves; and they were not
afraid of us.''

8th.— At eleven o'clock the general called the *Indians*
together, the *Cherokees* and *Catawbas* being prefent; he
fpake to them in a kind and loving manner, and bid them
heartily welcome to his camp, and expreffed his joy to fee
them, and defired them to give his compliments to all their
kings and captains:— He defired them that had any love
for the *Englijh* nation, to withdraw from the *French*;
for if he fhould find them among the *French*, he muft
treat them as enemies, as he fhould advance with a large
army very foon, and cannot wait longer on account of
the winter feafon. After that he drank the king's health,
and all that wifh well to the *Englijh* nation; then he
drank king *Beaver's, Shingas*; and all the warrior's
healths, and recommended us (the meffengers) to their
care; and defired them to give credit to what we fhould
fay. After that we went to another houfe with the general
alone; and he fhewed them the belt, and faid, he would
furnifh them with a writing, for both the belt and ftring;
and after a little difcourfe more, our *Indians* parted in
love, and well fatisfied. And we made all neceffary prep-
arations for our journey.

9th.— Some of the colonels and chief commanders
wondered how I came through fo many difficulties, and
how I could rule and bring thefe people to reafon, making
no ufe of gun or fword. I told them, it is done by no
other means than by faith. Then they afked me, if I had
faith to venture myfelf to come fafe through with my
companions. I told them, it was in my heart to pray for
them, ''you know that the Lord has given many promifes

to his fervants, and what he promifes, you may depend
upon, he will perform.''— Then they wifhed us good
fuccefs. We waited till almoft noon for the writing of
the general. We were efcorted by an hundred men,
rank and file, commanded by captain *Hajelet*;[54] we paffed
through a tract of good land, about fix miles on the old
trading path, and came to the creek again, where there
is a large fine bottom, well timbered; from thence we
came upon a hill, to an advanced breaft work, about
ten miles from the camp, well fituated for ftrength,
facing a fmall branch of the aforefaid creek; the hill
is fteep down, perpendicular about twenty feet, on the
fouth fide; which is a great defence; and on the weft
fide the breaft-work about feven feet high, where we
encamped that night:[55] our *Indian* companions heard
that we were to part in the morning, and that twelve men
were to be fent with us, and the others, part of the company, to go towards fort *Duquefne*. Our *Indians* defired
that the captain would fend twenty men, inftead of
twelve; that if any accident fhould happen, they could be
more able to defend themfelves in returning back; ''for
we know, fay they, the enemy will follow the fmalleft
party.'' It began to rain. Within five miles from the
breaft-work we departed from captain *Hajelet*; he kept
the old trading path to the *Ohio*. Lieutenant *Hays*[56]

[54] Captain John Haslett was an officer of the Pennsylvania provincial troops,
of which there was in Forbes's army, a contingent of two thousand and seven
hundred. Probably this was the same officer who commanded Delaware troops
in the Revolution, and after conspicuous bravery at Long Island was killed in
the battle of Princeton.— ED.

[55] The camping-place for this night, at the advanced breast-work, is identified
as on the Nine Mile Run, in Unity Township, Westmoreland County, being
still locally known as "Breast-work Hill."— ED.

[56] Lieutenant William Hays, who was later killed on his return from escort-
ing Post, belonged to the Royal Americans, having been commissioned December 11, 1756.— ED.

was ordered to accompany us to the *Alleghenny* river[87]
with fourteen men. We went the path that leads along
the *Loyal Hanning* creek, where there is a rich fine bottom, land well timbered, good fprings and fmall creeks.
At four o'clock we were alarmed by three men, in *Indian*
drefs; and preparation was made on both fides for defence. *Ifaac Still* fhewed a white token, and *Pefquitomen*
gave an *Indian halloo*; after which they threw down their
bundles, and ran away as faft as they could. We afterwards took up their bundles, and found that it was a
fmall party of our men, that had been long out. We
were forry that we had fcared them; for they loft their
bundles with all their food. Then, I held a conference
with our *Indians*, and afked them, if it would not be
good, to fend one of our *Indians* to *Logftown* and *fort
Duquefne*, and call the *Indians* from thence, before we
arrive at *Kufhkufhking*. They all agreed it would not
be good, as they were but meffengers; it muft be done by
their chief men. The wolves made a terrible mufic this
night.

11th.— We ftarted early, and came to the old *Shawanefe* town, called *Keckkeknepolin*,[88] grown up thick with
weeds, briars and bufhes, that we fcarcely could get
through. *Pefquitomen* led us upon a fteep hill, that our
horfes could hardly get up; and *Thomas Hickman's*
horfe ftumbled, and rolled down the hill like a wheel; on
which he grew angry, and would go no further with us,
and faid, he would go by himfelf: It happened we found

---

[87] The Ohio, as it is called by the Sennecas. Alleghenny is the name of
the fame river in the Delaware language. Both words fignify the fine, or fair
river.— [C. T. ?]

[88] The Indian town which Post calls Keckkeknepolin was usually known as
Blackleg's Town, being situated at the mouth of Loyalhanna Creek, where it
flows into the Kiskiminitas.— ED.

a path on the top of the hill.   At three o'clock we came
to *Kijkemeneco*, an old *Indian* town, a rich bottom, well
timbered, good fine *Englijh* grafs, well watered, and
lays wafte fince the war began.⁸⁸ We let our horfes
feed here, and agreed that lieutenant *Hays* might go back
with his party; and as they were fhort of provifions, we,
therefore, gave them a little of ours, which they took very
kind of us.   *Thomas Hickman* could find no other road,
and came to us again a little afhamed; we were glad to
fee him; and we went about three miles farther, where we
made a large fire.   Here the *Indians* looked over their
prefents, and grumbled at me; they thought, if they had
gone the other way by *Shamokin*, they would have got
more.   Captain Bull fpoke in their favour againft me.
Then I faid to them, ''I am afhamed to fee you grumble
about prefents; I thought you were fent to eftablifh a
peace.''   Though I confefs I was not pleafed that the
Indians were fo flightly fitted out from *Eajton*, as the
general had nothing to give them, in the critical circum-
ftances he was in, fit for their purpofe.

12th.— Early in the morning, I fpoke to the *Indians* of
my company, ''Brethren, you have now paffed through
the heart of the country back and forward, likewife
through the midft of the army, without any difficulty
or danger; you have feen and heard a great deal.   When
I was among you, at *Alleghenny*, you told me, I fhould
not regard what the common people would fay, but only
hearken to the chiefs; I fhould take no bad ftories along.
I did accordingly; and when I left *Alleghenny* I dropt all

---

⁸⁸ Heckewelder says that the word "Kiskiminitas" means "make daylight,"
and was due to the impatient exclamation of some eager warrior encamped
on the spot. The town here mentioned was in Armstrong County, on a creek
of the same name, about seven miles from where it flows into the Allegheny
River.— ED.

evil reports, and only carried the agreeable news, which
was pleafing to all that heard it. Now, brethren, I beg
of you to do the fame, and to drop all evil reports, which
you may have heard of bad people, and only to obferve
and keep what you have heard of our rulers, and the
wife people, fo that all your young men, women and
children, may rejoice at our coming to them, and may
have the benefit of it.''

They took it very kindly. After awhile they fpoke in
the following manner to us, and faid, ''Brethren, when
you come to *Kujhkujhking*, you muft not mind the
prifoners, and have nothing to do with them. Mr. *Poft*,
when he was firft there, liftened too much to the prifoners;
the *Indians* were almoft mad with him for it, and would
have confined him for it; for, they faid, he had wrote
fomething of them.''

As we were hunting for our horfes, we found *Thomas
Hickman's* horfe dead, which rolled yefterday down the
hill. At one o'clock we came to the *Alleghenny*, to an old
Shawano town, fituated under a high hill on the eaft,
oppofite an ifland of about one hundred acres, very rich
land, well timbered.⁹⁰ We looked for a place to crofs
the river, but in vain; we then went fmartly to work, and
made a raft; we cut the wood, and carried it to the water
fide, The wolves and owls made a great noife in the
night.

13th.— We got up early, and boiled fome chocolate

---

⁹⁰ When he parted from Captain Haslett, Post left the regular westward
Indian trail to the Forks of the Ohio. In order to avoid Fort Duquesne, and
to reach the Indian towns beyond the Allegheny, he followed a northward
branch of the same that led down the Loyalhanna and Kiskiminitas creeks.
The Indian town at the mouth of Kiskiminitas Creek had always been insig-
nificant, lying between Kittanning on the north, and Shannopin's Town on
the south.— ED

for breakfaſt, and then began to finiſh our rafts; we cloathed ourſelves as well as we could in *Indian* dreſs; it was about two o'clock in the afternoon, before we all got over to the other ſide, near an old *Indian* town. The *Indians* told us, we ſhould not call Mr. *Bull, captain,* their young men would be mad that we brought a warrior there. We went up a ſteep hill, good land, to the creek *Cowewanick*,[91] where we made our fire. They wanted to hunt for meat, and looked for a road. Captain *Bull* ſhot a ſquirrel, and broke his gun. I cut fire wood, and boiled ſome chocolate for ſupper. The others came home, and brought nothing. *Peſquitomen* wanted to hear the writing from the general, which we read to them, to their great ſatiſfaction. This was the firſt night we ſlept in the open air. Mr. *Bull* took the tent along with him. We diſcourſed a good deal of the night together.

14th.— We roſe early, and thought to make good progreſs on our way. At one o'clock *Thomas Hickman* ſhot a large buck; and, as our people were hungry for meat, we made our camp there, and called the water *Buck run.* In the evening we heard the great guns fire from *fort Duqueſne.* Whenever I looked towards that place, I felt a diſmal impreſſion, the very place ſeemed ſhocking and dark. *Peſquitomen* looked his things over, and found a white belt, ſent by the commiſſioners of trade,[92] for the *Indian* affairs. We could find no writing concerning the belt, and did not know what was the ſignification thereof: They ſeemed much concerned to know it.

---

[91] Connequeneſſing Creek, whoſe name, according to Heckewelder, ſignifies "a long ſtraight courſe."— ED.

[92] Perſons appointed by law to manage the *Indian* trade, for the public; the private trade, on account of its abuſes, being aboliſhed.—[C. T. ?]

15th.— We arofe early, and had a good day's journey: we paffed thefe two days through thick bufhes of briars and thorns; fo that it was very difficult to get through. We croffed the creek *Paquakonink*; the land is very indifferent. At twelve o'clock we croffed the road from *Venango* to *fort Duquefne*. We went weft towards *Kufhkufhking*, about fixteen miles from the fort. We went over a large barren plain, and made our lodging by a little run. *Pefquitomen* told us, we muft fend a meffenger, to let them know of our coming, as the *French* live amongft them; he defired a ftring of wampum; I gave him three hundred and fifty. We concluded to go within three miles of *Kufhkufhking*, to their fugar cabbins,[93] and to call their chiefs there. In difcourfe, Mr. Bull told the *Indians*, the *Englifh* fhould let all the prifoners ftay amongft them, that liked to ftay.

16th.— We met two *Indians* on the road, and fat down with them to dinner. They informed us that no body was at home, at *Kufhkufhking*; that one hundred and fixty, from that town, were gone to war againft our party. We croffed the above mentioned creek; good land, but hilly. Went down a long valley to *Beaver* creek, through old *Kufhkufhking*,[94] a large fpot of land, abcut three miles long; they both went with us to the town; one of them rode before us, to let the people in the town know of our coming; we found there but two men, and fome women. Thofe, that were at home, received us kindly.

---

[93] Where they boil into fugar the juice of a tree that grows in thofe rich lands.— [C. T. ?]

[94] Irvine says (*Pennsylvania Archives*, xi, p. 518) that the Indians termed all the land along Beaver and Mahoning creeks for twenty-five miles, Kuskuskies. Old Kuskusking was located between the mouths of Neshanock and Mahoning creeks on the Shenango, about where the town of New Castle, Lawrence County, now stands.— ED.

Pejquitomen defired us to read the meffage to them that were there.

17th.— There were five *Frenchmen* in the town; the reft were gone to war. We held a council with *Delaware George*, delivered him the ftring and prefents, that were fent to him; and informed him of the general's fentiments, and what he defired of them; upon which he agreed, and complied to go with Mr. *Bull*, to the general. Towards night *Keckkenepalin* came home from the war, and told us the difagreeable news, that they had fallen in with that party, that had guided us; they had killed Lieutenant *Hays*, and four more, and took five prifoners, the others got clear off. They had a fkirmifh with them within twelve miles of *fort Duquefne*. Further he told us, that one of the captives was to be burnt, which grieved us. By the prifoners they were informed of our arrival; on which they concluded to leave the *French*, and to hear what news we brought them. In the evening they brought a prifoner to town. We called the *Indians* together, that were at home, and explained the matter to them, and told them, as their own people had defired the general to give them a guide to conduct them fafe home and by a misfortune, your people have fallen in with this party, and killed five and taken five prifoners; and we are now informed that one of them is to be burnt; "Confider, my brethren, if you fhould give us a guide, to bring us fafe on our way home, and our parties fhould fall in with you, how hard you would take it."

They faid, "Brother, it is a hard matter, and we are forry it hath happened fo." I anfwered, "Let us therefore fpare no pains to relieve them from any cruelty." We could fcarce find a meffenger, that would undertake to go to *Sawcung*, where the prifoner was to be bu[r]nt.

We promifed to one named *Compafs*, 500 black wampum, and Mr. *Hays* gave him a fhirt and a dollar, on which he promifed to go. We fent him as a meffenger, By a ftring of wampum I fpoke thefe words, "Brethren, confider the meffengers are come home with good news, and three of your brethren, the *Englifh*, with them. We defire you would pity your own young men, women and children, and ufe no hardfhips towards the captives, as having been guiding our party."

Afterwards the warriors informed us, that their defign had not been to go to war, but that they had a mind to go to the general and fpeak with him; and on the road the *French* made a divifion among them, that they could not agree; after which they were difcovered by the *Cherokees* and *Catawbas*, who fled, and left their bundles, where they found an *Englifh* colour. So *Kekeujcung* told them he would go before them to the general, if they would follow him; but they would not agree to it; and the *French* perfuaded them to fall upon the *Englifh* at *Loyal-hanning*;[56] they accordingly did, and as they were driven back, they fell in with that party, that guided us, which they did not know. They feemed very forry for it.

18th.— Captain *Bull* acted as commander, without letting us know any thing, or communicating with us. He and *George* relieved a prifoner from the warriors, by what means I do not know. When the warriors were

---

[56] Kekeuscung's name fignified "the healer." He was accounted a great warrior, and often joined the Six Nations against the Cherokees. The traditional hostility between the latter Indians and those around the Allegheny rendered difficult the attempt to conciliate the Delawares while the Cherokees were in the English army.

The attack here mentioned on the English camp at Loyalhanna, was repulsed by Colonel Mercer and the Virginian troops. On their return they fired by mistake upon their own re-enforcements, and nearly killed their leader, Washington.— ED.

met, he then called us firſt to ſit down, and to hear what
they had to ſay. The *Indian* that delivered the priſoner
to *Bull* and *George*, ſpoke as follows:

"My brethren, the *Engliſh* are at ſuch a diſtance from
us, as if they were under ground, that I cannot hear them.
I am very glad to hear from you ſuch good news; and I
am very ſorry that it happened ſo, that I went to war.
Now I let the general know, he ſhould conſider his young
men, and if you ſhould have any of us, to ſet them at
liberty, ſo as we do to you.

Then *Peſquitomen* ſaid, "As the Governor gave theſe
three meſſengers into my boſom, ſo I now likewiſe, by
this ſtring of wampum, give *Bull* into *Delaware George's*
boſom, to bring him ſafe to the general." Mr. *Bull*
ſat down with the priſoner, who gave him ſome intelligence in writing; at which the *Indians* grew very jealous
and aſked them what they had to write there? I wrote
a letter to the general by Mr. *Bull.* In the afternoon
Mr. *Bull*, *Delaware George*, and *Kejkenepalen* ſet out for
the camp. Towards night they brought in another
priſoner. When Mr. *Bull* and company were gone, the
Indians took the ſame priſoner, whom Mr. *Bull* had
relieved, and bound him and carried him to another
town, without our knowledge. I a thouſand times
wiſhed Mr. *Bull* had never meddled in the affair, fearing
they would exceedingly puniſh, and bring the priſoner to
confeſſion of the contents of the writing.

19th.— A great many of the warriors came home.
The *French* had infuſed bad notions into the *Indians*, by
means of the letters, they found upon Lieutenant *Hays*,
who was killed, which they falſely interpreted to them,
viz. That, in one letter it was wrote, that the general
ſhould do all that was in his power to conquer the *French*,

and, in the mean time the meffengers to the *Indians*
fhould do their utmoft to draw the Indians back, and
keep them together in conferences, till he, the general,
had made a conqueft of the *French*, and afterwards he
fhould fall upon all *Indians*, and deftroy them. And,
that, if we fhould lofe our lives, the *Englifh* would carry
on the war, fo long as an *Indian*, or *Frenchman* was alive.
Thereupon the French faid to the Indians;

"Now you can fee, my children, how the *Englifh* want
to deceive you, and if it would not offend you, I would go
and knock thefe meffengers on the head, before you
fhould be deceived by them." One of the *Indian*
captains fpoke to the *French* and faid, "To be fure it
would offend us, if you fhould offer to knock them on the
head. If you have a mind to go to war, go to the *Englifh* army, and knock them on the head, and not thefe
three men, that come with a meffage to us."

After this fpeech the *Indians* went all off, and left the
French. Neverthelefs it had enraged fome of the young
people, and made them fufpicious; fo that it was a precarious time for us. I faid, "Brethren, have good
courage, and be ftrong; let not every wind difturb your
mind; let the *French* bring the letter here; for, as you
cannot read, they may tell you thoufands of falfe ftories.
We will read the letter to you. As *Ifaac Still*⁰⁰ can read,
he will tell you the truth.

After this all the young men were gathered together,
Ifaac Still being in company. The young men faid,
"One that had but half an eye could fee that the *Englifh* only intended to cheat them; and that it was beft
to knock every one of us meffengers on the head."

⁰⁰ An *Indian* with an *Englifh* name. An *Indian* fometimes changes his
name with an *Englifhman* he refpects; it is a feal of friendfhip, and creates
a kind of relation between them.— [C. T. ?]

Then *Ijaac* began to fpeak and faid, "I am afhamed to hear fuch talking from you; you are but boys like me; you fhould not talk of fuch a thing. There have been thirteen nations at *Eafton*, where they have eftablifhed a firm peace with the *Englifh*; and I have heard that the Five Nations were always called the wifeft; go tell them that they are fools, and cannot fee; and tell them that you are kings, and wife men. Go and tell the *Cayuga* chiefs fo, that are here; and you will become great men." Afterwards they were all ftill, and faid not one word more.

20th.— There came a great many more together in the town, and brought *Henry Often*, the fergeant, who was to have been burnt. They hallooed the war halloo; and the men and women beat him till he came into the houfe.[97] It is a grievous and melancholy fight to fee our fellow mortals fo abufed. *Ijaac Still* had a long dif-courfe with the *French* captain; who made himfelf great, by telling how he had fought the *Englifh* at *Loyal-Han-ning*. *Ijaac* rallied him, and faid he had feen them fcalp horfes, and take others for food. The firft he denied, but the fecond he owned. *Ijaac* ran the captain quite down, before them all. The *French* captain fpoke with the two *Cayugas*; at laft the *Cayugas* fpoke very fharp to him, fo that he grew pale, and was quite filent.

Thefe three days paft was precarious time for us. We were warned not to go far from the houfe; becaufe the people who came from the flaughter, having been driven back, were poffeffed with a murdering fpirit; which led them as in a halter, in which they were catched, and with bloody vengeance were thirfty and drunk. This

[97] When a prifoner is brought to an *Indian* town, he runs a kind of gauntlet thro' the mob; and every one, even the children, endeavour to have a ftroke at him; but as foon as he can get into any of their huts, he is under protection, and refrefhments are adminiftered to him.—[C. T. ?]

afforded a melancholy profpect. *Ijaac Still* was himfelf dubious of our lives. We did not let Mr. *Hays* know of the danger. I faid, "As God hath ftopped the mouth of the lions, that they could not devour *Daniel*, fo he will preferve us from their fury, and bring us through." I had a difcourfe with Mr. *Hays* concerning our meffage, and begged him he would pray to God for grace and wifdom, that he would grant us peace among this people. We will remain in ftillnefs, and not look to our own credit. We are in the fervice of our king and country. This people are rebellious in heart.

Now we are here to reconcile them again to the General, Governor, and the *Englijh* nation; to turn them again from their errors. And I wifhed that God would grant us his grace, whereby we may do it; which I hope and believe he will do. Mr. *Hays* took it to heart and was convinced of all; which much rejoiced me. I begged *Ijaac Still* to watch over himfelf and not to be difcouraged; for I hoped the ftorm would foon pafs by.

In the afternoon all the captains gathered together in the middle town; they fent for us, and defired we fhould give them information of our meffage. Accordingly we did. We read the meffage with great fatisfaction to them. It was a great pleafure both to them and us. The number of captains and counfellors were fixteen. In the evening meffengers arrived from *jort Duquejne*, with a ftring of wampum from the commander; upon which they all came together in the houfe where we lodged. The meffengers delivered their ftring, with thefe words from their father, the *French* King:

"My children, come to me, and hear what I have to fay. The *Englijh* are coming with an army to deftroy both you and me. I therefore defire you immediately, my children, to haften with all the young men; we will drive the *Englifh* and deftroy them. I, as a father, will tell you always what is beft.'' He laid the ftring before one of the captains. After a little converfation, the captain ftood up and faid; ''I have juft heard fomething of our brethren the *Englifh*, which pleafeth me much better. I will not go. Give it to the others, may be they will go.'' The meffenger took up again the ftring and faid, ''He won't go, he has heard of the *Englifh*.''[88] Then all cried out, ''yes, yes, we have heard from the *Englifh*.'' He then threw the ftring to the other fire place, where the other captains were; but they kicked it from one to another, as if it was a fnake. Captain *Peter* took a ftick, and with it flung the ftring from one end of the room to the other,[89] and faid, ''Give it to the *French* captain, and let him go with his young men; he boafted much of his fighting; now let us fee his fighting. We have often ventured our lives for him; and had hardly a loaf of bread, when we came to him; and now he thinks we fhould jump to ferve him.'' Then we faw the *French* captain mortified to the uttermoft; he looked as pale as death. The Indians difcourfed and joked till midnight; and the *French* captain fent meffengers at midnight to *fort Duquefne*.

21ft.— We were informed that the general was within twenty miles of *fort Duquefne*. As the *Indians* were afraid the *Englifh* would come over the river *Ohio*, I fpoke with fome of the captains, and told them that, ''I fuppofed the general intended to furround the *French*,

---

[88] *i. e.* He has liftened to the *Englifh* meffengers.—[C. T. ?]

[89] Kicking the ftring about, and throwing it with a ftick, not touching it with their hands, were marks of diflike of the meffage, that accompanied it.—[C. T. ?]

and therefore muft come to this fide the river; but we
affure you that he will not come to your towns to hurt
you.'' I begged them to let the *Shawaneje* at *Logjtown,*
know it, and gave them four ftrings of 300 wampum,
with this meffage; ''Brethren, we are arrived with good
news, waiting for you; we defire you to be ftrong, and
remember the ancient friendfhip your grandfathers had
with the *Englijh*. We wifh you would remember it, and
pity your young men, women and children, and keep
away from the *French*; and if the *Englijh* fhould come
to furround the *French*, be not afraid. We affure you
they won't hurt you.''

22d.— *Kittiujkund* came home, and fent for us, being
very glad to fee us. He informed us, the general was
within fifteen miles of the *French jort*; that the *French*
had uncovered their houfes, and laid the roofs round the
fort to fet it on fire, and made ready to go off, and would
demolifh the fort, and let the *Englijh* have the bare
ground; faying; ''they are not able to build a ftrong fort
this winter; and we will be early enough in the fpring
to deftroy them. We will come with feventeen nations
of *Indians*, and a great many *French*, and build a ftone
fort.

The Indians danced round the fire till midnight, for
joy of their brethren, the *Englijh*, coming. There went
fome fcouting parties towards the army. Some of the
captains told me, that *Shamokin Daniel*, who came
with me in my former journey, had fairly fold me to the
French; and the *French* had been very much difpleafed
that the *Indians* had brought me away.

23d.— The *liar* raifed a ftory, as if the *Englijh* were
divided into three bodies, to come on this fide the river.
They told us the *Cayugas*, that came with us, had faid

fo. We told the *Cayugas* of it; on which they called
the other *Indians* together; denied that they ever faid fo;
and faid, they were fent to this place from the *Five
Nations*, to tell them to do their beſt endeavors to ſend
the *French* off from this country; and when that was done
they would go and tell the general to go back over the
mountains.

I fee the *Indians* concern themfelves very much about
the affair of land; and are continually jealous, and afraid
the *Engliſh* will take their land. I told them to be ſtill
and content themſelves, ''for there are fome chiefs
of the *Five Nations* with the army; they will fettle the
affair, as they are the chief owners of the land; and it will
be well for you to come and ſpeak with the general
yourſelves.''

Iſaac Still aſked the *French* captain, whether it was
true, that *Daniel* had fold me to the *French*? He owned
it, and faid, I was theirs, they had bought me fairly; and,
if the *Indians* would give them leave, he would take me.

24th.— We hanged out the *Engliſh* flag, in ſpite of the
French; on which our priſoners folded their hands, in
hopes that their redemption was nigh, looking up to
God, which melted my heart in tears, and prayers to
God, to hear their prayers, and change the times, and the
fituation, which our priſoners are in, and under which
they groan. ''O Lord, faid they, when will our redemption come, that we ſhall be delivered, and return home?''
— And if any accident happeneth, which the *Indians*
diſlike, the priſoners all tremble with fear, faying, ''Lord,
what will become of us, and what will be the end of our
lives?'' So that they often wiſh themſelves rather under
the ground, than in this life. King Beaver came home,
and called us to his houſe, and faluted us in a friendly

manner; which we, in like manner, did to him. Afterwards I fpoke by four ftrings of 350 wampum, and faid, as followeth:

"I have a falutation to you, and all your people, from the general, the governor, and many other gentlemen. Brother, it pleafes me that the day is come to fee you and your people. We have warmed ourfelves by your fire, and waited for you, and thank you, that you did come home. We have good news of great importance; which we hope will make you, and all your people's hearts glad. By thefe ftrings I defire you would be pleafed to call all your kings and captains, from all the towns and nations; fo that they all may hear us, and have the benefit thereof, while they live, and their children after them."

Then he faid, "As foon as I heard of your coming, I rofe up directly to come to you." Then there came another meffage, which called me to another place, where fix kings of fix nations were met together. I fent them word, they fhould fit together a while, and fmoke their pipes, and I would come to them. King Beaver faid further,

"Brother, it pleafeth me to hear that you brought fuch good news; and my heart rejoices already at what you faid to me. It rejoices me that I have now heard of you." I faid, "Brother, you did well, that you firft came here, before you went to the kings; as the good news we brought is to all nations, from the rifing of the fun to the going down of the fame; that want to be in peace and friendfhip with the *Englifh*. So it will give them fatisfaction, when they hear it." The *French* captain told us, that they would demolifh the fort; and he thought the *Englifh* would be to-day at the place.

25th.— *Shingas* came home, and faluted us in a

friendly manner, and fo did *Beaver*, in our houfe; and
then they told us, they would hear our meffage; and we
perceived that the *French* captain had an inclination to
hear it. We called *Beaver* and *Shingas*, and informed
them, that all the nations, at *Eafton*, had agreed with the
governor, that every thing fhould be kept fecret from the
ears and eyes of the *French*. He faid, ''it was no matter,
they were beaten already. It is good news, and if he
would fay any thing, we would tell him what friendfhip
we have together.'' Accordingly they met together, and
the *French* captain was prefent. The number confifted
of about fifty.

King *Beaver* firft fpoke to his men, ''Hearken, all you
captains and warriors, here are our brethren, the *Englifh*; I wifh that you may give attention, and take notice
of what they fay. As it is for our good, that there may
an everlafting peace be eftablifhed, although there is
a great deal of mifchief done, if it pleafeth God to help
us, we may live in peace again.''

Then I began to fpeak by four ftrings to them, and
faid,

''Brethren, being come here to fee you, I perceive your
bodies are all ftained with blood, and obferve tears and
forrows in your eyes: With this ftring I clean your
body from blood, and wipe and anoint your eyes with the
healing oil, fo that you may fee your brethren clearly.
And as fo many ftorms have blown fince we laft faw one
another, and we are at fuch a diftance from you, that you
could not rightly hear us as yet, I, by this ftring, take a
foft feather, and with that good oil, our grandfathers
ufed, open and clear your ears, fo that you may both
hear and underftand what your brethren have to fay to
you. And by thefe ftrings I clear your throat from the

duſt, and take all the bitterneſs out of your heart, and
clear the paſſage from the heart to the throat, that you
may ſpeak freely with your brethren, the *Englijh*, from
the heart.''

Then *Iſaac Still* gave the pipe, ſent by the *Friends*,[100]
filled with tobacco, and handed round, after their cuſtom,
and ſaid:

"Brethren, here is the pipe, which your grandfathers
uſed to ſmoke with, when they met together in councils of
peace.   And here is ſome of that good tobacco, prepared
for our grandfathers from God:— When you ſhall taſte
of it, you ſhall feel it through all your body; and it will
put you in remembrance of the good councils, your grandfathers uſed to hold with the *Englijh*, your brethren, and
that ancient friendſhip, thay had together.''

King *Beaver* roſe, and thanked us firſt, that we had
cleared his body from the blood, and wiped the tears
and ſorrow from his eyes, and opened his ears, ſo that
now he could well hear and underſtand.   Likewiſe he
returned thanks for the *pipe and tobacco*, that we brought,
which our grandfathers uſed to ſmoke. He ſaid,—
"When I taſted that good tobacco, I felt it all through
my body, and it made me all over well.''

Then we delivered the meſſages, as followeth:

Governor *Denny's* anſwer to the meſſage of the *Ohio
Indians*, brought by *Frederick Poſt, Peſquitomen* and
Thomas Hickman.

"By this ſtring, my *Indian* brethren of the United
Nations and *Delawares*, join with me, in requiring of
the *Indian* councils, to which theſe following meſſages

---

[100] The *Quakers* of *Philadelphia*, who firſt ſet on foot theſe negociations of
peace; and for whom the *Indians* have always had a great regard.— [C. T. ?]
Comment by Ed. See on this subject *Pennsylvania Archives*, iii, p. 581.

fhall be prefented, to keep every thing private from the eyes and ears of the *French*.'' A ftring.

''Brethren, we received your meffage by *Pejquitomen* and *Frederick Poft*, and thank you for the care you have taken of our meffenger of peace, and that you have put him in your bofom, and protected him againft our enemy, *Onontio*, and his children, and fent him fafe back to our council fire, by the fame man, that received him from us.'' A ftring.

''Brethren, I only fent *Poft* to peep into your cabbins, and to know the fentiments of your old men, and to look at your faces, to fee how you look. And I am glad to hear from him, that you look friendly; and that there ftill remain fome fparks of love towards us. It was what we believed before hand, and therefore we never let flip the chain of friendfhip, but held it faft, on our fide, and it has never dropt out of our hands. By this belt we defire that you will dig up your end of the chain of friend-fhip, that you fuffered, by the fubtlety of the *French*, to be buried.'' A belt.

''Brethren, it happened that the governor of *Jerfey* was with me, and a great many *Indian* brethren, fitting in council at *Eafton*, when your meffengers arrived; and it gave pleafure to every one that heard it; and it will afford the fame fatisfaction to our neighboring governors, and their people, when they come to hear it. I fhall fend meffengers to them, and acquaint them with what you have faid.

''Your requefting us to let the king of *England* know your good difpofitions we took to heart, and fhall let him know it; and we will fpeak in your favor to his majefty, who has, for fome time paft, looked upon you as his loft children. And we can affure you, that, as a tender father over all his children, he will forgive what is paſt, and receive you again into his arms.'' A belt.

''Brethren, if you are in earneſt to be reconciled to us, you will keep your young men from attacking our country and killing and carrying captive our back inhabitants; And will likewiſe give orders, that your people may be kept at a diſtance from *Fort Duqueſne*; that they may not be hurt by our warriors, who are ſent by our king to chaſtiſe the *French*, and not to hurt you. Conſider the commanding officer of that army treads heavy, and would be very ſorry to hurt any of his *Indian* brethren.'' A large belt.

''And brethren, the chiefs of the *United Nations*, with their couſins, our brethren, the *Delawares*, and others now here, jointly with me ſend this belt, which has upon it two figures, that repreſent all the *Engliſh*, and all the *Indians*, now preſent, taking hands, and delivering it to *Peſquitomen*: and we deſire it may be likewiſe ſent to the *Indians*, who are named at the end of theſe meſſages;[101] as they have all been formerly our very good friends and allies; and we deſire they will all go from among the *French* to their own towns, and no longer help the *French*.''

''*Brethren on the Ohio*, if you take the belts we juſt now gave you, in which all here join, *Engliſh* and *Indians*, as we do not doubt you will; then, by this belt, I make a road for you, and invite you to come to *Philadelphia*, to your firſt old council fire, which was kindled when we firſt ſaw one another; which fire we will kindle up again, and remove all diſputes, and renew the old and firſt treaties

---

[101] "Saſtaghretſy, Anigh Kalicken, Atowateany, Towigh, Towighroano, Geghdageghroano, Oyaghtanont, Siſaghroano, Stiaggeghroano, Jenontady-nago."—[C. T.?]

of friendſhip. This is a clear and open road for you; fear, therefore, nothing, and come to us with as many as can be of the *Delawares, Shawaneſe*, or of the *Six Nations*: We will be glad to ſee you; we deſire all tribes and nations of *Indians*, who are in alliance with you, may come. As ſoon as we hear of your coming, of which you will give us timely notice, we will lay up proviſions for you along the road.''

A large white belt, with the figure of a man, at each end, and ſtreaks of black, repreſenting the road from the *Ohio* to *Philadelphia*.

''Brethren, the *Six Nation* and *Delaware* chiefs join with me in thoſe belts, which are tied together, to ſignify our union and friendſhip for each other; with them we jointly take the *tomahawks* out of your hands, and bury them under ground.

''We ſpeak aloud, ſo as you may hear us; you ſee we all ſtand together, joined hand in hand.'' Two belts tied together.

''General *Forbes* to the *Shawaneſe*, and *Delawares*, on the *Ohio*.

''Brethren, I embrace this opportunity by our brother, *Peſquitomen*, who is now on his return home with ſome of your uncles, of the *Six Nations*, from the treaty of *Eaſton*, of giving you joy of the happy concluſion of that great council, which is perfectly agreeable to me; as it is for the mutual advantage of our brethren, the *Indians*, as well as the *Engliſh* nation.

''I am glad to find that all paſt diſputes and animoſities are now finally ſettled, and amicably adjuſted; and I hope they will be for ever buried in oblivion, and that you will now again be firmly united in the intereſt of your brethren, the *Engliſh*.''

"As I am now advancing, at the head of a large army, againſt his majeſty's enemies, the *French*, on the *Ohio*, I muſt ſtrongly recommend to you to ſend immediate notice to any of your people, who may be at the *French* fort, to return forthwith to your towns; where you may ſit by your fires, with your wives and children, quiet and undiſturbed, and ſmoke your pipes in ſafety. Let the *French* fight their own battles, as they were the firſt cauſe of the war, and the occaſion of the long difference, which hath ſubſiſted between you and your brethren, the *Engliſh*; but I muſt entreat you to reſtrain your young men from croſſing the *Ohio*, as it will be impoſſible for me to diſtinguiſh them from our enemies; which I expect you will comply with, without delay; leſt, by your neglect thereof, I ſhould be the innocent cauſe of ſome of our brethren's death. This advice take and keep in your own breaſts, and ſuffer it not to reach the ears of the *French*.

"As a proof of the truth and ſincerity of what I ſay, and to confirm the tender regard I have for the lives and welfare of our brethren, on the *Ohio*, I ſend you this ſtring of wampum.

"I am, brethren and warriors,
    "Your friend and brother,
                              "JOHN FORBES."

"Brethren, kings *Beaver* and *Shingas*, and all the warriors, who join with you:

"The many acts of hoſtility, committed by the *French* againſt the *Britiſh* ſubjects, made it neceſſary for the king to take up arms, in their defence, and to redreſs their wrongs, which have been done them; heaven hath favoured the juſtice of the cauſe, and given ſucceſs to his fleets and armies, in different parts of the world. I have received his commands, with regard to what is to be done on the *Ohio*, and fhall endeavour to act like a foldier by driving the *French* from thence, or deftroying them.

"It is a particular pleafure to me to learn, that the *Indians*, who inhabit near that river, have lately concluded a treaty of peace with the *Englifh*; by which the ancient friendfhip is renewed with their brethren, and fixed on a firmer foundation than ever. May it be lafting and unmoveable as the mountains. I make no doubt but it gives you equal fatisfaction, and that you will unite your endeavours with mine, and all the governors of thefe provinces, to ftrengthen it: The clouds, that, for fome time, hung over the *Englifh*, and their friends, the *Indians* on the *Ohio*, and kept them both in darknefs, are now difperfed, and the chearful light now again fhines upon us, and warms us both. May it continue to do fo, while the fun and moon give light.

"Your people, who were fent to us, were received by us with open arms; they were kindly entertained, while they were here; and I have taken care that they fhall return fafe to you; with them come trufty meffengers, whom I earneftly recommend to your protection; they have feveral matters in charge; and I defire you may give credit to what they fay; in particular, they have a large belt of wampum, and by this belt we let you know, that it is agreed by me, and all the governors, that there fhall be an everlafting peace with all the *Indians*, eftablifhed as fure as the mountains, between the *Englifh* nation and the *Indians*, all over, from the fun rifing to the fun fetting; and as your influence on them is great, fo you will make it known to all the different nations, that want to be in friendfhip with the *Englifh*; and I hope, by your means and perfuafions, many will lay hold on this belt, and

immediately withdraw from the *French*; this will be
greatly to their own intereſt and your honor, and I ſhall
not fail to acquaint the great king of it: I ſincerely wiſh
it, for their good; for it will fill me with concern, to find
any of you joined with the *French*; as in that caſe, you
muſt be ſenſible I muſt treat them as enemies; however,
I once more repeat, that there is no time to be loſt; for I
intend to march with the army very ſoon; and I hope to
enjoy the pleaſure of thanking you for your zeal, and of
entertaining you in the fort ere long.   In the mean time
I wiſh happineſs and proſperity to you, your women
and children.

"I write to you as a warrior ſhould, that is, with can-
dour and love, and I recommend ſecrecy and diſpatch.

"I am, kings *Beaver* and *Shingas*,

"And brother warriors,

"Your aſſured friend and brother,

"JOHN FORBES."

"From my camp at LOYALHANNON,⇐ F̄ ⁞ ┊ ·⁞⹁. ˙⹁
     Nov. 9, 1758."

The meſſages pleaſed, and gave ſatisfaction to all the
hearers, except the *French* captain. He ſhook his head
with bitter grief, and often changed his countenance.
Iſaac Still ran down the *French* captain with great
boldneſs, and pointed at him ſaying, "There he ſits."
Afterwards *Shingas* roſe up and ſaid:

"Brethren, now we have rightly heard and underſtood
you, it pleaſeth me and all the young men, that hear it;
we ſhall think of it, and take it into due conſideration;
and when we have conſidered it well, then we will give
you an anſwer, and ſend it to all the towns and nations,
as you deſired us."

We thanked them and wifhed them good fuccefs in
their undertaking; and wifhed it might have the fame
effect upon all other nations, that may hereafter hear it,
as it had on them. We went a little out of the houfe.
In the mean time *Ifaac Still* demanded the letter, which
the *French* had falfely interpreted, that it might be read in
public. Then they called us back, and I, *Frederick
Poft*, found it was my own letter, I had wrote to the
general. I therefore ftood up, and read it, which Ifaac
interpreted. The *Indians* were well pleafed, and took
it as if it was written to them; thereupon they all faid:
"We always thought the *French* report of the letter was a
lie; they always deceived us:" Pointing at the *French*
captain; who, bowing down his head, turned quite pale,
and could look no one in the face. All the *Indians*
began to mock and laugh at him; he could hold it no
longer, and went out. Then the *Cayuga* chief delivered
a ftring, in the name of the *Six Nations*, with thefe
words:

"Coufins, hear what I have to fay; I fee you are forry,
and the tears ftand in your eyes. I would open your ears,
and clear your eyes from tears, fo that you may fee, and
hear what your uncles, the *Six Nations*, have to fay.
We have eftablifhed a friendfhip with your brethren,
the *Englifh*. We fee that you are all over bloody, on
your body; I clean the heart from the duft, and your eyes
from the tears, and your bodies from the blood, that you
may hear and fee your brethren, the *Englifh*, and appear
clean before them, and that you may fpeak from the
heart with them." Delivered four ftrings.

Then he fhewed to them a ftring from the *Cherokees*,
with thefe words:

"Nephews, we let you know, that we are exceedingly

glad that there is fuch a firm friendfhip eftablifhed, on
fo good a foundation, with fo many nations, that it will
laft for ever; and, as the *Six Nations* have agreed with
the *Englifh*, fo we wifh that you may lay hold of the fame
friendfhip.   We will remind you, that we were formerly
good friends.   Likewife you let you know, that the *Six
Nations* gave us a *tomahawk*, and, if any body offended
us, we fhould ftrike him with it; likewife they gave me a
knife, to take off the fcalp.   So we let you know, that we
are defirous to hear very foon from you, what you deter-
mine.   It may be we fhall ufe the hatchet very soon,
therefore I long to hear from you.''

Then the council broke up.   After a little while meffengers arrived, and *Beaver* came into our houfe, and
gave us the pleafure to hear, that the *Englifh* had the
field, and that the *French* had demolifhed and burnt the
place entirely, and went off; that the commander is gone
with two hundred men to *Venango*, and the reft gone
down the river in battoes, to the lower *Shawaneje* town,
with an intention to build a fort there; they were feen
yefterday paffing by *Sawcung*.

We ended this day with pleafure and great fatisfaction
on both fides: the *Cayuga* chief faid, he would fpeak
further to them tomorrow.

26th.— We met together about ten o'clock.   Firft,
King *Beaver* addreffed himfelf to the *Cayuga* chief, and
faid;

''My uncles, as it is cuftomary to anfwer one another,
fo I thank you, that you took fo much notice of your
coufins, and that you have wiped the tears from our eyes,
and cleaned our bodies from the blood; when you fpoke
to me I faw myfelf all over bloody; and fince you cleaned
me I feel myfelf quite pleafant through my whole body,

and I can fee the fun fhine clear over us." Delivered four ftrings.

He faid further, "As you took fo much pains, and came a great way through the bufhes, I, by this ftring, clean you from the fweat, and clean the duft out of your throat, fo that you may fpeak what you have to fay from your brethren, the *Englifh*, and our uncles, the *Six Nations*, to your coufins, I am ready to hear."

Then *Petiniontonka*, the *Cayuga* chief, took the belt with eight diamonds,[102] and faid;

"Coufins, take notice of what I have to fay; we let you know what agreement we have made with our brethren, the *Englifh*. We had almoft flipt and dropt the chain of friendfhip with our brethren, the *Englifh*; now we let you know that we have renewed the peace and friendfhip with our brethren, the *Englifh*; and we have made a new agreement with them. We fee that you have dropt the peace and friendfhip with them. We defire you would lay hold of the covenant, we have made with our brethren, the *Englifh*, and be ftrong. We likewife take the *tomahawk* out of your hands, that you received from the white people; ufe it no longer; fling the *tomahawk* away; it is the white people's; let them ufe it among themfelves; it is theirs, and they are of one colour; let them fight with one another, and do you be ftill and quiet in *Kufhkufhking*. Let our grandchildren, the *Shawanefe*, likewife know of the covenant, we eftablifhed with our friends, the *Englifh*, and also let all other nations know it."

Then he explained to them the eight diamonds, on the belt, fignifying the five united nations, and the three

[102] Diamond figures, formed by beads of wampum, of different colours. —[C. T. ?]

younger nations, which join them; thefe all united with the *Englijh*. Then he proceeded thus:

"Brethren," (delivering a belt with eight diamonds, the second belt) "we hear that you did not fit right; and when I came I found you in a moving pofture, ready to jump towards the funfet; fo we will fet you at eafe, and quietly down, that you may fit well at *Kujhkujhking*; and we defire you to be ftrong; and if you will be ftrong, your women and children will fee from day to day the light fhining more over them; and our children and grand children will fee that there will be an everlafting peace eftablifhed. We defire you to be ftill; we do not know as yet, what to do; towards the fpring you fhall hear from your uncles what they conclude; in the mean time do you fit ftill by your fire at *Kujhkujhking*."

In the evening the devil made a general difturbance, to hinder them in their good difpofition. It was reported that they faw three *Catawba Indians* in their town; and they roved about all that cold night, in great fear and confufion. When I confider with what tyranny and power the prince of this world rules over this people, it breaks my heart over them, and that their redemption may draw nigh, and open their eyes, that they may fee what bondage they are in, and deliver them from the evil.

27th.— We waited all the day for an anfwer. *Beaver* came and told us, "They were bufy all the day long." He faid, "It is a great matter, and wants much confideration. We are three tribes, which muft feparately agree among ourfelves; it takes time before we hear each agreement, and the particulars thereof." He defired us to read our meffage once more to them in private; we told them, we were at their fervice at any time; and then we

explained him the whole again. There arrived a meffenger
from *Sawcung*, and informed us that four of their people
were gone to our camp, to fee what the *Englifh* were
about; and that one of them climbing upon a tree was
difcovered by falling down; and then our people fpoke to
them; three refolved to go to the other fide, and one came
back and brought the news, which pleafed the company.
Some of the captains and counfellors were together; they
faid, that the *French* would build a ftrong fort, at the
lower *Shawaneje* town. I anfwered them, ''Brethren,
if you fuffer the French to build a fort there, you muft
fuffer likewife the *Englifh* to come and deftroy the place;
Englifh will follow the *French*, and purfue them, let it
coft whatever it will; and wherever the *French* fettle, the
Englifh will follow and deftroy them.''

They faid, ''We think the fame, and would endeavour
to prevent it, if the *Englifh* only would go back, after
having drove away the *French*, and not fettle there.'' I
faid, ''I can tell you no certainty in this affair; it is beft for
you to go with us to the general, and fpeak with him. So
much I know, that they only want to eftablish a trade with
you; and you know yourfelves that you cannot do without
being fupplied with fuch goods as you ftand in need of;
but, brethren, be affured you muft entirely quit the
French, and have no communication with them, elfe they
will always breed difturbance and confufion amongft
you, and perfuade your young people to go to war againft
our brethren, the *Englifh*.''

I spoke with them further about *Venango*, and faid,
''I believed the *Englifh* would go there, if they fuffered
the *French* longer to live there. This fpeech had much
influence on them, and they faid; ''We are convinced of
all that you have faid; it will be fo.'' I found them in-

clined to fend off the *French* from *Venango*; but they
wanted firft to know the difpofition of the *Englijh*, and
not to fuffer the *French* to build any where.

28th.— King *Beaver* arofe early before the break of
day, and bid all his people a good morning, defired them
to rife early and prepare victuals; for they had to anfwer
their brethren, the *Englijh*, and their uncles, and therefore they fhould be in a good humor and difpofition.
At ten o'clock they met together; *Beaver* addreffed himfelf to his people, and faid,

"Take notice all you young men and warriors to what
we anfwer now: it is three days fince we heard our
brethren, the *Englijh*, and our uncles; and what we
have heard of both, is very good; and we are all much
pleafed with what we have heard. Our uncles have
made an agreement, and peace is eftablifhed with our
brethren, the *Englijh*, and they have fhook hands with
them; and we likewife agree in the peace and friendfhip,
they have eftablifhed between them." Then he fpoke
to the *French* captain *Canaquais*, and faid,

"You may hear what I anfwer; it is good news, that
we have heard. I have not made myfelf a king. My
uncles have made me like a queen, that I always fhould
mind what is good and right, and whatever I agree with,
they will affift me, and help me through. Since the
warriors came amongft us, I could not follow that which
is good and right; which has made me heavy; and fince
it is my duty to do that which is good, fo I will endeavour
to do and to fpeak what is good, and not let myfelf be
difturbed by the warriors."

Then he fpoke to the *Mingoes*, and faid,

"My uncles, hear me; It is two days fince you told me,
that you have made peace and friendfhip, and fhook

hands with our brethren, the *Englijh*. I am really very
much pleafed with what you told me; and I join with
you in the fame; and, as you faid, I fhould let the *Shawaneje* and *Delamaitanoes* know of the agreement, you have
made with our brethren, the *Englijh*, I took it to heart,
and fhall let them know it very foon.'' He delivered a
ftring.

"Look now, my uncles, and hear what your coufins
fay: you have fpoke the day before yefterday to me. I
have heard you. You told me, you would fet me at
Kujhkujhking eafy down. I took it to heart; and I
fhall do fo, and be ftill, and lay myfelf eafy down, and
keep my match-coat clofe to my breaft. You told me,
you will let me know in the next fpring, what to do; fo I
will be ftill, and wait to hear from you.'' Gave him a
belt.

Then he turned himfelf to us, and gave us the following
anfwers. Firft, to the general;

"Brother, by thefe ftrings I would defire, in a moft
kind and friendly manner, you would be pleafed to hear
me what I have to fay, as you are not far off.

"Brother, now you told me you have heard of that
good agreement, that has been agreed to, at the treaty
at Eafton; and that you have put your hands to it, to
ftrengthen it, fo that it may laft for ever. Brother, you
have told me, that after you have come to hear it, you
have taken it to heart, and then you fent it to me, and let
me know it. Brother, I would defire you would be
pleafed to hear me, and I would tell you, in a moft foft,
loving and friendly manner, to go back over the mountain,
and to ftay there; for, if you will do that, I will ufe it for
an argument, to argue with other nations of *Indians*.
Now, brother, you have told me you have made a road

clear, from the fun-fet to our firft old council fire, at
Philadelphia, and therefore I fhould fear nothing, and
come into that road.   Brother, after thefe far *Indians*
fhall come to hear of that good and wide road, that you
have laid out for us, then they will turn and look at the
road, and fee nothing in the way; and that is the reafon
that maketh me tell you to go back over the mountain
again, and to ftay there; for then the road will be clear, and
nothing in the way.''

Then he addreffed himfelf to the Governor of *Pennfyl-*
vania, as follows;

''Brother, give good attention to what I am going to
fay; for I fpeak from my heart; and think nothing the lefs
of it, though the ftrings be fmall.[108]

''Brother, I now tell you what I have heard from you
is quite agreeable to my mind; and I love to hear you.   I
tell you likewife, that all the chief men of *Allegheny* are
well pleafed with what you have faid to us; and all my
young men, women and children, that are able to underftand, are well pleafed with what you have faid to me.

''Brother, you tell me that all the Governors of the
feveral provinces have agreed to a well eftablifhed and
everlafting peace with the *Indians*; and you likewife tell
me, that my uncles, the *Six Nations*, and my brethren
the *Delawares*, and feveral other tribes of *Indians* join
with you in it, to eftablifh it, fo that it may be everlafting;
you likewife tell me, you have all agreed on a treaty of
peace to laft for ever; and for thefe reafons I tell you,
I am pleafed with what you have told me.

''Brother, I am heartily pleafed to hear that you never
let flip the chain of friendfhip out of your hands, which

---

[108] Important matters fhould be accompanied with large ftrings, or belts;
but fometimes a fufficient quantity of wampum is not at hand.—[C. T. ?]

our grandfathers had between them, fo that they could agree as brethren and friends in any thing.

"Brother, as you have been pleafed to let me know of that good and defirable agreement, that you and my uncles and brothers have agreed to, at the treaty of peace, I now tell you I heartily join and agree in it, and to it; and now I defire you to go on fteadily in that great and good work, you have taken in hand; and I will do as you defire me to do; that is, to let the other tribes of *Indians* know it, and more efpecially my uncles, the *Six Nations*, and the *Shawaneje*, my grandchildren, and all other nations, fettled to the weftward.

"Brother, I defire you not to be out of patience, as I have a great many friends at a great diftance; and I fhall ufe my beft endeavours to let them know it as foon as poffible; and as foon as I obtain their anfwer, fhall let you know it." Then he gave fix ftrings all white.

In the evening arrived a meffenger from *Sackung*, *Netodwehement*, and defired they fhould make all the hafte to difpatch us, and we fhould come to *Sackung*; for, as they did not know what is become of thofe three, that went to our camp, they were afraid the *Englifh* would keep them, till they heard what was become of us, their meffengers.

29th.— Before day break *Beaver* and *Shingas* came, and called us into their council. They had been all the night together. They faid; "Brethren, now is the day coming, you will fet off from here. It is a good many days fince we heard you; and what we have heard is very pleafing and agreeable to us. It rejoices all our hearts; and all our young men, women and children, that are capable to underftand, are really very well pleafed with what they have heard; it is fo agreeable to us, that we

never received fuch good news before; we think God has
made it fo; he pities us, and has mercy on us. And now,
brethren, you defire that I fhould let it be known to all
other nations; and I fhall let them know very foon.
Therefore *Shingas* cannot go with you. He muft go
with me, to help me in this great work; and I fhall fend
nobody, but go myfelf, to make it known to all nations.''

Then we thanked them for their care; and wifhed him
good fuccefs on his journey and undertaking: and, as
this meffage had fuch a good effect on them, we hoped
it would have the fame on all other nations, when they
came to hear it. I hoped that all the clouds would pafs
away, and the chearful light would fhine over all nations;
fo I wifhed them good affiftance and help on their
journey. Farther, he faid to us;

''Now we defire you to be ftrong;[184] becaufe I fhall
make it my ftrong argument with other nations; but as we
have given credit to what you have faid, hoping it is true,
and we agree to it; if it fhould prove the contrary, it
would make me fo afhamed, that I never could lift up
my head, and never undertake to fpeak any word more
for the intereft of the *Englifh*.''

I told them, ''Brethren, you will remember that it was
wrote to you by the general, that you might give credit
to what we fay; fo I am glad to hear of you, that you give
credit; and we affure you, that what we have told you is
the truth; and you will find it fo.''

They faid further, ''Brethren, we let you know, that
the *French* have ufed our people kindly, in every refpect;
they have ufed them like gentlemen, efpecially thofe that
live near them. So they have treated the chiefs. Now we

[184] The word, *wifhickfey*, tranflated, *be ftrong*, is of a very extenfive fignifica-
tion be ftrong, be fteady, purfue to effect what you have begun, &c.—[C. T. ?]

defire you to be ftrong; we wifh you would take the fame
method, and ufe our people well: for the other *Indians*
will look upon us;[105] and we do not otherwife know how
to convince them, and to bring them into the *Englifh*
intereft, without your ufing fuch means as will convince
them.   For the *French* will ftill do more to keep them to
their intereft.''

I told them, ''I would take it to heart, and inform the
Governor, and other gentlemen of it; and fpeak to them
in their favour.''   Then they faid, ''It is fo far well, and
the road is cleared; but they thought we fhould fend
them another call, when they may come.''   I told them;
''We did not know when they would have agreed with
the other nations.   Brother, it is you, who muft give us
the firft notice when you can come; the fooner the better;
and fo foon as you fend us word, we will prepare for you
on the road.''   After this we made ready for our journey.

Ketiufhund, a noted *Indian*, one of the chief counfellors,
told us in fecret, ''That all the nations had jointly agreed
to defend their hunting place at *Alleghenny*, and fuffer
nobody to fettle there; and as thefe *Indians* are very
much inclined to the *Englifh* intereft, fo he begged us
very much to tell the Governor, General, and all other
people not to fettle there.   And if the *Englifh* would
draw back over the mountain, they would get all the
other nations into their intereft; but if they ftaid and
fettled there, all the nations would be againft them; and
he was afraid it would be a great war, and never come to
a peace again.''

I promifed to inform the Governor, General, and all
other people of it, and repeated my former requeft to
them, not to fuffer any *French* to fettle amongft them.

---

[105] *i. e.* They will obferve how we are dreffed.— [C. T. ?]

After we had fetched our horfes, we went from *Kujhkujhking*, and came at five o'clock to *Saccung*, in company with twenty *Indians*. When we came about half
way, we met a meffenger from fort *Duquejne*, with a
belt from *Thomas King*,[106] inviting all the chiefs to
Saccung. We heard at the fame time, that Mr. *Croghn*
and *Henry Montour* would be there to day. The meffenger was one of thofe three, that went to our camp;
and it feemed to rejoice all the company; for fome of
them were much troubled in their minds, fearing that the
Englijh had kept them, as prifoners, or killed them. In
the evening we arrived at *Saccung*, on the *Beaver* creek.
We were well received. The king provided for us.
After a little while we vifited Mr. *Croghn* and his company.

30th.— In the morning the *Indians* of the town vifited
us. About eleven o'clock about forty came together;
when we read the meffage to them; Mr. *Croghn*, *Henry
Montour* and *Thomas King* being prefent. They were
all well pleafed with the meffage. In the evening we
came together with the chiefs, and explained the fignifica-
tion of the belts; which lafted till eleven o'clock at night.

December 1jt.— After hunting a great while for our
horfes, without finding them, we were obliged to give
an *Indian* three hundred wampum for looking for them.
We bought corn for four hundred and fifty wampum for
our horfes. The Indians met together to hear what Mr.
Croghn had to fay. *Thomas King* fpoke by a belt, and
invited them to come to the general; upon which they all
refolved to go.

In the evening the captains and counfellors came together, I and *Ifaac Still* being prefent; they told us, that

[106] Thomas King was an Oneida Indian, who had taken a prominent part
in the treaty at Easton (October, 1758).— ED.

they had formerly agreed not to give any credit to any meſſage, ſent from the Engliſh by *Indians*; thinking, if the *Engliſh* would have peace with them, they would come themſelves; "So ſoon, therefore, as you came, it was as if the weather changed; and a great cloud paſſed away, and we could think again on our ancient friendſhip with our brethren, the *Engliſh*. We have thought ſince that time, more on the *Engliſh* than ever before, although the *French* have done all, in their power, to prejudice our young men againſt the *Engliſh*. Since you now come the ſecond time, we think it is God's work; he pities us, that we ſhould not all die; and if we ſhould not accept of the peace offered to us, we think God would forſake us."

In diſcourſe, they ſpoke about preaching, and ſaid, "They wiſhed many times to hear the word of God; but they were always afraid the *Engliſh* would take that opportunity to bring them into bondage." They invited me to come and live amongſt them; ſince I had taken ſo much pains in bringing a peace about between them and the *Engliſh*. I told them, "It might be, that when the peace was firmly eſtabliſhed, I would come to proclaim the peace and love of God to them."

In the evening arrived a meſſage, with a ſtring of wampum, to a noted *Indian*, *Ketiuſcund*, to come to *Wenango*, to meet the *Unami* chief, *Quitahicung* there; he ſaid that a *French Mohock* had killed a *Delaware* Indian; and when he was aſked why he did it? He ſaid the *French* bid him do it.

2d.— Early before we ſet out, I gave 300 wampums to the *Cayugas*, to buy ſome corn for their horſes; they agreed that I ſhould go before to the general, to acquaint him of their coming. The *Beaver* creek being very high,

it was almoſt two o'clock in the afternoon, before we came
over the creek; this land ſeems to be very rich. I, with
my companion, *Kekiuſcund's* ſon, came to Log's-town,
ſituated on a hill. On the eaſt end is a great piece of
low land, where the old *Logs-town* uſed to ſtand. In the
new *Logs-town* the *French* have built about thirty houſes
for the *Indians*. They have a large corn ńeld on the
ſouth ſide, where the corn ſtands ungathered. Then
we went further through a large tract of fine land, along
the river ſide. We came within eight miles of *Pittſburg*,[107] where we lodged on a hill, in the open air. It
was a cold night; and I had forgot my blanket, being
packed upon Mr. Hays's horſe. Between *Saccung* and
Pittſburg, all the *Shawanos* towns are empty of people.

3d.— We ſtarted early, and came to the river by *Pittſburg*; we called that they ſhould come over and fetch
us; but their boats having gone adrift, they made a raft
of black oak palliſadoes, which ſunk as ſoon as it came
into the water. We were very hungry, and ſtaid on that
iſland, where I had kept council with the *Indians*, in
the month of Auguſt laſt; for all I had nothing to live on,
I thought myſelf a great deal better off now, than at that
time, having now liberty to walk upon the iſland according to pleaſure; and it ſeemed as if the dark clouds were
diſperſed.

While I waited here, I ſaw the general march off from
Pittſburg; which made me ſorry, that I could not have
the pleaſure of ſpeaking with him. Towards evening
our whole party arrived: upon which they fired from the

---

[107] It is probable that Croghan brought Post the news of the change of
name from Fort Duquesne to Pittsburg. He apparently uses the new term
with much relish. The day after the English occupation of Fort Duquesne,
General Forbes wrote to Governor Denny, dating his letter "Fort Duquesne,
or now Pittsburg."— *Pennsylvania Colonial Records*, viii, p. 232.— ED.

fort with twelve great guns; and our *Indians* faluted again three times round with their fmall arms. By accident fome of the *Indians* found a raft hid in the bufhes, and Mr. Hays, coming laft, went over firft with two Indians. They fent us but a small allowance; fo that it would not ferve each round. I tied my belt a little clofer, being very hungry, and nothing to eat.[108] It fnowed, and we were obliged to fleep without any fhelter. In the evening they threw light balls from the fort; at which the *Indians* ftarted, thinking they would fire at them; but feeing it was not aimed at them, they rejoiced to fee them fly fo high.

4th.— We got up early, and cleared a place from the fnow, cut fome fire wood, and hallooed till we were tired. Towards noon Mr. *Hays* came with a raft, and the *Indian* chiefs went over: he informed me of Colonel *Bouquet's*[109] difpleafure with the *Indians'* anfwer to the

[108] As it often happens to the *Indians*, on their long marches, in war, and fometimes in their hunting expeditions, to be without victuals for feveral days, occafioned by bad weather and other accidents, they have the cuftom in fuch cafes; which *Poft* probably learned of them, viz. girding their bellies tight, when they have nothing to put in them; and they fay it prevents the pain of hunger.—[C. T. ?]

[109] Colonel Henry Bouquet, a Swifs officer, who had served with distinction in the armies of Sardinia and Holland, was engaged to enter the regiment of Royal Americans, and came to America in 1756. The following year he was in command in South Carolina; but early in 1758 was summoned north to aid Forbes in his march through Pennsylvania. Bouquet commanded the advance, and prepared the road, ordered the stations for reserve supplies, and by careful management contributed much to the success of the campaign. Upon Forbes's retiring, Bouquet was left in command at Fort Pitt, where he remained fulfilling the arduous and exacting duties of his frontier service until late in 1762, when he was relieved by Captain Ecuyer, and returned to Philadelphia. On the news of the siege of Fort Pitt (1763), Bouquet organized a relief expedition, which inflicted a severe defeat upon the Indians at Bushy Run. The following year, the Indian country was invaded, Bouquet's expedition to the Muskingum proving a complete success. Relieved from his Western command, he was promoted to the rank of brigadier-general and placed in command of all

general, and his defire that they fhould alter their mind, in infifting upon the general's going back; but the *Indians* had no inclination to alter their mind. In the afternoon fome provifion was fent over, but a fmall allowance. When I came over to the fort, the council with the *Indians* was almoft at an end. I had a difcourfe with Colonel *Bouquet* about the affairs, difpofition and refolution of the *Indians*.

I drew provifion for our journey to fort *Ligonier*, and baked bread for our whole company: towards noon the *Indians* met together in a conference. Firft king *Beaver* addreffed himfelf to the *Mohocks*, defiring them to give their brethren an anfwer about fettling at *Pittfburg*. The *Mohocks* faid, "They lived at fuch a diftance, that they could not defend the *Englifh* there, if any accident fhould befal them; but you, coufins, who live clofe here, muft think what to do." Then *Beaver* faid by a ftring:

"What this meffenger has brought is very agreeable to us; and as our uncles have made peace with you, the *Englifh*, and many others nation, fo we likewife join, and accept of the peace offered to us; and we have already anfwered by your meffenger, what we have to fay to the general, that he fhould go back over the mountains; we have nothing to fay to the contrary."

Neither Mr. *Croghn* nor *Andrew Montour* would tell Colonel *Bouquet* the *Indians'* anfwer. Then Mr. *Croghn*,

the troops in the southern British colonies of America. He died at Pensacola, February, 1766, at the early age of forty-seven. He was not only a soldier of ability and vigor, but a man of most attractive and charming character, beloved by superiors and subordinates. The collection of his letters in the British Museum is a chief source for the history of the West during this period. See calendar in *Canadian Archives*, 1889; extracts in *Michigan Pioneer and Historical Collections*, xix, pp. 27-295; also *Bouquet's Expedition against the Ohio Indians* (Cincinnati, 1868).— ED.

Colonel *Armjtrong* and Colonel *Bouquet* went into the
tent by themfelves, and I went upon my bufinefs. What
they have further agreed I do not know; but when they
had done, I called king *Beaver, Shingas,* and *Kekeujcund,*
and faid,

"Brethren, if you have any alteration to make, in the
anfwer to the general, concerning leaving this place, you
will be pleafed to let me know." They faid, they would
alter nothing, "We have told them three times to leave
the place and go back; but they infift upon ftaying here;
if, therefore, they will be deftroyed by the *French* and
the *Indians,* we cannot help them."

Colonel *Bouquet* fet out for *Loyalhannon*: The *Indians*
got fome liquor between ten and eleven o'clock. One
Mohock died; the others fired guns three times over him;
at the laft firing one had accidentally loaded his gun with
a double charge: this gun burft to pieces, and broke his
hand clean off; he alfo got a hard knock on his breaft;
and in the morning at nine o'clock he died, and they
buried them in that place, both in one hole.

6th.— It was a cold morning; we fwam our horfes
over the river, the ice running violently. Mr. *Croghn*
told me that the *Indians* had fpoke, upon the fame
ftring that I had, to Colonel *Bouquet,* and altered their
mind; and had agreed and defired that 200 men fhould
ftay at the fort. I refufed to make any alteration in
the anfwer to the general, till I myfelf did hear it of the
Indians; at which Mr. *Croghn* grew very angry. I told
him I had already fpoke with the *Indians*; he faid, it
was a d — d lie; and defired Mr. *Hays* to enquire of the
Indians, and take down in writing what they faid. Accordingly he called them, and afked them, if they had
altered their fpeech, or fpoke to Colonel *Bouquet* on that

ſtring they gave me. *Shingas* and the other counſellor
ſaid, they had ſpoken nothing to Colonel *Bouquet* on the
ſtring they gave me, but what was agreed between the
Indians at *Kuſhkuſhking*. They ſaid, Mr. *Croghn* and
Henry Montour had not ſpoke and acted honeſtly and
uprightly; they bid us not alter the leaſt, and ſaid, "We
have told them three times to go back; but they will not
go, inſiſting upon ſtaying here. Now you will let the
governor, general, and all people know, that our deſire
is, that they ſhould go back, till the other nations have
joined in the peace, and then they may come and build
a trading houſe."

They then repeated what they had ſaid the 5th inſtant.
Then we took leave of them, and promiſed to inform the
general, governor, and all other gentle people of their
diſpoſition; and ſo we ſet out from *Pittſburg*, and came
within fifteen miles of the breaſt-work; where we encamped. It ſnowed, and we made a little cabbin of hides.

7th.— Our horſes were fainting, having little or no
food. We came that day about twenty miles, to another
breaſt-work; where the whole army had encamped on a
hill; the water being far to fetch.

8th.— Between *Pittſburg* and fort *Ligonier* the country
is hilly, with rich bottoms, well timbered, but ſcantily
watered. We arrived at fort *Ligonier* in the afternoon,
about four o'clock; where we found the general very ſick;
and therefore could have no opportunity to ſpeak with him.

9th.— We waited to ſee the general; they told us he
would march the next day, and we ſhould go with him.
Captain *Sinclair* wrote us a return for proviſions for
four days.

10th.— The general was ſtill ſick; ſo that he could not
go on the journey.

11th.— We longed very much to go farther; and therefore fpoke to Major *Halket*,[110] and defired him to enquire of the general, if he intended to fpeak with us, or, if we might go; as we were in a poor condition, for want of linen, and other neceffaries. He defired us to bring the *Indians'* anfwer, and our journal to the general. Mr. *Hays* read his journal to Major *Halket* and Governor *Glen*.[111] They took memorandums, and went to the general.

12th.— They told us we fhould ftay till the general went.

14th.— The general intended to go; but his horfes could not be found. They thought the *Indians* had carried them off. They hunted all day for the horfes, but could not find them. I fpoke to Colonel *Bouquet* about our allowance being fo fmall, that we could hardly fubfift; and that we were without money; and defired him to let us have fome money, that we might buy neceffaries. Provifions, and every thing is exceeding dear. One pound of bread coft a fhilling; one pound of fugar four fhillings, a quart of rum feven fhillings and fix pence, and fo in proportion. Colonel Bouquet laid our matters before the general; who let me call, and excufed himfelf, that his diftemper had hindered him from fpeaking with me; and promifed to help me in every thing I fhould want, and ordered him to give me fome

[110] Major Halket was the son of Sir Peter Halket, who was killed, together with another son, at the battle of Monongahela (1755). When Major Halket accompanied the detachment sent by Forbes to bury the bones of the victims of that disaster, he recognized the skeletons of his father and brother and at the sight fainted with grief and horror.— ED.

[111] James Glen had been governor of South Carolina (1744-55), but was superseded in the latter year by Governor Lyttleton. His presence at Forbes's camp is perhaps explained by the fact that he was interested in the Cherokee Indian trade.— ED.

money. He faid farther, that I often fhould call; and
when he was alone he would fpeak with me.

16th.— Mr. *Hays*, being a hunting, was fo lucky as to
find the general's horfes, and brought them home; for
which the general was very thankful to him.

17th.— Mr. *Hays*, being defired by Màjor *Halket* to
go and look for the other horfes, went, but found none.

18th.— The general told me to hold myfelf ready, to
go with him down the country.

20th.— After we had been out two days, to hunt
for our horfes, in the rain, we went again to day, and were
informed, they had been feen in a loft condition; one
laying on the hill, and the other ftanding; they had been
hoppled together; but a perfon told us, he had cut the
hopples. When we came home we found the horfes;
they having made home to the fort.

22d.— It was cold and ftormy weather.

23d.— I hunted for our horfes, and having found them,
we gave them both to the king's commiffary; they not
being able to carry us farther.

The fergeant *Henry Ojten*, being one of the company
that guided us, as above mentioned, and was that fame
prifoner, whom the *Shawanos* intended to burn alive,
came to day to the fort. He was much rejoiced to fee us,
and faid, ''I thank you a thoufand times for my deliver-
ance from the fire; and think it not too much to be at
your fervice my whole life time.'' He gave us intelligence
that the *Indians* were, as yet, mightily for the *Englifh*.
His mafter had offered to fet him at liberty, and bring him
to *Pittfburg* if he would promife him ten gallons of rum;
which he did; and he was brought fafe to *Pittfburg*.
Delaware George is ftill faithful to the *Englifh*; and was
very helpful to procure his liberty. *Ifaac Still, Shingas*

and *Beaver* are gone with the meffage to the nations living further off. When the *French* had heard that the garrifon, at *Pittfburg*, confifted only of 200 men, they refolved to go down from *Venango*, and deftroy the *Englifh* fort. So foon as the *Indians* at *Kufhkufhking*, heard of their intention, they fent a meffage to the *French*, defiring them to draw back; for they would have no war in their country. The friendly *Indians* have fent out parties with that intention, that if the *French* went on, in their march towards the fort, they would catch them, and bring them to the *Englifh*. They fhewed to *Often* the place, where eight *French Indian* fpies had lain near the fort. By their marks upon the place they learned that thefe eight were gone back, and five more were to come **to the fame place again. He told us further, that the *Indians* had fpoke among themfelves, that if the *Englifh* would join them, they would go to *Venango*, and deftroy the *French* there. We hear that the friendly *Indians* intend to hunt round the fort, at *Pittfburg*, and bring the garrifon frefh meat. And upon this intelligence the general fent Captain *Wedderholz*[112] with fifty men, to reinforce the garrifon at *Pittfburg*.**

25th.— The people in the camp prepared for a *Chriftmas* frolick; but I kept *Chriftmas* in the woods by myfelf.

26th.— To day an exprefs came from *Pittfburg* to inform the general, that the French had called all the *Indians* in their intereft together, and intended to come and deftroy them there.

---

[112] Captain Nicholas Wedderholz (Weatherholt) was a militia officer in command of a German company from Northumberland County, which was enlisted December 16, 1755, and "discontinued" in 1760. It is said that every man in his company was of German descent. During the Indian troubles of 1763, Weatherholt raised another company, which did not, however, see active service.— Ed.

27th.— Towards noon the general fet out; which caufed a great joy among the garrifon, which had hitherto lain in tents, but now being a fmaller company, could be more comfortably lodged. It fnowed the whole day. We encamped by a *beaver dam*, under *Laurel Hill*.

28th.— We came to *Stony Creek*, where Mr. *Quickfell* is ftationed. The general fent Mr. *Hays*, exprefs, to fort *Bedford* (*Rays Town*) and commanded him to fee, if the place for encampment, under the *Allegheny* mountain, was prepared; as alfo to take care that refrefhments fhould be at hand, at his coming. It was ftormy and fnowed all the day.

29th.— On the road I came up with fome waggons; and found my horfes with the company; who had taken my horfe up, and intended to carry the fame away. We encamped on this fide, under the *Allegheny* hill.

30th.— Very early I hunted for my horfes, but in vain, and therefore was obliged to carry my faddle bags, and other baggage on my back. The burden was heavy, the roads bad; which made me very tired, and came late to *Bedford*; where I took my old lodging with Mr. *Frazier*. They received me kindly, and refrefhed me according to their ability.

31ft.— This day we refted, and, contrary to expectation, preparation was made for moving further to-morrow. Mr. *Hays*, who has his lodging with the commander of that place, vifited me.

January 1ft. 1759.— We fet out early. I got my faddle bags upon a waggon; but my bed and covering I carried upon my back; and came that day to the crofling of *Juniata*: where I had poor lodgings, being obliged to fleep in the open air, the night being very cold.

2d.— We fet out early. I wondered very much that

the horfes, in these flippery roads, came fo well with the waggons over thefe fteep hills. We came to fort *Littleton*; where I drew provifions; but could not find any who had bread, to exchange for flour. I took lodging in a common houfe. Mr. *Hays* arrived late.

3d.— We rofe early. I thought to travel the neareft road to *Shippen's Town*, and therefore defired leave of the general to profecute my journey to *Lancafter*, and wait for his excellency there; but he defired me to follow in his company. It fnowed, freezed, rained, and was ftormy the whole day. All were exceeding glad that the general arrived fafe at fort *Loudon*. There was no room in the fort for fuch a great company; I, therefore, and fome others went two miles further, and got lodgings at a plantation.

4th.— I and my company took the upper road; which is three miles nearer to *Shippen's town*, where we arrived this evening. The flippery roads made me, as a traveller, very tired.

5th.— To day I ftaid here for the general. Mr. *Hays* went ten miles further, to fee fome of his relations. In the afternoon *Ifrael Pemberton* came from *Philadelphia* to wait upon the general.[113]

6th.— I came to-day ten miles to Mr. *Miller's*, where I

---

[113] Israel Pemberton was a member of a prominent Quaker family, and a merchant of Philadelphia. Very active in political affairs, and influential with the Indians because of his Quaker principles and trade-relations, he was one of the leading members of the "Friendly Association," formed to put down war with the Indians. In 1759 he sent for the association £1,000 worth of goods to be distributed to the Ohio Indians at Pittsburg. Pemberton, with other leading Quakers, was much disliked by the borderers, who called him "King Wampum," and placed his life in jeopardy during the Paxton riots (1763). Neither did Pemberton find favor with the "Sons of Liberty," and the patriot party of the Revolution. In 1777 he, with two brothers, was banished to Virginia on the charge of aiding the British enemy.— ED.

lodged, having no comfortable place in *Shippen's town;* all the houfes being crowded with people.

7th.— They made preparation, at Mr. *Millers,* for the reception of the general; but he, being fo well to-day, refolved to go as far as *Carlifle.* I could fcarce find any lodging there. *Henry Montour* was fo kind as to take me in his room.

8th.— I begged the general for leave to go to *Lancafter,* having fome bufinefs, which he at laft granted. I went to captain Sinclair for a horfe, who ordered me to go to the chief juftice of the town; who ought to procure one for me, in the province fervice. According to this order I went; but the juftice told me, that he did not know how to get any horfe; if I would go and look for one, he fhould be glad if I found any. But having no mind to run from one to another, I refolved to walk, as I had done before: and fo travelled along, and came about ten miles that day to a tavern keeper's, named *Chefnut.*

9th.— To-day I croffed the *Sufquahanna* over the ice, and came within thirteen miles of *Lancafter.* It was flippery and heavy travelling.

10th.— It rained all the day. I arrived at three o'clock in the afternoon, in *Lancafter*; and was quite refrefhed, to have the favour to fee my brethren.

IV

JOURNAL OF CAPTAIN THOMAS MORRIS, OF HIS MAJESTY'S
XVII REGIMENT OF INFANTRY; DETROIT, SEPTEMBER
25, 1764

Reprint from the author's *Miscellanies in Prose and Verse*
(London, 1791), pp. 1-39

INTRODUCTORY NOTE

The journal of Captain Thomas Morris is notable from two points of view. First, because of its rarity — the volume in which it is found, *Miscellanies in Prose and Verse* (London, printed for James Ridgway, 1791), being a treasure much prized by the collector of valuable Americana. In the second place, the journal is of importance to historical students because of the light it throws upon conditions in the West at this critical moment (1766), and the proof it furnishes that Pontiac's influence was still paramount among the Western Indians, that Bradstreet had been completely duped, and that native hostility to British sovereignty over the Western tribes was deep-seated, and would take many years wholly to uproot.

Incidentally, also, the journal possesses considerable dramatic interest. Dealing with a single episode, told in the first person by the chief participant, and he a person of literary tastes, the thrilling incidents — repeated escapes from torture and death, the flight through the woods, and the final refuge at Detroit — all depicted graphically, yet simply, hold one's attention unflagging to the end. The side touches are in keeping with the principal incidents: the contrast between the author's situation and his calm enjoyment of Shakespeare's tragedy, so curiously preserved for him from the loot of some English officer's baggage; the appearance of the white charger that had borne its master Braddock to sudden death in the Monongahela Valley nine years before; the

gratitude and fidelity of the Canadian Godefroy, evinced
to so good a purpose; the pomp and pride of the red-
coated brave who wore on his back his reward for services
to Sir William Johnson; the honor of Pontiac and the
Miami chief, who protected with difficulty the sacred
person of an ambassador; the roguery of the Loretto
Indian, who deserted his chief and so speedily suffered
therefor — all these circumstances heighten and pro-
long the reader's interest, and add vividness to the narrative.

Our knowledge of the author's life is but slight. He
came of a race of soldiers, his father and grandfather before
him having served as captains of the same regiment in which
he was an officer. His early education was considerable;
and fifteen months had been spent in Paris familiarizing
himself with the language and literature of its people.
His tastes were always those of a scholar and a lover of
literature; he being of that class of British soldiers of
which Wolfe was so conspicuous an example, whose
recreations took the line of literary appreciation and performance. Morris came to America in 1758, as a lieutenant in the 17th regiment of infantry, in which he had
been commissioned three years previous. Although this
was Forbes's command, Morris saw service at Louisburg
in 1758, and was with Amherst in the campaign around
Lake Champlain in the following year. In 1761, he was
promoted to a captaincy and assigned to the garrison of
Fort Hendrick, at Canajoharie in the Mohawk Valley —
the home of the famous Mohawk chiefs, Hendricks and
Brant. It was doubtless there that he acquired that
knowledge of the Mohawk temperament which he exhibits
in the opening pages of his journal. While stationed at
this lonely outpost he addressed his friend "Dicky"

Montgomery in a parody of one of Horace's odes, which possesses more historical interest than literary merit.[1] It is evident from his dedication of certain odes to "ceux des Français, qui ont connu l'auteur au siége de la Martinique," that Morris accompanied General Monckton upon that expedition in 1762.

After his adventures along the Maumee, related in the present journal, he remained at Detroit for some time, and returned to England with his regiment in 1767. At this time occurred his meeting with the soldier whom he had previously encountered as an Indian prisoner, under circumstances of great danger and distress, near the treacherously-destroyed Fort Miami.

What we know of Morris's later life is comprised in his "Preamble" to the volume containing this journal. Having retired from the army in 1775, he lost his property by means of speculative ventures. For the sake of his children, he appealed to the king for a pension, on the ground of past services, especially those detailed in the Maumee journal. A copy of the journal was annexed to the petition, but the latter failed of effect. The narrative here reprinted was laid aside until encouragement from a "refpectable gentleman of my acquaintance, a man of letters in whofe judgment I place implicit faith" determined him to print some of his literary efforts and to include the journal to "complete the volume." He expresses the hope that the recital of his adventures "might poffibly, fome time or other, procure a friend or protector to one of my children." "This is a plain and fimple tale," he concludes, "accounting for my prefumption in offering to the public an old ftory relating to one whofe wifh ufed to be, to lie concealed in domeftic

[1] Simms, *Frontiersmen of New York* (Albany, 1882), i, pp. 438, 439.

life; a wish, in which he has been amply gratified by the very obliging silence of some of his nearest connexions.''

It is evident, therefore, that the journal, unlike most of the others we publish in this volume, was dressed up for publication, and purposely given a dramatic turn. The official report of the expedition, as sent to Bradstreet, together with letters from Morris to his superior, are in the British Public Record Office, still unpublished.[2]

The small volume of *Miscellanies*, from which we extract the journal, contains in addition thereto an essay on dramatic art, translations of two of Juvenal's satires, and five odes which are accompanied by transliterations into French prose. Morris had already published two collections of songs — in 1786, and in 1790. In 1792, appeared his *Life of Reverend David Williams*; and four years later a versified tale, *Quashy, or the Coal Black Maid*, which has been described as ''a negroe love story which bears reference to the slave-trade, and is here but indifferently told.''[3] With the publication in 1802, of *Songs, Political and Convivial*, Captain Thomas Morris passes from public view.

The character of the man throws the incidents of this hazardous journey into still stronger relief. Here is no frontiersman like Weiser and Croghan, familiar with the hardships of the wilderness; no missionary, like Post, seeking rewards not measured by earthly laurels and success; not even a bluff, practical soldier like Bradstreet, who dispatched him on his venturesome mission. Morris was a man of the great world, a fashionable dilettante, dabbling in literature and the dramatic art.

---

[2] Parkman, *Conspiracy of Pontiac*, ii, p. 195.

[3] *Monthly Review*, March, 1797, p. 381.

Parkman comments on his round English face — as
shown in the portrait which appears on the frontispiece
to his *Miscellanies*, and which we republish as frontispiece to the present volume — and the lack of resolu-
tion and courage therein expressed. Yet upon his
memorable embassy he displayed no want of either.
Probably it was his familiarity with the French language
that led to his being chosen for the task; he entered
upon it with commendable zeal, and attempted to carry
out his orders at every risk.

Doubtless the adventure appealed to that latent fondness for experiences, that men of the literary temperament frequently possess. In his essay on dramatic art
he says, "If the world ever afforded me a pleaſure
equal to that of reading Shakeſpear at the foot of a
water-fall in an American deſert, it was Du Menil's performance of tragedy." Morris evinced a steadiness of
courage, endurance, and hardihood, fortitude under disaster, and an unflinching determination to do his duty,
as well as a power of attaching men to his service, that
would do credit to any man. For a victim of Indian
cruelties, his magnanimity was a still rarer quality. He
bore no grudge against his savage tormentors, speaking
of them as "an innocent, much-abuſed, and once happy
people." His appreciation of the qualities of the French
Canadians, and his remarks upon their conduct of Indian
affairs show keen observation, astuteness, and a judgment free from prejudice. As an author, wit, man of
affairs, courageous soldier, magnanimous foe, we may
apply to him in earnest the epithet levied in jest by the
reviewer of his first volume of songs — the "inimitable
Captain Morris."

                                        R. G. T.

JOURNAL OF CAPTAIN THOMAS MORRIS OF HIS MAJESTY'S XVII REGIMENT OF INFANTRY

General Bradſtreet, who commanded an army ſent againſt thoſe Indian nations who had cut off ſeveral Engliſh garriſons, of which we had taken poſſeſſion after the ſurrender of Canada, having too haſtily determined to ſend an officer to take poſſeſſion alſo of the Illinois country in his Britannic Majeſty's name, ſent his Aid de Camp to ſound me on the occaſion. His Aid de Camp deſired me to recommend ſome officer with qualities he deſcribed. I named every one that I could recollect; but he always anſwered me ſhortly: "No, no; he won't do." I then began to ſuſpect that he might have a deſign on myſelf. Accordingly I ſaid: "If I thought my ſervices would be acceptable"— He interrupted me: "That is what is wanted." I replied: "Why did you not ſay ſo at firſt?" He ſaid, with an oath: "It is not a thing to be aſked of any man." I anſwered: "If the General thinks me the propereſt perſon, I am ready." I was immediately conducted to the General; and while I was at dinner with him, he ſaid, in his frank manner: "Morris, I have a French fellow here, my priſoner, who expects to be hanged for treaſon; he ſpeaks all the Indian languages, and if you think he can be of uſe to you, I'll ſend for him, pardon him, and ſend him with you." I anſwered: "I am glad you have thought of it, Sir; I wiſh you would." The priſoner, whoſe name was

Godefroi,[4] was accordingly fent for; and, as foon as he entered the tent, he turned pale, and fell on his knees, begging for mercy. The General telling him that it was in his power to hang him, concluded with faying: "I give thee thy life; take care of this gentleman." The man expreffed a grateful fenfe of the mercy fhewn him, and protefted that he would be faithful: and indeed his behaviour afterwards proved that he was fincere in his promife. As General Bradftreet had pardoned him on my account, he confidered me as his deliverer. Little minds hate obligations; and thence the tranfition is eafy to the hatred of their benefactor: this man's foul was of another make, and, though in a low ftation, a noble pride urged him to throw a heavier weight of obligation on him to whom he thought he was indebted for his liberty, if not his life; and I had the fingular fatisfaction of owing thofe bleffings to one who fancied he owed the fame to me.

While I was preparing to fet out, the boats being almoft loaden with our provifions and neceffaries, the Aid de Camp told me, that if the Indian deputies, who were expected to arrive at the camp that evening, did not come, the Uttawaw [Ottawa] village,[5] where I was to lie that night, would be attacked at three o'clock in the morning;

---

[4] Jacques Godefroy was a prominent habitant of Detroit, who had been employed by Major Gladwin to seek an interview with Pontiac on behalf of the English cause. From this mission he had returned unsuccessful. Later, dispatched to the Illinois with four other Canadians, they had not only pillaged an English trader, but aided the Indians to capture Fort Miami. As Godefroy had taken the oath of allegiance to the British crown in 1760, he was arrested and sentenced to be hanged on the charge of treason. After this journey with Morris he continued to live at Detroit, much respected and esteemed, and one of the richest of the French colony. His son leaned toward the American side in the Revolution, and assisted George Rogers Clark.— Ed.

[5] This was Pontiac's village on the Maumee. See Croghan's Journal of 1765, *ante*.— Ed.

"but that," added he, "will make no difference in your affairs." I was aftonifhed that the General could think fo: but I made no reply to him, and we talked of other matters. However, as I was ftepping into my boat, fome canoes appeared, and I came on fhore again, and found they were the Indian deputies who were expected. This I thought a very happy incident for me; and having received proper powers and inftructions I fet out in good fpirits from Cedar Point,* in Lake Erie, on the 26th of Auguft, 1764, about four o'clock in the afternoon, at the fame time that the army proceeded for Detroit. My efcort confifted of Godefroi, and another Canadian, two fervants, twelve Indians, our allies, and five Mohawks, with a boat in which were our provifions, who were to attend us to the fwifts of the Miamis river, about ten leagues diftant, and then return to the army. I had with me likewife Warfong, the great Chippawaw chief, and Attawang, an Uttawaw chief, with fome other Indians of their nations, who had come the fame day to our camp with propofals of peace. We lay that night at the mouth of the Miamis river.

I was greatly delighted on obferving the difference of temper betwixt thefe Indian ftrangers and thofe of my old acquaintance of the five nations. Godefroi was employed in interpreting to me all their pleafantries; and I thought them the moft agreeable ralliers I had ever met with. As all men love thofe who refemble themfelves, the fprightly manners of the French cannot fail to recommend them to thefe favages, as our grave deportment is an advantage to us among our Indian neighbors; for it is certain that a referved Englifhman differs not more from a lively Frenchman than does a ftern Mohawk

* Cedar Point was near the entrance to the Maumee River.— ED.

from a laughing Chippawaw. The next day (27th) we
arrived at the Swifts,[7] fix leagues from the mouth of the
river, and the Uttawaw chief fent to his village for
horfes. Soon after a party of young Indians came to us
on horfeback, and the two Canadians and myfelf having
mounted, we proceeded, together with the twelve Indians
my efcort, who were on foot, and marched in the front,
the chief carrying Englifh colours, towards the village,
which was two leagues and a half diftant. On our ap-
proaching it, I was aftonifhed to fee a great number of
white flags flying; and, paffing by the encampment of the
Miamis, while I was admiring the regularity and contriv-
ance of it, I heard a yell, and found myfelf furrounded
by Pondiac's army, confifting of fix hundred favages,
with tommahawks in their hands, who beat my horfe, and
endeavoured to separate me from my Indians, at the
head of whom I had placed myfelf on our difcovering the
village. By their malicious fmiles, it was eafy for me
to guefs their intention of putting me to death. They
led me up to a perfon, who ftood advanced before two
flaves (prifoners of the Panis nation, taken in war and
kept in flavery[8]) who had arms, himfelf holding a fufee
with the butt on the ground. By his drefs, and the air
he affumed, he appeared to be a French officer: I afterwards found that he was a native of old France, had been
long in the regular troops as a drummer, and that his
war-name was St. Vincent. This fine dreffed half
French, half Indian figure defired me to difmount; a
bear-fkin was fpread on the ground, and St. Vincent and
I fat upon it, the whole Indian army, circle within circle,

---

[7] See note on Maumee Rapids, Croghan's *Journals, ante.*— ED.

[8] On Indian slavery, see "The Panis; Canadian Indian Slavery," in Canadian
Institute *Proceedings*, 1897.— ED

ftanding round us. Godefroi fat at a little diftance from
us; and prefently came Pondiac, and fquatted himfelf,
after his fafhion, oppofite to me. This Indian has a
more extenfive power than ever was known among that
people; for every chief ufed to command his own tribe:
but eighteen nations, by French intrigue, had been
brought to unite, and chufe this man for their commander,
after the Englifh had conquered Canada; having been
taught to believe that, aided by France, they might make
a vigorous pufh and drive us out of North America.
Pondiac afked me in his language, which Godefroi interpreted, ''whether I was come to tell lies, like the reft of
my countrymen.'' He faid, ''That Ononteeo (the
French king) was not crufhed as the Englifh had reported,
but had got upon his legs again,'' and prefented me a
letter from New Orleans, directed to him, written in
French, full of the moft improbable falfehoods, though
beginning with a truth. The writer mentioned the
repulfe of the Englifh troops in the Miffiffippi, who
were going to take poffeffion of Fort Chartres,[1] blamed
the Natchez nation for their ill conduct in that affair,
made our lofs in that attack to be very confiderable, and
concluded with affuring him, that a French army was
landed in Louifiana, and that his father (the French
king) would drive the Englifh out of the country. I
began to reafon with him; but St. Vincent hurried me
away to his cabin; where, when he talked to me of the
French army, I afked him if he thought me fool enough
to give credit to that account; and told him that none but

---

[1] The reference here is to the defeat and retreat of Major Arthur Loftus,
who left Pensacola early in February, 1764, with a detachment of the 22nd
infantry to proceed to the Illinois, and take possession for the English. On
the nineteenth of March he was ambushed and fired upon near Tunica Bend
on the Mississippi, and obliged to retreat to New Orleans.— ED.

the fimple Indians could be fo credulous. Attawang, the Uttawaw chief, came to feek me, and carried me to his cabin. The next day (28th) I went to the grand council, and addreffed the chiefs. When I mentioned that their father, the king of France, had ceded thofe countries to their brother the king of England, (for fo the two kings are called by the Indians) the great Miamis chief ftarted up and fpoke very loud, in his fingular language, and laughed. Godefroi whifpered me, that it was very lucky that he received my intelligence with contempt and not anger, and defired me to fay no more, but fit down, and let my chief fpeak; accordingly I fat down, and he produced his belts, and fpoke. I have called the Miamis tongue a fingular language; becaufe it has no affinity in its found with any other Indian language which I have heard. It is much wondered whence this nation came; who differ as much from all the other nations in their fuperftitious practices, as in their fpeech, and manner of encamping.[10] As they left the Uttawaw villages before me on their way home, we traced their encampments, where we faw their offerings of tobacco, made by every individual each morning, ranged in the niceft order, on long flips of bark both on the fhore, and on rocks in the river. They carry their God in a bag, which is hung in the front of their encampment, and is vifited by none but the prieft; if any other perfon prefumes to advance between the front of the encampment and that fpirit in the bag, he is put to death: and I was told that a drunken French foldier, who had done fo, was with great difficulty faved. When the council was

[10] The Miamis were of Algonquian stock; but the early French writers noted their peculiarities and special customs. See *Wisconsin Historical Collections*, xvi, p. 376; also index thereto.— Ed.

over, St. Vincent changed his note, and told me that if
I could enfure to him his pardon, he would go to Detroit.
I anfwered him, "that it was not in my power to promife
it." However, as I found that I could not well do without him, I contrived to make him my friend. Pondiac
faid to my chief: "If you have made peace with the
Englifh, we have no bufinefs to make war on them.
The war-belts came from you." He afterwards faid
to Godefroi: "I will lead the nations to war no more;
let 'em be at peace, if they chufe it: but I myfelf will never
be a friend to the Englifh. I fhall now become a wan-
derer in the woods; and if they come to feek me there,
while I have an arrow left, I will fhoot at them." This I
imagined he faid in defpair, and gave it as my opinion,
that he might eafily be won to our intereft; and it afterwards proved fo. He made a fpeech to the chiefs, who
wanted to put me to death, which does him honour;
and fhews that he was acquainted with the law of nations:
"We muft not," faid he, "kill ambaffadors: do we not
fend them to the Flat-heads, our greateft enemies,[11] and
they to us? Yet thefe are always treated with hofpitality."
The following day (29th) the Mohawk, who commanded
the Indians in the provifion-boat, ftole away, without
taking my letter to General Bradftreet, as he had been
ordered, having, the night before, robbed us of almoft
every thing, and fold my rum (two barrels) to the Uttawaws. The greater part of the warriors got drunk; and
a young Indian drew his knife, and made a ftroke at me;
but Godefroi feized his arm, threw him down, and took
the knife from him. He certainly faved my life, for I

[11] The Northern tribes, especially the Iroquois, termed the Cherokees,
Chickasaws, etc., "Têtes plattes" (Flat-heads). The enmity between the
Northern and the Southern Indians was traditional.— ED.

was fitting, and could not have avoided the blow though
I faw it coming. I was now concealed under my matrefs,
as all the young Indians were determined to murder me,
was afterwards obliged to put on Indian fhoes and cover
myfelf with a blanket to look like a favage, and efcape by
fording the river into a field of Indian corn with St. Vincent, Godefroi, and the other Canadian. Pondiac
afked Godefroi, who returned to the village to fee what
was going on, ''what he had done with the Englifh man.''
And being told, he faid, ''you have done well.'' Attawang came to fee me, and made his two fons guard me.
Two Kickapoo chiefs came to me, and fpoke kindly,
telling me that they had not been at war with the Englifh
for feven years. Two Miamis came likewife, and told
me that I need not be afraid to go to their village. A
Huron woman however abufed me becaufe the Englifh
had killed her fon. Late at night I returned to Attawang's cabin, where I found my fervant concealed under
a blanket, the Indians having attempted to murder him;
but they had been prevented by St. Vincent. There
was an alarm in the night, a drunken Indian having
been feen at the fkirt of the wood. One of the Delaware
nation, who happened to be with Pondiac's army, paffing
by the cabin where I lay, called out in broken Englifh:
''D — d fon of a b — ch.'' All this while I faw none of
my own Indians: I believe their fituation was almost
as perilous as my own. The following day (30th) the
Miamis and Kickapoos fet out on their return home, as
provifions were growing fcarce. An Indian called the
little chief, told Godefroi that he would fend his fon with
me, and made me a prefent of a volume of Shakefpear's
plays; a fingular gift from a favage. He however begged
a little gunpowder in return, a commodity to him much

more precious than diamonds. The next day (31ft) I
gave Attawang, who was going to Detroit, a letter for
General Bradftreet,[12] and to one of my fervants whom I
fent along with this chief, I gave another for his Aid de
Camp. And now, having purchafed three horfes and
hired two canoes to carry our little baggage, I fet out
once more, having obtained Pondiac's confent, for the
Illinois country, with my twelve Indians, the two Canadians, St. Vincent's two flaves, and the little chief's fon
and nephew. There was fcarcely any water in the channel of the river, owing to the great drought, fo that the
canoes could hardly be dragged along empty in fome
places. We paffed by the ifland where is Pondiac's
village, and arrived at a little village confifting of only
two pretty large cabins, and three fmall ones, and here
we encamped: that is, we lay on the ground; and as a
diftinguifhed perfonage, I was honoured by having a few
fmall branches under me, and a fort of bafket-work
made by bending boughs with their ends fixed in the
earth, for me to thruft my head under to avoid the mufke-
toes or large gnats with which that country is infefted.
The day following (Auguft 1ft)[13] arrived St. Vincent and
Pondiac. The latter gave the former the great belt,
forty years old, on which were defcribed two hundred
and ten villages. St. Vincent joined us, and we fet forward, and arrived at another village of the Uttawaws,
the laft of their villages we had to pafs. One of the
chiefs of this village gave me his hand, and led us into the
cabin for ftrangers, where was Katapelleecy, a chief of

---

[12] A letter to Bradstreet from Morris, dated September 2, 1764, is quoted
by Wallace, *History of Illinois and Louisiana under French Rule* (Cincinnati,
1893), p. 352, *note.*— ED.

[13] Reference to the date of starting (*ante*, p. 303) shows that this should read
September 1.— ED.

very great note, who gave his hand to all my fellow-travellers, but not to me. This man was a famous dreamer, and told St. Vincent that he had talked with the great fpirit the preceding night; and had he happened to dream any thing to my difadvantage the night I lay there, it had been over with me.[14] The Indian who gave me his hand, went into the upper range of beds, and came down dreffed in a laced fcarlet coat with blue cuffs, and a laced hat. I wondered more at the colour of the cloaths than at the finery; and was told that it was a prefent from the Englifh, and that this Indian had conducted Sir William Johnfon to Detroit.[15] The next morning (2d) he told me the Englifh were liars; that if I fpoke falfe-hoods he fhould know it, and afked why the General defired to fee the Indians at Detroit, and if he would cloathe them. I affured him that the General fought their friendfhip; and gave him, at his own requeft, a letter of recommendation to him. We then continued our route towards the Miamis country, putting our baggage into the canoes, but the greater part of us went by land, as the water was fo fhallow, that thofe who worked the canoes were frequently obliged to wade and drag them along. We met an Indian and his wife in a canoe return-ing from hunting; and bought plenty of venifon ready dreffed, fome turkeys, and a great deal of dried fifh for a fmall quantity of powder and fhot. The following day (3d) we were over-taken by Pondiac's nephew and two other young Uttawaws, who, with the Chippawaws before-mentioned, made the party twenty-four. We met an

[14] On the influence of dreams over the actions of Indians, see Long's *Travels*, vol. ii of this series.— ED.

[15] The journey of Sir William Johnson to Detroit, here referred to, took place July 4 – October 30, 1761. For the diary of this voyage. see Stone, *Life and Times of Sir William Johnson*, ii, pp. 429-477.— ED.

Indian who, as we afterwards found, had been defpatched
to Pondiac with belts from the Shawanefe and Delawares;
but he would not ftop to talk to us. This day I faw made
the moft extraordinary meal to which I ever was or ever
can be witnefs. Till thefe laft named Indians joined us
we had killed nothing but a very large wild cat, called a
pichou,[16] which indeed was very good eating: but this
day we eat two deer, fome wild turkeys, wild geefe, and
wild ducks, befides a great quantity of Indian corn. Of
the wild ducks and Indian corn we made broth; the
Indians made fpoons of the bark of a tree in a few minutes,
and, for the firft time, I eat of boiled wild duck. When
we marched on after dinner, I could perceive no frag-
ments left. What an Indian can eat is fcarcely credible
to thofe who have not feen it. Indeed the Frenchmen,
who had been ufed to favage life, expreffed their afton-
ifhment at the quantity which had been devoured. The
next day (4th) we found plenty of game, having fufficient
time to hunt for it, as the canoes were for the greateft
part of the day dragged along, there not being water
fufficient to float them. The day after (5th) we met an
Indian on a handfome white horfe, which had been
General Braddock's, and had been taken ten years before
when that General was killed on his march to Fort du
Quefne, afterwards called Fort Pitt, on the Ohio. The
following day (6th) we arrived at a rocky fhoal, where the
water was not more than two or three inches deep, and
found a great number of young Indians fpearing fifh
with fticks burnt at the end and fharpened; an art at
which they are very dexterous; for the chief, who fteered
my canoe with a fetting-pole (no oars being ufed the
whole way), whenever he faw a fifh, ufed to ftrike it

[16] Pichou is the Canadian name for the loup-cervier, or *lynx canadensis*.— ED.

through with his pole, though the end had been blunted
and made as flat and broad as a fhilling, pin it to the
ground, then lift it out of the water, and fhake it into the
boat. I never faw him mifs a fifh which he took aim at.
The day after, on the feventh of September, in the morning we got into eafy water, and arrived at the meadow
near the Miamis fort, pretty early in the day. We were
met at the bottom of the meadow by almoft the whole
village, who had brought fpears and tommahawks, in
order to defpatch me; even the little children had bows
and arrows to fhoot at the Englifhman who was come
among them; but I had the good fortune to ftay in the
canoe, reading the tragedy of Anthony and Cleopatra,
in the volume of Shakefpear which the little chief had
given me, when the reft went on fhore, though perfectly
ignorant of their intention, I pufhed the canoe over to
the other fide of the river, where I faw a man cutting
wood. I was furprifed to hear him fpeak Englifh. On
queftioning him I found he was a prifoner, had been one
of Lieutenant Holmes's garrifon at the Miamis Fort,
which officer the Indians had murdered, a young fquaw
whom he kept having enticed him out of the garrifon
under a pretext of her mother's wanting to be bled.
They cut off his head, brought it to the fort, and threw
it into the corporal's bed,[17] and afterwards killed all the
garrifon except five or fix whom they referved as victims
to be facrificed when they fhould lofe a man in their wars
with the Englifh. They had all been killed except this
one man whom an old fquaw had adopted as her fon.
Some years afterwards, when I lay on board a tranfport

[17] Holmes had warned Gladwin of the conspiracy among the Indians;
nevertheless, he himself fell a victim thereto. See Parkman, *Conspiracy of
Pontiac*, i, pp. 189, 278.— ED.

in the harbour of New York, in order to return to Europe,
Sir Henry Moore, then governor of that province,[18] came
to bid me adieu, and was rowed on board by this very
man among others. The man immediately recollected
me; and we felt, on feeing each other, what thofe only
can feel who have been in the like fituations. On our
arrival at the fort, the chiefs affembled, and paffed me
by, when they prefented the pipe of friendfhip; on which
I looked at Godefroi, and faid: "Mauvais augure pour
moi." A bad omen for me. Nor was I miftaken; for
they led my Indians to the village, on the other fide of the
water, and told me to ftay in the fort with the French
inhabitants; though care had been taken to forbid them
to receive me into their houfes, and fome ftrings of
wampum, on which the French had fpoken to fpare my
life, had been refufed. We wondered at this treatment,
as we expected that I fhould be civilly received; but foon
learned that this change of temper was owing to the
Shawanefe and Delawares, a deputation of fifteen of
them having come there with fourteen belts and fix
ftrings of wampum; who, in the name of their nations,
and of the Senecas, declared they would perifh to a man
before they would make peace with the Englifh: feven
of them had returned to their villages; five were gone to
Wyaut [Ouiatonon]; and three had fet out the morning I
had arrived for St. Joseph;[19] (a fortunate circumftance
for me, for they had determined to kill me). The Shawanefe and Delawares begged of the Miamis either to put

<hr/>

[18] Sir Henry Moore was the only colonist appointed governor of New York,
having been born in Jamaica in 1713. After serving as governor of that island,
and by his bravery and wisdom averting serious peril during a slave insurrec-
tion, he was rewarded with a baronetcy and the governorship of New York
(1764). He filled this position with acceptability, dying at his post in 1769.— ED.

[19] For these forts, see Croghan's *Journals, ante*.— ED.

us to death (the Indians and myfelf) or to tie us and fend
us prifoners to their villages, or at leaft to make us return.
They loaded the Englifh with the heavieft reproaches;
and added, that while the fun fhone they would be at
enmity with us. The Kiccapoos, Mafcoutins, and
Wiatanons, who happened to be at the Miamis village
declared, that they would difpatch me at their villages,
if the Miamis fhould let me pafs. The Shawanefe
and Delawares concluded their fpeeches with faying:
"This is the laft belt we fhall fend you, till we fend the
hatchet: which will be about the end of next month
(October)." Doubtlefs their defign was to amufe
**General Bradftreet with fair language, to cut off his
army at Sandufky, when leaft expected, and then to
fend the hatchet to the nations: a plan well laid; but of
which it was my good fortune to prevent them from
attempting the execution. To return to myfelf: I remained in the fort, and two Indian warriors (one of
whom was called Vifenlair) with tommahawks in their
hands, feized me, one by each arm; on which I turned
to Godefroi, the only perfon who had not left me, and
cried out to him, feeing him ftand motionlefs and pale:
"Eh bien! Vous m'abandonnez donc?" Well then!
You give me up? He anfwered: "Non, mon capitaine,
je ne vous abandonnerai jamais," No, my captain, I
will never give you up; and followed the Indians, who
pulled me along to the water-fide, where I imagined they
intended to put me into a canoe; but they dragged me
into the water. I concluded their whim was to drown
me, and then fcalp me; but I foon found my miftake, the
river being fordable. They led me on till we came near
their village; and there they ftopped and ftripped me.
They could not get off my fhirt, which was held by the**

wrift bands, after they had pulled it over my head; and in
rage and defpair I tore it off myfelf.   They then bound
my arms with my fafh, and drove me before them to a
cabin, where was a bench, on which they made me fit.
The whole village was now in an uproar.   Godefroi prevailed with St. Vincent, who had followed us to the water-
fide, but had turned back, to come along with him; and
encouraged Pondiac's nephew and the little chief's fon
to take my part.   St. Vincent brought the great belt, and
Pondiac's nephew fpoke.   Nanamis, an Indian, bid
Godefroi take courage, and not quit me.   Godefroi told
le Cygne, a Miamis chief, that his children were at
Detroit; and that, if they killed me, he could not tell
what might befal them.   He fpoke likewife to le Cygne's
fon, who whifpered his father, and the father came and
unbound my arms, and gave me his pipe to fmoke.
Vifenlair, upon my speaking, got up and tied me by the
neck to a poft.   And now every one was preparing to
act his part in torturing me.   The ufual modes of torturing prifoners are applying hot ftones to the foles of
the feet, running hot needles into the eyes, which latter
cruelty is generally performed by the women, and fhooting
arrows and running and pulling them out of the fufferer in
order to fhoot them again and again: this is generally
done by the children.   The torture is often continued
two or three days, if they can contrive to keep the prifoner
alive fo long.   Thefe modes of torture I fhould not have
mentioned, if the gentleman who advifed me to publifh
my journal, had not thought it neceffary.   It may eafily
be conceived what I muft have felt at the thought of
such horrors which I was to endure.   I recollect perfectly what my apprehenfions were.   I had not the
fmalleft hope of life; and I remember that I conceived

myfelf as it were going to plunge into a gulf, vaft, im-
meafurable; and that, in a few moments after, the thought
of torture occafioned a fort of torpor and infenfibility;
and I looked at Godefroi, and feeing him exceedingly
diftreffed, I faid what I could to encourage him: but he
defired me not to fpeak. I fuppofed that it gave offence
to the favages, and therefore was filent; when Pacanne,
king of the Miamis nation, and juft out of his minority,
having mounted a horfe and croffed the river, rode up to
me. When I heard him calling out to thofe about me,
and felt his hand behind my neck, I thought he was going
to ftrangle me out of pity: but he untied me, faying (as
it was afterwards interpreted to me) I give that man his
life. "If you want meat (for they fometimes eat their
prifoners) go to Detroit, or upon the lake (meaning go
face your enemies the Englifh) and you'll find enough.
What bufinefs have you with this man's flefh, who is
come to fpeak to us?" I fixed my eyes fteadfaftly on
this young man, and endeavoured by looks to exprefs my
gratitude. An Indian then prefented me his pipe; and I
was difmiffed by being pufhed rudely away. I made
what hafte I could to a canoe, and paffed over to the
fort, having received on my way a fmart cut of a fwitch
from an Indian on horfeback. Mr. Levi, a Jew trader,
and fome foldiers, who were prifoners, came to fee me.
Two very handfome young Indian women came likewife,
feemed to compaffionate me extremely, and afked
Godefroi a thoufand queftions. If I remember right,
they were the young king's fifters. Happy Don Quixote,
attended by princeffes! I was never left alone, as the
wretches, who ftripped and tied me, were always lurking
about to find an opportunity to ftab me. I lay in the
houfe of one L'Efperance, a Frenchman. The next day

my Indians fpoke on their belts. The two wretches ftill fought an opportunity to kill me. The day following the Miamis returned their anfwer: "That we muft go back;" fhewed the belts of the Senecas, Shawanefe, and Delawares; gave my Indians a fmall ftring of white wampum; and told them: "to go and inform their chiefs of what they had feen and heard." While the council fat I was concealed in L'Efperance's garret, as Godefroi was obliged to attend it. Being determined at all events to get into the Illinois country if poffible, St. Vincent and I agreed, that he fhould endeavour to gain le Cygne and the young king to attend me to Wyaut: but, in the middle of the night, St. Vincent came and awoke me, told me that two Frenchmen were juft arrived from St. Jofeph, and that the Delewares, who were there, were coming back to the Miamis village. He advifed me to fend for my chief immediately, and tell him, for his own fafety as well as mine, to try to get leave to go away in the morning, (for the Miamis had appointed the next day but one for our departure). This was accordingly done, and leave obtained. I went to vifit le Cygne, who told me, "that he would have been glad to have attended me to Wyaut; but that he could not think of leading me to my death: for that there were fo many tommahawks lifted up there, that he fhould have trembled to have gone himfelf." I gave notes to Pacanne and Pondiac's nephew, fetting forth that they had faved my life, and entreating all Englifhmen to ufe them kindly. (Pacanne fhewed his paper to Colonel Croghan, when he made his tour through the Indian country, and the Colonel was pleafed to bring him to Detroit, and, at a private meeting appointed for that purpofe, fent for me, and gave me a very handfome prefent to lay at his feet). We gave

all our blankets and fhirts to thofe Indians who had done
us fervice; and hearing that the chiefs were in council, and
talked of not allowing me to return with my party, but
of detaining me prifoner; and my Indians themfelves
appearing uneafy, having left my money and baggage
with one Capucin, a Frenchman, I hurried away about
noon, vexed at heart that I had not been able to execute
the orders I had received. I gave General Bradftreet's
letter for Monfieur St. Ange, the French commandant at
Fort Chartres, to St. Vincent, to deliver to that officer;
and figned a certificate which he was pleafed to put into
my hands, fpecifying that, on many occafions, he had
faved my life. Fear lent wings to my Indians this day;
and we continued our march till it was quite dark, being
apprehenfive of an attack. We fet out very early the
next morning; and as nothing worthy of obfervation
happened, my thoughts were taken up during this day's
journey in admiring the fine policy of the French with
refpect to the Indian nations; of which, from among
a thoufand, I fhall felect two remarkable inftances,
which I mention as not only worthy of imitation, but to
wear out of the minds of fuch of my countrymen as have
good fenfe and humanity the prejudices conceived
againft an innocent, much-abufed, and once happy
people; who have as deep a fenfe of the juftice and benevo-
lence of the French, as of the wrongs and haughty treat
ment which they have received from their prefent mafters.
The firft of thefe is the encouragement given by the
French court to marriages betwixt its fubjects and
Indian women; by which means Lewis got admiffion into
their councils, and all their defigns were known from
their very birth. Add to this, that the French fo entirely
won their affections by this ftep, that to this hour the

favages fay, that the French and they are one people.
The next inftance is, the prohibiting the fale of fpirituous
liquors to Indians, under pain of not receiving abfolution:
it is what the French call a *cas refervé*; none but a bifhop
can abfolve a perfon guilty of it. This prevented many
mifchiefs too frequent among the unfortunate tribes of
favages, who are fallen to our lot. From drunkennefs
arife quarrels, murders, and what not? for there is nothing, however fhocking and abominable, that the moft
innocent of that innocent people are not madly bent on
when drunk. From impofing on the drunken Indian in
trade, abufing his drunken wife, daughter, or other
female relation, and other fuch fcandalcus practices
arife ftill greater evils. When fuch things are done
(and they are done) can we wonder that the Indians feek
revenge? The ill conduct of a few diffolute pedlars has
often coft the lives of thoufands of his Majefty's moft
induftrious fubjects, who were juft emerging from the
gloom of toil and want, to the fair profpect of eafe and
contentment. The following day, while we were fhooting at fome turkeys, we difcovered the cabins of a hunting
party on the oppofite fide of the Miamis river; the men
were in the woods; but a fquaw came over to us, who
proved to be the wife of the little chief. Godefroi told
her that I was gone to the Ilinois country with her fon.
She informed us that the Indians were not returned
from Detroit; and added that there were four hundred
Delawares and three hundred Shawanefe (as fhe had
been told) at the Uttawaw villages, who wanted to go
and fet fire to that place. We were fure that this piece
of news about the Shawanefe and Delawares was falfe,
as the Uttawaws themfelves wanted provifions: but my
Indians believed it, and it ferved to bring them over at

once to my way of thinking, which was, to pafs through the woods, and avoid the villages of the Uttawaws. They were all much alarmed, but in particular the Huron of Loretto. This regenerate monfter of the church, this Chriftian favage,[20] who fpoke French fluently, had the cruelty and infolence to tell me, that as I could not march as faft as the reft, I muft take an old man and a boy (both lame) and make the beft of my way: that the chief would go with me, and he would conduct the other[s], who were eleven in number, and all able men. I fpoke to him with gentlenefs, and begged that he would not think of feparating from us; on which he faid fomething, that I did not underftand, in his language which refembles that of the five nations, and of courfe was underftood by my chief, and which vexed him fo much, that he told me, "I might go by myfelf;" but I found means to pacify him. I now told Godefroi, who was of himfelf fo determined, that he would of courfe go with me. Upon this the Huron gave us very grofs language; and indeed fuch ftubborn impudence I never faw. He told the chief that if he fuffered me to take my horfes with me, we fhould be difcovered, but I obtained the chief's confent to take them a little way. I then propofed going into the wood to fettle the diftribution of our provifions and ammunition; but the Huron would liften to nothing: fo leaving him and his party, confifting of ten, with my beft horfe, which he faid he would turn loofe as foon as he fhould get a little way further, I ftruck into the wood

---

[20] One of the earliest Jesuit missions in Canada was to the Hurons, for whom (1673) a village was built at Loretto, ten miles from Quebec, on a seigniory belonging to the Jesuit order. Remnants of the Loretto Hurons are still to be found at the old village. The French had employed these "praying Indians" in their wars; it will be seen that the English were following the same policy.— Ed.

with Godefroi, the chief, the old Indian, and the Indian boy; Godefroi and myfelf on horfeback. We went North Eaft from twelve o'clock till two; from two to five we went North; and finding a pool of water, we took up our lodgings there. The next day we continued our route North, North Eaft, being as nearly as we could guefs in the courfe of the Miamis river. We endured great thirft all this day. About three o'clock we reached the fwamps, which, by the drynefs of the feafon, might have paffed for meadows, and not finding any water, about five o'clock we made a hole, two feet deep, with our hands, (for we had no kind of tool fit for that ufe) where fome tall, broad grafs grew; and getting good water, though very muddy, we made a fire, and determined to pafs the night by the fide of our little well. We travelled in the fwamps the following day till half an hour after one o'clock, at which time we came to open woods, having found water in two places on our way; but we could find none when we wanted to repofe ourfelves at the clofe of day. We therefore fet to work, as the day before, and made a hole four feet deep in a place which muft be a fwamp in the wet feafon: but it was three hours before we got a draught of what I might rather call watery mud than muddy water. We were forced from want of water to ftew a turkey in the fat of a racoon; and I thought I had never eaten any thing fo delicious, though falt was wanting: but perhaps it was hunger which made me think fo. We heard four fhots fired very near us juft before dark; we had a little before difcovered the tracks of Indians, and they undoubtedly had difcovered ours, and, fuppofing us friends, fired to let us know were they were. Thefe fhots alarmed our chief, and he told me that I muft leave my horfes behind. I bid Godefroi drive them to fome little diftance from us, and let them go: accordingly he went towards the place where we had left them, as if he intended to do fo; but, unknown to me, wifely deferred it till morning, hoping our chief would change his mind. This night the chief, feeing me writing by the light of the fire, grew jealous, and afked if I was counting the trees. The next morning the chief being a little intimidated, inftead of going Eaft North Eaft, as agreed on the night before, in order to draw near the Miamis river, went due North; by which means he led us into the moft perplexed wood I ever faw. He had my compafs, which I afked him for, and wanted to carry about me, as he very feldom looked at it; but this gave great offenfe, and he told me I might go by myfelf. In fhort, he was grown captious beyond meafure. In order to pleafe him, we had put his pack on one of our horfes; but we were forced to take it off again, as a loaded horfe could not force its way through the thick wood we were in. I found fuch a difficulty in leading my horfe (for it was impoffible to ride) through this part of the foreft, that I called out to the party for God's fake to ftop till I could fee them, or I fhould never fee them more: at that time I could not be more than fifteen yards behind them. They had hurried on in purfuit of a rattle-fnake. The chief now told me again, that I muft let my horfes go; but Godefroi convinced me, that I could not reach Detroit without them. I therefore refolved, if he perfifted, to quit him, to take Godefroi with me, and to kill one of my horfes for a supply of food, for we had very little ammunition left, and no provifions. However the chief grew good-humoured by Godefroi's management; and as he now thought himfelf out of danger, changed his courfe, going Eaft North Eaft. We

foon got into a fine open wood, where there was room
to drive a coach and fix. Here we halted to refrefh ourfelves by fmoaking our pipes, having nothing to eat, the
old Indian, who always ranged as we travelled on, having
found no game that morning. As I had not been ufed
to fmoaking, I defired to have fumach leaves only,
without tobacco; but, after a few whiffs, I was fo giddy,
that I was forced to defift: probably an empty ftomach
was the chief caufe of this unpleafant effect of fmoaking.
Soon after we came into extenfive meadows; and I was
affured that thofe meadows continue for a hundred and
fifty miles, being in the winter drowned lands and marfhes.
By the drynefs of the feafon they were now beautiful
paftures: and here prefented itfelf one of the moft delightful profpects I ever beheld; all the low grounds being
meadow, and without wood, and all the high grounds
being covered with trees, and appearing like iflands;
the whole fcene feemed an elyfium. Here we found good
water, and fat down by it, and made a comfortable meal
of what the old Indian had killed, after we left our halting-
place. We afterwards continued our route, and at
five o'clock difcovering a fmall rivulet, which gave us all,
and me in particular, inexpreffible pleafure, we made a
fire by the fide of it, and lay there all night. The day
following, we croffed the tracks of a party of men running
from the Uttawaw villages directly up into the woods, which
we imagined to be thofe of the Huron's party who might
have loft their way; as it proved. I laughed and joked
a good deal with Godefroi on this occafion; for when
the Huron left us, I afked in a fneering manner, "if he
had any commands, in cafe I fhould get before him to
Detroit;" and he anfwered me in the fame tone, "if when
you arrive, you don't find me there, you may fafely fay

that I am gone to the devil." Soon after, to our great joy, we fell into the path leading from the Uttawaw villages to Detroit, and ftruck into a by-path to avoid meeting Indians; but unluckily ftumbled on that which led from the great path to Attawang's village. We met three Hurons on horfeback, who told us, that peace was concluded, that the Uttawaws had returned the day before to their villages, and that General Bradftreet was to be at Cedar-Point that night on his way to Sandufky. One of thefe Indians had been prefent when I was prifoner at Attawang's village; and though I was dreffed like a Canadian, and fpoke French to Godefroi to prevent difcovery, recollected me to be the Englifhman he had feen there. I gave him a letter from St. Vincent to Pondiac which I had promifed to deliver. They then took their leave of us; and as foon as they were out of fight, we turned into the great path, and putting our Indians on our horfes, Godefroi and I walked at a very great rate. We arrived at the Pootiwatamy village[11] at a quarter paft three, where I had the pleafure of feeing Englifh colours flying. I wanted to avoid the village; but the chief, being very hungry (for we had eat nothing that day) fell into a paffion, and afked what we were afraid of. He knew he ran no rifk here. I was a little vexed, and mounting my horfe bid him follow. I went to the village, where I bought a little Indian corn and a piece of venifon; and then Godefroi and I rode on till it was dark, in hopes of reaching Detroit the next day; and finding water, made a fire near it, and paffed the night there, having left our fellow-travellers to fleep with the Pootiwatamies; who, as none of them knew me, were

---

[11] See Croghan's *Journals, ante,* for note upon the location of this Potawatomi village.— ED.

told by Godefroi that I was gone to the country of the
Ilinois, and that he growing tired of the journey, and
wanting to fee his children, was on his return home.
The next morning we fet out at the dawn of day; and,
to fave ourfelves the trouble of making a raft, took the
upper road, though the journey was much longer that
way, hoping to find the river fordable, in which we were
not difappointed. We travelled this day a great way,
and our horfes were fo much fatigued, that they were
hardly able to carry us towards the clofe of the day. We
found frefh horse-dung on the road, which Godefroi having curioufly examined, knew that fome Indians had juft
paffed that way; and by their tracks he was fure they
were before us. He therefore made an excufe to halt
for about an hour, endeavouring to conceal the truth
from me; but I was no ftranger to his real motive. However, about feven o'clock we arrived at Detroit; whence I
was fifty leagues diftant when I left the Miamis river and
ftruck into the woods: and by the circuit I was obliged
to make to avoid purfuit, I made it at leaft fourfcore
leagues, or two hundred and forty miles. The Huron
and his people did not arrive till many days after, and in
three different parties. They had loft their way; were
obliged to divide themfelves into fmall bodies in order to
feek for game; had fuffered extremely by fatigue and
hunger; one having died by the way, and all the reft being
very ill when they reached Detroit. The Huron I imagined
would have died. I gave him, as well as all the others,
all the affiftance in my power; but could not help re-
proaching him with his barbarity to me, and reminding
him, "that the Great Spirit had protected one whom he
had abandoned, and punifhed him who had bafely
deferted his fellow-warrior." Immediately after my

arrival at Detroit, I fent an exprefs to General Bradftreet, with an account of my proceedings, and to warn
him of the dangerous fituation he was in, being advanced
fome miles up the Sandufky river, and furrounded with
treacherous Indians. The moment he received my
letter, he removed, falling down the river, till he reached
Lake Erie: by this means he difappointed their hopes of
furprifing his army. This army however fuffered extremely afterwards, and great numbers were loft in
traverfing the defert, many of their boats having in the
night been dafhed to pieces againft the fhore, while the
foldiers were in their tents. The boats were unfortunately too large to be drawn out of the water. The centi-
nels gave the alarm on finding the fudden fwell of the
lake, but after infinite labour, from the lofs of boats, a
large body of men were obliged to attempt to reach Fort
Niagara by land, many of whom perifhed. It is worthy
of remark, that, during this violent fwell of the waters,
foldiers ftood on the fhore with lighted candles, not a
breath of wind being perceived. This phænomenon
often happens. Another curious fact refpecting the waters
of thefe lakes is, that they rife for feven years and fall
for feven years; or in other words, there is a feven years
tide. I have read fomewhere, that the Cafpian fea
overflows its banks once in fifteen years. This, however,
is denied elfewhere. But, if the former opinion be
really the cafe, as the American lakes and the Cafpian
sea are in parts of the earth almoft oppofite to each
other, it might be worth while to enquire, whether, when
they are at the lowest in one place, they are at the higheft
in that which is oppofite, or both rife and fall at the fame
time?

The Natchez nation, mentioned in the letter to Pondiac, which he fhewed me, and who were blamed by the reft of the Indian army for having fired too foon on the Englifh who were fent to take poffeffion of Fort Chartres by way of the Miffiffippi river, no doubt did it by defign, that the troops might have an opportunity of retreating; for the French had formerly endeavoured to extirpate that nation, and had nearly fucceeded in the undertaking, a fmall number only having efcaped the maffacre.[21] It is not probable fuch an action could ever be forgiven; efpecially by favages. This nation have a perpetual fire; and two men are appointed to watch it. It has been conjectured that their anceftors were deferters from the Mexicans who worfhip the fun.

The Miamis nation, of whom I have fpoken fo much, and into whofe hands I fell after leaving Pondiac's army at the Uttawaw villages, are the very people who have lately defeated the Americans in three different battles; and when the laft accounts from that country reached us, they were encamped on the banks of the Ohio, near the falls or cataracts of that river.[22]

---

[21] The Natchez War, with its sequel in the Chickasaw campaigns, was the most disastrous series of Indian troubles in the early history of French Louisiana. The Natchez secretly rose, and treacherously massacred the garrison of Fort Rosalie, November 29, 1729. During the two succeeding years Governor Périer twice invaded their territory, and inflicted so severe a chastisement that the nation as such ceased to exist, its remnant taking refuge among the Chickasaws.— ED.

[22] This paragraph was obviously interpolated just before the publication of the journal (1791), for the three different battles to which Morris here refers were those of Harmar's campaign in 1790, when three several detachments of the latter's army were at different times overpowered in the Miami territory. The defeat of St. Clair (November 4, 1791), by the same tribesmen, doubtless was too recent an event for the information to have reached England, and been embodied in a publication of that year.— ED.

It may not be improper to mention, that if I could have completed the tour intended, viz. from Detroit to New Orleans, thence to New York, and thence to Detroit again, whence I fet out, it would have been a circuit little fhort of five thoufand miles.

DETROIT, September 25, 1764.

Important
Historical Publications
OF
The Arthur H. Clark Company

Full descriptive circulars will be mailed
on application

The Philippine Islands
1493-1898

Being the history of the Philippines from their discovery to the present time

EXPLORATIONS by early Navigators, descriptions of the Islands and their Peoples, their History, and records of the Catholic Missions, as related in contemporaneous books and manuscripts, showing the political, economic, commercial, and religious conditions of those Islands from their earliest relations with European Nations to the end of the nineteenth century.

Translated, and edited and annotated by E. H. BLAIR *and* J. A. ROBERTSON, *with introduction and additional notes by* E. G. BOURNE.

With Analytical Index and Illustrations. Limited edition, 55 volumes, large 8vo, cloth, uncut, gilt top. Price $4.00 net per volume.

> "Students desiring to know the true inwardness of this far-reaching event in American History, must inevitably hereafter turn first to Dr. Doughty's scholarly and well-considered volumes."— *American Historical Review.*

The Siege of Quebec and the Battle of the Plains of Abraham

By A. DOUGHTY, Litt. D. (Laval), Joint Librarian of the Legislature, Quebec, in collaboration with G. W. PARMELEE, D.C. L., Secretary of the Department of Public Instruction, Quebec

With Plans, Portraits, and Views

THIS is the first ample history of the campaign of 1759, and the most extensive and important monograph that has so far been written on any episode in the annals of New France. But the interest of the subject outstrips all bounds that are merely local. Montcalm's defeat and the English occupation of Quebec were great events in the history of the whole continent. In the world-struggles between England and France they rank even before the battle of Plassey.

A LIMITED EDITION of 525 sets was printed, of which only 19 remain for sale. Complete in 6 volumes, small quarto, handsomely printed, and bound in blue cloth. Price $50.00, net.

> "Indispensable to every future historian of the Seven Years' War in America. . . . The cartography of the campaign has been largely supplemented by Mr. Doughty's discoveries. . . . The mechanical features of these volumes deserve high praise."— *New York Evening Post.*

> "Merits the thanks of all those interested in probably the most famous incident of our history." — Sir JOHN G. BOURINOT, K.C.M.G., LL.D., Litt.D.

> "A hundred and one writers have treated this well-worn subject, but it has been left for Messrs. Doughty and Parmelee to go over the whole ground and present us with a final and authoritative record."
> — *The Daily Chronicle*, London, England.

"The bare title hardly conveys an idea of the interesting lore embraced in this admirably carried out study of the roads and their part in the development of the country."—*Boston Globe*.

The Historic Highways of America
by Archer Butler Hulbert

A series of monographs on the History of America as portrayed in the evolution of its highways of War, Commerce, and Social Expansion.

Comprising the following volumes:

Sixteen volumes, crown 8vo, cloth, uncut, gilt tops. A LIMITED EDITION only printed direct from type, and the type distributed. Each volume handsomely printed in large type on Dickinson's hand-made paper, and illustrated with maps, plates, and facsimiles.

Published a volume each two months, beginning September, 1902.

PRICE, volumes 1 and 2, $2.00 net each; volumes 3 to 16, $2.50 net each.

FIFTY SETS PRINTED ON LARGE PAPER, each numbered and *signed by the author*. Bound in cloth, with paper label, uncut, gilt tops. Price, $5.00 net per volume.

"The history of American trails and carries in colonial times; of paths, roads, and highways in our national beginnings; and of our great lake, river, and railroad traffic in later times is and has been of the first importance in our social and political history. Mr. Hulbert has shown himself abundantly able to investigate the subject and put in good form the results of his labors."
— Professor WILLIAM M. SLOANE, *Princeton University*.

"Mr. Hulbert has evidently mastered his subject, and has treated it very ably and enthusiastically. History is too frequently a mere collection of dry bones, but here we have a book which, when once begun, will be read eagerly to the end, so vividly does the author bring scenes and personages before us."— *Current Literature*.

"As in the prior volumes, the general effect is that of a most entertaining series. The charm of the style is evident."—*American Historical Review*.

"His style is effective . . . an invaluable contribution to the makings of American History."— *New York Evening Post*.

"Should fill an important and unoccupied place in American historical literature."
—*The Dial*.

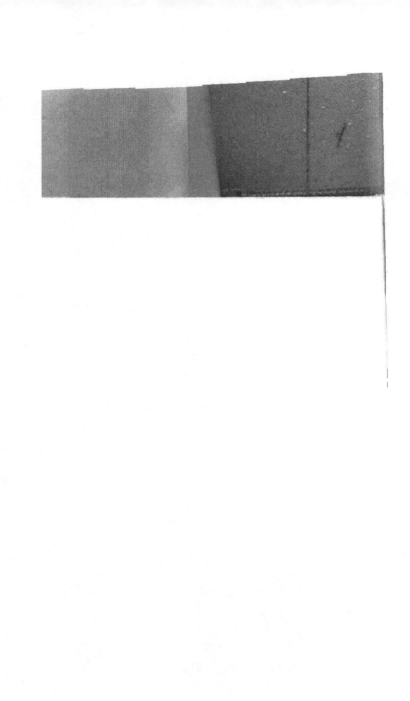

CPSIA information can be obtained
at www.ICGtesting.com
Printed in the USA
LVHW051004211218
600889LV00008B/245/P